Praise for Joseph J. Ellis's

THE QUARTET

"Customary, graceful prose. . . . [Ellis's] portraits . . . show his sure touch—highlighting Washington's dignity, Hamilton's energy, Madison's learning and Jay's diplomacy."
—*The New York Times Book Review*

"Ellis shows the extraordinary capacity of these four leaders to understand the events, discuss them dispassionately, explain them to the American people, reach compromise, rise above pettiness and sacrifice personal wealth, power and popularity for the long-term public good. Given the rarity of these qualities today, Ellis's book is a compelling reminder of the political virtues that created the American republic." —*Minneapolis Star Tribune*

"This is more than just a reinterpretation of a vital transition in our history; it is a reflection of new material from an episode that occurred two and a quarter centuries ago. . . . Having set forth the analysis, Ellis plunges into the narrative. His is an inviting voice and his story compelling, built around irresistible figures who, as the annual publishing lists amply display, retain their appeal in our own time." —*The Boston Globe*

"Ellis lives and breathes the Founders, and he deploys his customary zip and trenchant scholarship in showing how four central figures—Washington, John Jay, Alexander Hamilton and James Madison—conceived and promoted a new political framework built on the Constitution." —*Newsday*

JOSEPH J. ELLIS

THE QUARTET

Joseph J. Ellis is the author of many works of American history, including *Founding Brothers: The Revolutionary Generation*, which was awarded the Pulitzer Prize; and *American Sphinx: The Character of Thomas Jefferson*, which won the National Book Award. He recently retired from his position as the Ford Foundation Professor of History at Mount Holyoke College and lives in Amherst, Massachusetts, with his wife and their youngest son.

www.josephellishistorian.com

Joseph J. Ellis is available for speaking engagements.
To inquire, please contact Penguin Random
House Speakers Bureau at
speakers@penguinrandomhouse.com
or visit www.prhspeakers.com.

THE QUARTET

THE QUARTET

*Orchestrating the
Second American Revolution,
1783-1789*

JOSEPH J. ELLIS

VINTAGE BOOKS
A Division of Penguin Random House LLC
New York

FIRST VINTAGE BOOKS EDITION, MAY 2016

Copyright © 2015 by Joseph J. Ellis

All rights reserved. Published in the United States by Vintage Books, a division
of Penguin Random House LLC, New York, and distributed in Canada by
Random House of Canada, a division of Penguin Random House Canada
Limited, Toronto. Originally published in hardcover in the United States by
Alfred A. Knopf, a division of Penguin Random House LLC, New York, in 2015.

Vintage and colophon are registered trademarks of
Penguin Random House LLC.

The Cataloging-in-Publication Data is on file at the Library of Congress.

Vintage Books Trade Paperback ISBN: 978-0-8041-7248-6
eBook ISBN: 978-0-385-35341-0

Author photograph © Peter W. Ellis
Book design by Betty Lew

www.vintagebooks.com

Printed in the United States of America
10 9 8 7 6 5 4 3 2 1

In memory of Pauline Maier

CONTENTS

Appendix B

Appendix C

PREFACE

PLURIBUS TO UNUM

$\mathcal{T}$he idea for this book first came to me while listening to twenty-eight middle school boys recite the Gettysburg Address from memory in front of their classmates and proud parents. My son Scott was teaching science at the Greenwood School in Putney, Vermont, and had invited me to judge the annual oratorical contest. I don't remember exactly when it happened, but at some point during the strenuous if repetitious effort to get Lincoln's words right, it dawned on me that the first clause in the first sentence of Lincoln's famous speech was historically incorrect.

Lincoln began as follows: "Four score and seven years ago our fathers brought forth on this Continent a new Nation." No, not really. In 1776 thirteen American colonies declared themselves independent states that came together temporarily to win the war, then would go their separate ways. The government they created in 1781, called the Articles of Confederation, was not really much of a government at all and was never intended to be. It was, instead, what one historian has called a "Peace Pact" among sovereign states that regarded themselves as mini-nations of their own, that came together voluntarily for mutual security in a domestic version of a League of Nations.[1]

And once you started thinking along these lines, there were reasons as self-evident as Jefferson's famous truths why no such thing as a coherent American nation could possibly have emerged after independence was won. Politically, a state-based framework followed naturally from the arguments that the colonies had been hurling at the British ministry for over a decade, which denied Parliament's right to tax them because that authority resided within the respective colonial legislatures, which represented their constituents in a more direct and proximate fashion than those distant members of Parliament could ever do. The resolution declaring independence, approved on July 2, 1776, clearly states that the former colonies were leaving the British Empire not as a single collective but rather as "Free and Independent States."[2]

Distance also made a huge difference. The vast majority of Americans were born, lived out their lives, and died within a thirty-mile geographic radius. It took three weeks for a letter to get from Boston to Philadelphia. Political horizons and allegiances, therefore, were limited—obviously no such things as radios, cell phones, or the Internet existed to solve the distance problem—so the ideal political unit was the town or county government, where representatives could be trusted to defend your interests because they shared them as your neighbors.[3]

Indeed, it was presumed that any faraway national government would represent a domestic version of Parliament, too removed from the interests and experiences of the American citizenry to be trusted. And distrusting such distant sources of political power had become a core ideological impulse of the movement for independence, often assuming quasi-paranoid hostility toward any projection of power from London and Whitehall, which was described as inherently arbitrary, imperious, and corrupt. And so creating a national government was the last thing on the minds of American revolutionaries, since such a distant source of political power embodied all the tyrannical tendencies that patriotic Americans believed they were rebelling against.[4]

In 1863 Lincoln had some compelling reasons for bending the arc of American history in a national direction, since he was then waging a civil war on behalf of a union that he claimed predated the existence of the states. This was a fundamental distortion of how history happened, though we may wish to forgive Lincoln, since it was the only way for him to claim the political authority to end slavery.

Truth be known, nationhood was never a goal of the war for independence, and all the political institutions necessary for a viable American nation-state were thoroughly stigmatized in the most heartfelt convictions of revolutionary ideology. The only thing holding the American colonies together until 1776 was their membership in the British Empire. The only thing holding them together after 1776 was their common resolve to leave that empire. Once the war was won, that cord was cut, and the states began to float into their own at best regional orbits. Any historically informed prophet who was straddling that postwar moment could have safely predicted that North America was destined to become a western version of Europe, a constellation of rival political camps and countries, all jockeying for primacy. That, at least, was the clear direction in which American history was headed.[5]

To say that "something happened" to change that direction is obviously inadequate. The beauty of the Lincoln version of the story is its presumption that a national ethos was already embedded in the political equation, albeit latently or implicitly, so that what we might call the second revolution of 1787–88 followed naturally from the first in 1776. But for all the political, ideological, and demographic reasons already noted, the transition from the Declaration of Independence to the Constitution cannot be described as natural. Quite the contrary, it represented a dramatic change in direction and in scale, in effect from a confederation of sovereign states to a nation-size republic, indeed the largest republic ever established.

So how do we explain such a seismic shift in the gravitational field of American political history? Well, the kind of bottom-up explanation that works so well to convey popular opposition to British imperial policy in the 1760s and 1770s will not work in the 1780s. Mobs did not appear, urging the creation of a fully empowered American nation. Quite the opposite: the dominant historical forces in the 1780s were centrifugal rather than centripetal, meaning that the vast majority of citizens had no interest in American nationhood; indeed, they regarded the very idea of a national government as irrelevant to their local lives and ominously reminiscent of the British leviathan they had recently vanquished. There was no popular insurgency for a national government because such a thing was not popular.

The obvious alternative explanation is top-down. All democratic cultures find such explanations offensive because they violate the hallowed conviction that, at least in the long run, popular majorities can best decide the direction that history should take. However true that conviction might be over the full span of American history— and the claim is contestable—it does not work for the 1780s, which just might be the most conspicuous and consequential example of the way in which a small group of prominent leaders, in disregard of popular opinion, carried the American story in a new direction.

There is an ironic precedent for this argument. During the first half of the twentieth century Charles Beard and his disciples, chiefly Merrill Jensen, created a school of thought, called the Progressive School, that dominated our understanding of the revolutionary era. While much of their work has not aged well, chiefly its claim that the founders were driven primarily by economic motives, two features of their story line remain abidingly relevant: first, that the founders must not be regarded as demigods with unique access to supernatural wisdom; and second, that the transition from the Articles of Confederation to the Constitution was orchestrated by a political elite that collaborated—to say "conspired" seems sinister, but it is what the Progressives meant—to replace a state-based confederation with a federal government that claimed to speak for the American people as a collective whole.[6]

In virtually every other respect, the narrative offered in the pages that follow veers in a different direction from the Progressive interpretation. My sense is that the most prominent leaders of this founding elite were driven by motives that were more political than economic, chiefly the desire to expand the meaning of the American Revolution so that it could function on a larger, indeed national, scale. The great conflict, as I see it, was not between "aristocracy" and "democracy," whatever those elusive categories might mean, but rather between "nationalists" and "confederationists," which is shorthand for those who believed that the principles of the American Revolution could flourish in a much larger political theater and those who did not. Finally, my version of the story regards the successful collaboration of this small cadre not as a betrayal of the core convictions of the American Revolution, but rather as a quite brilliant rescue.[7]

My argument is that four men made the transition from confederation to nation happen. They are George Washington, Alexander Hamilton, John Jay, and James Madison. If they are the stars of the story, the supporting cast consists of Robert Morris, Gouverneur Morris (no relation), and Thomas Jefferson. Readers can and should decide for themselves, but my contention is that this political quartet diagnosed the systemic dysfunctions under the Articles, manipulated the political process to force a calling of the Constitutional Convention, collaborated to set the agenda in Philadelphia, attempted somewhat successfully to orchestrate the debates in the state ratifying conventions, then drafted the Bill of Rights as an insurance policy to ensure state compliance with the constitutional settlement. If I am right, this was arguably the most creative and consequential act of political leadership in American history.

It made a huge difference that all four of the political collaborators identified here possessed impeccable revolutionary credentials. (The posture of Progressive historians has always seemed somewhat odd on this score, since the men they accused of hijacking the American Revolution were all central players in making the victory over Great Britain happen.) If the overarching issue at stake was what direction the American Revolution should take after independence was won, no one could accuse them of failing to grasp the almost mystical meaning of "The Cause." And since Washington was the one-man embodiment of all the semi-sacred reverberations that term conveyed, his endorsement of the national agenda provided a crucial veneer of legitimacy for their bold and slightly illegal project. It also helped that all four of them had served in the Continental Army or the Continental (then Confederation) Congress, which meant that they had experienced the war for independence from a higher perch than most of their contemporaries. They were accustomed, as Hamilton put it, to "think continentally" at a time when the allegiances and perspectives of most Americans were confined within local and state borders. Indeed, the very term *American Revolution* implies a national ethos that in fact did not exist in the population at large.

Perhaps the best way to understand the term *American Revolution* is to realize that it describes a two-tiered political process. The first American Revolution achieved independence. It was a mere, or perhaps not so mere, colonial rebellion. It also created a series of mini-republics in the former colonies, now states, but it did so in ways that were inherently incompatible with any national political agenda.

The second American Revolution modified the republican framework existent in the states in order to create a nation-size republic. The overly succinct way to put it is that the American Revolution did not become a full-fledged revolution until it became more expansively American. Or even more succinctly, the first phase of the American Revolution was about the rejection of political power; the second phase was about controlling it. More practically, the United States could not become the dominant model for the liberal state in the modern world until the second American Revolution of 1787–88.

Several ongoing editorial projects have made it possible to recover the thoughts, doubts, fears, and anxieties of the founding generation more fully than ever before, to include the four men featured in these pages. Though Jay is somewhat of an exception, the most prominent founders are the focus of massive multivolume collections over the last half century that provide the fullest documentation of any political elite in recorded history. The recently published correspondence of the delegates of the Continental and the Confederation Congress has provided an equally exhaustive account of the inherent disarray within that flimsy framework called the Articles of Confederation. It now seems abundantly clear, more so than ever before, that by 1787 the confederation was on the verge of dissolution. And the full record of all the debates in the state ratifying conventions, which has been proceeding at a stately pace and is nearing completion, offers a level of documentation on the ratification process that almost defies comprehension in its state-by-state specificity.[8]

My immersion in this extraordinarily rich body of primary evidence has made me even more aware that the second American Revolution occurred in a chronological place that must be recovered on its own terms before it can be evaluated by ours. In effect, we must be prepared to perform an exercise in anthropology over time rather than space. The residents of late-eighteenth-century America lacked access to many of our modern values, meaning that they lived in a premodern world that is forever lost to us. That world was predemocratic, pre-Darwin, pre-Freud, pre-Einstein, pre-Keynes, and pre–Martin Luther King, Jr. The distinctive mentality of that world makes it dangerous to solicit their advice or wisdom in response to our current controversies (i.e.: What would George Washington say about our invasion and occupation of Iraq?). Such efforts resemble the futile attempt to plant cut flowers. But the same interpretive problem also flows in the opposite direction. Viewing and judging the founding generation through the lens of our own values is inherently presumptive and presentistic, much like evaluating the child-rearing practices of indigenous tribes in Samoa by the standards of Dr. Spock.

There are two especially salient danger zones where our modern presumptions can most easily lead us astray. The first is our creedal conviction that democracy is the political gold standard against which all responsible governments must be measured. The second is our political certainty, in truth recently arrived at, that racial equality is morally superior to any race-based alternative. Neither of those modern assumptions would have been either comprehensible or credible to the founding generation.

The term *democracy* remained an epithet until the third decade of the nineteenth century. It meant mob rule, the manipulation of majority opinion by demagogues, and shortsighted political initiatives on behalf of the putative "people" that ran counter to the long-term interests of the "public." In the 1780s *democracy* meant the refusal to pay taxes to reduce the federal debt incurred in the war, the preference for an inflated currency that privileged debtors over creditors, the illegal confiscation of loyalist estates, and the repudiation of any political authority that subordinated local interests to some larger, national agenda.

It is true that the first American Revolution gave newfound credence to egalitarian assumptions that fed the democratic ethos and eventually undermined the hierarchical assumptions of colonial America. But it took fifty years for democratic values to become hegemonic, and the second American Revolution predated that development. The democratic society that Alexis de Tocqueville described in the 1830s was still aborning in the 1780s. The operative word for the revolutionary generation was *republic* rather than *democracy*. And therefore we should expect to see them searching for a way to harness the primal energies of popular opinion within a multitiered political architecture that filtered the swoonish swings "of the people" through layers of deliberation controlled by what Jefferson called "the natural aristocracy." That filtration process was what the Constitution was all about, which does not make that seminal document antidemocratic so much as predemocratic.[9]

Race and slavery present even more daunting interpretive challenges. There is no way to finesse the fact that slavery was built into the American founding, just as it was built into the economy of all the states south of the Potomac. Historians who prefer to downplay that awkward reality thereby obscure the most consequential and tragic choice the founders were forced to make. Although most of the prominent founders, and all the men featured here, fully recognized that slavery was incompatible with the values of the American Revolution, they consciously subordinated the moral to the political agenda, permitting the continuance and expansion of slavery as the price to pay for nationhood. This decision meant that tragedy was also built into the American founding, and the only question we can ask is whether it was a Greek tragedy, meaning inevitable and unavoidable, or a Shakespearean tragedy, meaning that it could have gone the other way, and the failure was a function of the racial prejudices the founders harbored in their heads and hearts.[10]

There is little doubt that the lost world of the founding was a more explicitly racist world than our own. The founders were truly remarkable for their ability to imagine a nation-size republic and a political framework that insisted on the separation of church and state, both of which were unprecedented social experiments that succeeded. But neither they nor the vast majority of white Americans were capable of imagining a biracial society. (Neither, for that matter, was such a staunch opponent of slavery as Harriet Beecher Stowe, who provided an appendix at the end of *Uncle Tom's Cabin* that described her plan for deporting all the freed slaves back to Africa.) We need to remind ourselves that racial integration in the United States was a mid-twentieth-century idea that few if any of the founders could have comprehended. Imposing our racial agenda on them is politically correct but historically irresponsible.

Given the parameters of the possible within which the founders were working, the republic they created has rather remarkably stood the test of time, indeed has lasted longer than any of them expected.

To end where we began, with Lincoln, the operative question that all the European pundits were asking back then was whether "any nation so conceived and so dedicated can long endure." After more than two centuries, the answer is abundantly clear. And now for how it happened.

THE QUARTET

Chapter 1

THE ARTICLES AND THE VISION

Certain I am that unless Congress speaks in a more decisive tone; unless they are vested with powers by the several states competent to the great purposes of War . . . , that our cause is lost. . . . I see one head gradually changing into thirteen.

George Washington to Joseph Jones
MAY 31, 1780

On March 1, 1781, three and a half years after they were endorsed by the Continental Congress, the Articles of Confederation were officially ratified when the last state, Maryland, gave its approval. The unseemly delay could be explained by the conspicuous fact that a war was going on, which inevitably deflected attention from all other business, but the specific reason was that the landless states, like Maryland, refused to ratify until all the states with extensive western claims—Virginia most prominently—agreed to cede their claims to Congress. The president of the Continental Congress, Samuel Huntington, declared the creation of a new political entity, called the Confederation Congress, which established "a perpetual Union between the thirteen United States." To mark the occasion, thirteen cannons were fired on the hill overlooking the Philadelphia harbor, and that salvo was answered by thirteen cannons from the frigate *John Paul Jones*. In the evening "a grand exhibition of fireworks was staged at the State House, and all the Vessels in the Harbor were decorated and illuminated."[1]

At almost the same time that Americans were celebrating their newly declared union, a pamphleteer in London, Josiah Tucker, predicted that any vision of an emergent American nation-state would prove to be a mirage, "one of the idlest, and most visionary Notions, that ever was conceived by the Writers of Romance." Tucker spoke for all those English and European pundits who regarded the very term *United States* as a comical oxymoron. The diversity of climates, competing regional interests, and long-standing political disagreements made it impossible to imagine that Americans could ever, as he put it, "be united into one compact Empire, under any species of Government whatsoever." What had brought them together in the summer of 1776 was their common desire to secede from that empire. If they failed in that effort—and the issue in the spring of 1781 remained uncertain—Americans would revert back to their identity as British subjects. If they succeeded, they would dissolve into a political stew of local, state, and regional principalities likely to end up fighting one another. "Their Fate," predicted Tucker, "seems to be—A DISUNITED PEOPLE, till the End of Time."[2]

A closer look at the recently ratified document that promoted all those salvos and illuminations reveals that Tucker's skepticism about any emergent American nation-state was not that far off the mark. For the Articles of Confederation were not, and were not intended to be, a political framework for a national government. Indeed, the Articles were not designed to establish any kind of government at all. As its name suggests, the Articles created a confederation of thirteen sovereign states that were nations themselves, entering, as Article III put it, "into a firm league of friendship with each other, for their common defence, the security of their liberties, and their mutual and general welfare." It was less a constitution than a diplomatic treaty among sovereign powers.[3]

The key provision was Article II: "Each state retains its sovereignty, freedom, and independence, and every power, jurisdiction, and right, which is not by this Confederation expressly delegated to the United States, in Congress assembled." Those powers, jurisdictions, and rights were quite few, chiefly to resolve border disputes between states, establish standard weights and measures and a common currency (though the states were not prohibited from printing their own money), and create "a common treasury" from funds raised by taxes on the states to pay for the war. Whether the states were legally obliged to pay the tax levies was left ambiguous. Article VIII vested authority in the state legislatures to comply "within the time agreed upon by the United States in Congress assembled." For three years the vast majority of states had failed to pay their share of taxes to support the Continental Army, leaving a legacy of confusion about where the power of the purse ultimately resided. In the absence of a clear resolution in the Articles, it effectively resided in the states.[4]

In at least two other aspects, it was clear that the political framework created by the Articles was not designed to function as a national government. First, the proper model for a republican government had been established in the state constitutions, almost all of which followed the guidelines proposed by John Adams in his *Thoughts on Government* (1776). The central ingredients in the Adams political recipe were a bicameral legislature, an elected or appointed governor, and an independent judiciary, an early version of the separation-of-powers doctrine later embodied in the federal Constitution. The structure of the Articles—a single-house legislature and an appointed but powerless president—dispensed with all the political wisdom that had accumulated in the states about a properly balanced republican government, because, in truth, that is not what the Articles were intended to be.[5]

Second, there was no way the Confederation Congress could claim to be a representative body. Article V put it succinctly: "In determining questions in the United States in Congress assembled, each State shall have one vote." This meant, in effect, that Rhode Island, the smallest state, had the same political power as Virginia. The one-state-one-vote principle represented a continuation of the practice followed in the Continental Congress, which had come into existence in 1774, before the debates over state constitutions occurred and before the commitment to proportional representation in the state legislatures had become an accepted, indeed essential, constitutional feature. By rejecting proportional representation, the architects of the Articles were making a clear statement that they did not intend the Confederation Congress to function as a national government once the war was won. The closest approximation in our own time is the European Union.[6]

—— ∞ ——

It was not always so. During the first fifteen months of the war, from the outbreak of hostilities at Lexington and Concord in April 1775 to the Declaration of Independence in July 1776, the Continental Congress had functioned as a provisional national government, exercising control over military strategy, diplomacy, and economic policy much in the manner of a fully empowered federal government. To be sure, these were heady times, when the all-consuming character of the political and military crisis literally forced the delegates in Congress to assume emergency powers, and to do so in a political environment so saturated with patriotism that dissent was tantamount to treason. In this exuberant moment, when all political disagreements were enveloped within the protective canopy of "The Cause," it became possible to believe that the wartime alliance was symptomatic of something much larger and more permanent. The Philadelphia physician and revolutionary gadfly Benjamin Rush said it out loud: "We are now a new Nation . . . dependent on each other—not totally independent states." The war for American independence had also become, at least in some minds, a war for American nationhood.[7]

But Rush's national vision proved to be a temporary infatuation. Until independence was officially declared on July 2, 1776, then announced to the world two days later, there was enormous pressure to sustain a united front. The cracks and fissures in that front appeared for all to see in late July and early August, when the delegates put themselves in a committee-of-the-whole format to debate the character and shape of the new government for the recently created United States. That debate proved to be a preview of coming attractions, exposing the latent sectional and ideological differences that would haunt the American experiment well into the next century.

The debate focused on a document written by a committee of

twelve delegates in June, prior to the vote on independence, and chaired by John Dickinson, the leader of the moderate faction in Congress. Called the Dickinson Draft, it is an elusive text that has caused several generations of historians to throw up their hands in frustration, because Dickinson attempted to synthesize the competing convictions of a large committee that harbored fundamentally different ideas about what the emergent American republic should look like. The Dickinson Draft is, in truth, one of the most revealing documents of the revolutionary era, not in spite of but because of its intellectual incoherence. For what Dickinson attempted to achieve was a political compromise between those who wanted a state-based confederation and those who wanted a federal government with enumerated powers over the states. In other words, Dickinson tried and failed to do in the summer of 1776 what James Madison and his Federalist colleagues succeeded in doing in the summer of 1787.[8]

No official record of the debate exists because none was kept. Fortunately, both John Adams and Thomas Jefferson kept extensive notes on the deliberations, which occurred between July 22 and August 20. This meant that they coincided with the looming British invasion of Long Island. Despite that distraction, the political issues at stake got the attention of the most prominent delegates, including John Adams and Benjamin Franklin. Ironically, Dickinson himself was absent, having gone to command his militia unit in New Jersey in anticipation of the British attack in New York.[9]

The debate exposed three fundamental disagreements: first, a sectional split between northern and southern states over slavery; second, a division between large and small states over representation; and third, a more general argument between proponents for a confederation of sovereign states and advocates for a more consolidated national union. There was considerable overlap between the second and third arguments, since defenders of the one-state-one-vote principle were implicitly rejecting the viability of a nation-size republic.

Slavery was too volatile a subject to be addressed directly; indeed, there was an unspoken policy of silence surrounding the topic based on the broadly shared sense that it, more than any other issue, possessed the potential to destroy the political consensus that had formed around independence. But slavery was too embedded in the economy of the southern states to avoid altogether, and it came up, albeit obliquely, during debate over Article XII of the Dickinson Draft, which proposed that "the expenses for the war and the general welfare shall be defrayed out of a Common Treasury, which shall be supplied by the several colonies in proportion to the Number of Inhabitants of every Age, Sex and Quality, except Indians." An argument then ensued over how to count "Inhabitants," which soon became an argument over slaves: Were they persons or property?[10]

The delegates from the southern states insisted that slaves were property, like horses and sheep, and therefore should not be counted as "Inhabitants." Franklin countered this claim with an edgy joke, observing that slaves, the last time he looked, did not behave like sheep: "Sheep will never make any insurrections." The South Carolina delegation, which did not find this funny, then issued the ultimate threat. If the northern states insisted on this point, "there is an End of the Confederation."

In response to this threat of a southern secessionist movement, Samuel Chase of Maryland urged all delegates to calm down, then proposed to insert "white" before "Inhabitants" in order to appease his southern brethren. But the northern delegates, led by Adams, objected strenuously to this change, accusing South Carolina of attempting to avoid its fair share of the tax burden to finance the war. In a thoroughly sectional vote, Chase's amendment was defeated.[11]

In the long view, which is to say looking down the road another eight decades or so, this debate proved prophetic. It was the first occasion when the intractable dilemma posed by slavery found its way into the public record. And in 1861 South Carolina acted on the same secessionist threat it first made in the summer of 1776. More immediately, both northern and southern delegates recognized the need to deflect the "Inhabitants" question, and they revised the Dickinson Draft so that each state would be billed "in proportion to the value of all land within each state," thereby skirting the slavery question but in the process producing a criterion for taxation that proved inherently immeasurable and infinitely manipulable by the state legislatures.

If the debate over slavery had enormous long-term implications, the debate over representation posed more pressing problems that defined the shape of the political settlement for the next decade. Here the argument was not sectional but rather between large and small states. Article XVIII of the Dickinson Draft proposed a continuation of the one-vote-per-state principle. Delegates from Massachusetts, Virginia, and Pennsylvania found that principle preposterous, indeed a recipe for chaos and endless bickering, because the disproportionate political power of the small states defied the economic realities: "Let the small colonies give equal Money and Men," Franklin argued, momentarily forgetting that the colonies were now states, "and then have an equal vote." Adams chimed in that the only sensible basis for representation was population, because any stable republican government needed to reflect the will of its citizenry.[12]

Both Franklin and Adams were thinking of a new government that was more potent and unified than a mere confederation. The most ardent advocate for such a vision was Rush, who projected a national picture of Americans as "a single people," no longer Virginians or Rhode Islanders, and the term *United States* as a singular rather than plural noun. The debate over representation had thus exposed the first serious split between nationalists and confederationists.

Delegates from the small states found Rush's national vision a political nightmare that merely exchanged the despotic power of Parliament for a domestic version of the same leviathan. Roger Sherman of Connecticut led the small-state delegation with a warning that his constituents would never surrender their liberties to some distant government that did not share their values. He could testify

that Connecticut would passionately embrace "The Cause," but once
the war was won, his country was Connecticut, and any loyalty that
extended beyond the borders of his state defied the local and at most
regional orientation of his constituents, which was "as far as we are
prepared to go."[13]

This was a revealing way to put it. Beneath the argument between
large and small states over representation lurked a more fundamental
disagreement about distance and scale. The vast majority of Americans lived and died locally. Representative government as they experienced it was a face-to-face affair. So that above and beyond—or
rather beneath and beyond—questions of political architecture lay
a residual psychological reality that was severely circumscribed and
that imposed geographic limits on the political imaginations of the
vast bulk of ordinary Americans. Feeding into the small-scale perspective were all the political arguments that colonists had thrown
at the British ministry from 1765 to 1775, stigmatizing parliamentary
power as illegitimate because it was distant and disconnected from
their local and state interests. The greater the distance, in effect, the
greater the distrust. The geographic boundaries of a state, as Sherman had so nicely put it, were as far as they were prepared to go. A
decade later, this apprehension about governments beyond immediate surveillance became the primal source of Antifederalist opposition to the Constitution, and it was unquestionably the perspective
of most American citizens.

Almost as an appendix to the debate between nationalists and
confederationists was the debate over the ill-defined western borders
of states, like Virginia, with claims that reached to the Mississippi
or, even more preposterously, to the Pacific. There was a consensus
in the Congress that these extravagant claims were based on colonial
charters that had been drafted before anyone realized the size of the
North American continent. (One map put the Alleghenies within
one hundred miles of the Pacific.) Admission to the Articles of Confederation required a state to cede its territorial claims to western

lands, but left ambiguous how that cession would occur and whether the state could determine its own borders. This alienated the "landless" states, which worried that large states like Virginia, Pennsylvania, and New York would become even larger upon arrival. In an effort to assure his colleagues from Maryland that the Old Dominion would behave responsibly, Thomas Jefferson insisted that "no Virginian intended to go to the South Seas," an apparent reference to the Pacific. But only Virginians found this assurance convincing.[14]

Knowing as we do that these huge political and constitutional questions over sovereignty, slavery, and size would define the history of the emerging American republic well into the next century, the belief that these problems could be solved in a few weeks of earnest effort during the summer of 1776 seems unrealistic in the extreme. Looking back from the edge of the grave over forty years later, Adams recalled that it was "a standing miracle" that the delegates could agree on anything:

> The colonies had grown up under conditions so different, there was so great a variety of religions, they were composed of so many different nations, their customs, manners, habits had so little resemblance, and their intercourse had been so rare, and their knowledge of each other so imperfect, that to unite them in the same principles in theory and the same system of action, was certainly a difficult enterprise.[15]

But that was not how he felt in the crucible of the moment. Adams was especially distraught to discover that the near-unanimous consensus on American independence was followed by almost total disagreement over how an independent American republic should be configured. "Thus we are sowing the Seeds of Ignorance, Corruption, and Injustice," he lamented, "in the fairest Field of Liberty ever appeared on Earth, even in the first attempts to cultivate it." It was distressing to realize that, beyond independence, there was no consensus on what being an American meant, or whether there was such a thing at all. For Adams it was especially distressing to witness such conspicuous failure "in the first formation of Government erected by the People themselves on their own Authority, without the poisonous Interposition of Kings and Priests." There was, to be sure, such a thing as "The Cause," but the glorious potency of that concept did not translate to "The People of the United States."[16]

—— ⌒∞∞⌒ ——

The debate over the Dickinson Draft was simultaneously revealing and inconclusive, the former because it exposed the severe limits that would be imposed on any robust expression of federal power, the latter because final resolutions on all the controversial questions had to be deferred. The delegates in the Continental Congress could not afford to sustain focus on the unresolved political issues because in late August and early September the Continental Army suffered a series of devastating defeats on Long Island and Manhattan that put its very survival at risk. It made no sense to debate the future shape of the American government if the Continental Army was annihilated, rendering any independent American future highly problematic.

Over the course of the next year, from the fall of 1776 to the fall of 1777, the primary focus of the Continental Congress, again for understandable reasons, remained the war. With the exception of George Washington's splendid victories at Trenton and Princeton, General William Howe and the British army dominated the battlefield, producing victories at Brandywine and Germantown that led to the capture and occupation of Philadelphia, which prompted the flight of the Continental Congress (as Adams put it, "like a covey of pigeons") to York, Pennsylvania. Revisions of the Dickinson Draft had to take a backseat to the pressing imperative of sustaining the Continental Army and not losing the war.

But despite those rather essential distractions, revisions of the Dickinson Draft proceeded apace. And all the revisions reduced the prospective power of any central government. Article XIX of the Dickinson Draft, for example, had contained language that might be interpreted to give the Confederation Congress authority over foreign policy. It was dropped. The Dickinson Draft gave the Congress ultimate authority in resolving questions about western borders. This was blurred. And the inherent ambiguity of the Dickinson Draft on the question of state versus federal sovereignty was clarified in an amendment by Thomas Burke of South Carolina: "Each state retains its sovereignty, freedom and independence, and every Power, Jurisdiction, and right, which is not by this confederation expressly delegated to the United States in Congress assembled."[17]

The final draft of the Articles of Confederation that was sent to the states in November 1777, then, had been cleansed of any language that envisioned the existence of an American nation-state after the war. To be sure, the Dickinson Draft had always been a tortured document that leaned toward a state-based confederation. And it was always clear that the vast majority of Americans did not regard the war for independence as a movement for American nationhood, to the extent they gave the matter any thought at all. The final draft of the Articles of Confederation, then, merely confirmed and institutionalized that conviction.

When the Articles were sent to the states, the letter accompanying the document urged ratification more as a wartime measure than as any commitment to a future American union. Failure to ratify, the letter warned, would send a signal of weakness to the British government, which would then redouble its military effort, thereby forcing America "to bid adieu to independence, to liberty, to safety." Even the states that swiftly ratified submitted amendments, nearly a hundred, most designed to protect local and state interests from federal encroachment. The Congress simply ignored them, but they constituted another sign that whatever pretensions for a national union might have existed in the early months of the war had wholly evaporated as the conflict drew to a close.[18]

Then there was the matter of the army, along with the Continental Congress the other institutional projection of collective commitment with national implications. As the war dragged on, the same centrifugal forces that moved political power from the Congress to the states also undermined popular support for the Continental Army. Over two hundred years later, when paintings, films, and histories remind us of the deplorable conditions endured by ordinary men to win American independence—and most of the images and words are utterly accurate—it is difficult to recover the combination of abuse and neglect directed at the Continental Army by most of the American citizenry at the time.[19]

There are two enormous and overlapping ironies at work here, which taken together represent a central paradox of the American Revolution: namely, the two institutions that made victory in the war for independence possible, the Continental Congress and the Continental Army, represented a consolidated kind of political and military power that defied the republican principles on which the American Revolution was purportedly founded. If we wished to push this line of argument to its logical limit, we would say that the ideological and emotional hostility to any conspicuous and centralized expression of political authority rendered a viable American nation inherently incompatible with the goals of the American Revolution.

The military side of this story had its origins in the fall of 1776. The American debacle on Long Island and Manhattan prompted a conference among Washington, his staff, and a delegation from the Congress. It was now clear for all to see that the Continental Army, as currently configured, was no match for the combined force of the British army and navy. Washington insisted, and the civilian delegates agreed, that there needed to be a "New Establishment," consisting of an American army three times larger than the current fifteen-thousand-man force, with enlistments to last three years or, better yet, "for the duration." Given the overall size of the American population, Washington argued that he was asking for only a fraction of what was demographically possible, meaning that the number of American males available for military service was several times larger than what was needed to overwhelm the British army. If provided with such a large, enduringly dedicated force, Washington and his staff believed they could end the war in a year.[20]

In October 1776 Congress approved all the requests. But when President John Hancock sent the troop quotas to the respective state legislatures, they were regarded as requests, and none of the states complied. What was militarily necessary was clear, but what was politically impossible was clearer. The states, after all, needed to protect their own people, best done with militia, often paid at a higher rate than soldiers in the Continental Army. As for the creation of a cadre of Continentals committed to service "for the duration," that smelled distinctly like a "standing army" in the British mode, which the American Revolution was designed to destroy. The hard core of the Continental Army was eventually comprised of misfits—indentured servants, recently arrived immigrants, emancipated slaves, unemployed artisans. The vast majority of "the soldiery," as Washington called them, were one-year enlistees who came and went like transients, an army of amateurs.

Washington's reports from the field became a litany of lamentations: bemoaning the lack of food, clothing, shoes, ammunition; warning that the one-year enlistments put the very survival of the army at risk on an annual basis; urging the necessity of a larger army of veteran troops who could assume the offensive instead of fighting a purely defensive war. But the unspoken and unattractive truth was that the marginal status of the Continental Army was reassuring for the vast majority of Americans, since a robust and professional army on the British model contradicted the very values it was supposedly fighting for. It had to be just strong enough to win the war, or perhaps more accurately not lose it, but not so strong as to threaten the republican goals the war was ultimately about.[21]

Beginning in 1780, Washington went on the offensive, claiming that the lack of support for the Continental Army was a direct consequence of the failure of the Continental Congress to impose its will on the states. "Certain I am," he warned, "that unless Congress speaks in a more decisive tone; unless they are vested with powers by the several states competent to the great purpose of War . . . , that our Cause is lost. . . . I see one head gradually changing into thirteen." Over and over he repeated the refrain that a confederation of sovereign states, almost by definition, lacked the unity of purpose necessary to win the war: "In a word, our measures are not under the influence and direction of one council, but thirteen, each of which is actuated by local views and politics." As a result, "we have become a many-headed Monster, a heterogeneous Mass, that never will Nor can steer to the same point." Though his own personal honor was obviously invested in the eventual triumph of American independence, he wanted it placed in the record that "if we fail for want of proper exertions in any of the State Governments, I trust the responsibility will fall where it ought, and that I shall stand justified to the Congress, to my Country, and to the World." If a potent Congress and powerful army were, in fact, incompatible with the principles on which the American Revolution was based, then everyone needed to realize that the war could not be won, and all those principles would prove meaningless.[22]

Despite his own personal preference for political unity vested in the Continental Congress, in 1777 Washington started writing a series of "Circular Letters to the States." It had become obvious that the power of the purse now resided in the state governments, and if he wanted to lobby for longer enlistments and money to give his troops shirts and shoes, the governors and legislatures of the states were the proper place to direct his attention. Doing so was itself a statement about the increasingly diffuse political realities that the protracted conflict had created. The survival of the Continental Army was now dependent on persuading thirteen provinces, each of them divided into multiple counties and towns, to act together.[23]

If there was any doubt in Washington's mind whether the center was going to hold—and there was—there was no doubt in anyone's mind about who was the one-man centerpiece of the American Revolution. Even before independence was declared, Washington had become the chief symbol of resistance to British rule.

It helped that he looked the part. Biographers do not agree about his height.* But all concur that he was a full head taller than the average male of his time, a physical specimen at just over two hundred pounds, who was also reputed to be the finest horseman in Virginia. In his youth he had earned fame during the French and Indian War for surviving the massacre at the Monongahela in 1755, when the British army under General Edward Braddock was ambushed outside modern-day Pittsburgh and Washington lived to tell the tale, despite bullet holes in his coat and hat and two horses shot out from under him. He then parlayed his military reputation into marriage with Martha Custis, the wealthiest widow in Virginia, which propelled him into the upper ranks of the Tidewater aristocracy.

He was a literate but not well-read man. Adams had gone to Harvard, Jefferson to William and Mary, but Washington had gone to war, meaning that his education possessed a more primal quality that aligned itself nicely with his commanding physical presence. He

---

* The tour guides at Mount Vernon say six foot two, but when measured for his casket after death he was listed at six foot three and a half inches.

was not well versed in the constitutional arguments about Parliament's limited authority over the American colonies, often deferring to his neighbor George Mason on such questions. His own encounter with British imperialism had been more personal and palpable, based on his experience with the London mercantile house Cary & Company, which he believed was bleeding him to death by charging extravagant fees for its services. For Washington, the imperious face of the British Empire was not Parliament but Robert Cary and his band of London merchants, whose profits were driving the entire planter class of Virginia into bankruptcy. Washington's towering ego could not stand the realization that his very fate was in the hands of British creditors an ocean away, who were manipulating interest rates—or so he believed—in a massive imperial swindle.

His hostility to British authority, then, had a personal edge. While he understood and endorsed the political arguments about American rights, such arguments struck him as abstractions. His grievances were more palpably economic and even emotional. He was similarly indisposed toward proposals by moderates in the Continental Congress to make plaintive appeals to the presumed generosity of George III, which struck him as deferential confessions of inferiority, a self-defeating tactic that did not accord with his own sense of superiority.

Not the kind of man to suffer fools gladly, he ran his plantation at Mount Vernon imperiously and assiduously, always on the lookout for laziness among his overseers; he was not someone you would want to work for. He had once applied for a commission in the British army and been turned down—imagine the course of American history if the British had accepted him—but he interpreted his rejection not as a measure of his worth but as a statement of British stupidity. Both physically and psychologically, he was a formidable figure, and at forty-three years he was at the peak of his powers.[24]

When he set out from his beloved Mount Vernon in May 1775 to attend the Continental Congress, he had no way of knowing that he would be appointed commander in chief of the Continental Army. (Or did he? Why else did he wear his military uniform, the only delegate to do so?) What he did know beyond much doubt was that the ten-year constitutional conflict with Great Britain was about to become a war; indeed, it had already started a month earlier at Lexington and Concord. While a majority of delegates in the Continental Congress continued to grope for a political solution to the crisis, Washington knew in his bones that none would be found. He left instructions with his plantation manager to remove his books and his wife, Martha (presumably not in that order), when British frigates came up the Potomac to burn Mount Vernon to the ground. Washington recognized from the start that he was risking everything he held dear by committing to American independence, and this over a year before Jefferson wrote the words that memorialized the patriotic pledge of "our lives, our fortunes, and our sacred honor."[25]

And honor, in a way that is difficult for our modern minds to fully appreciate, animated his every thought and feeling. When he accepted the appointment as head of what soon would be called the Continental Army on June 16, 1775, he gave a speech making two points: he did not believe himself qualified for the position; and he would serve without pay. That evening he wrote his brother-in-law in the same vein:

> I am now embarked on a tempestuous Ocean from whense, perhaps no friendly harbor is to be found. . . . It is an honor I wished to avoid. . . . I can answer but for three things, a firm belief in the justice of our Cause—close attention to the prosecution of it—and the strictest integrity—If these cannot supply the places of Ability and Experience the cause will suffer & more than probably my character along with it, as reputation derives its principal support from success.[26]

He demonstrated the same pattern of postured reticence on two subsequent occasions: when he agreed to chair the Constitutional Convention and when he accepted the office of president. The pattern suggests that he had a problem acknowledging his own ambitions, always insisting that the summons to serve originated outside his own soul. But the decision to head the American army was especially poignant, because he knew that the British army and navy, taken together, was the most formidable military power on the planet, and the prospects for American success were dubious at best. There was no question in his mind about the moral supremacy of the American cause, but he was at the core a rock-ribbed realist who realized that a fervent belief in the worthiness of a cause was no guarantee of its ultimate triumph. He was lashing his life and, even more psychologically important to him, his honor to a vessel that was sailing into uncharted and troubled waters.

From the beginning, then, the war for Washington was an all-or-nothing wager. There were, to be sure, enormous political considerations at stake. He announced from the start that he regarded the Continental Army as subservient to civilian control, as embodied in the Continental Congress. This was done without much pondering, almost breezily, a decision that becomes significant only when one realizes that Julius Caesar, Oliver Cromwell, Napoleon Bonaparte, and Simon Bolívar never managed to make it.

There were also pressing strategic questions about how to conduct the war. It took him more than a year to gain control over his own aggressive instincts, which nearly proved a fatal liability in the New York campaign. Eventually he realized that a defensive strategy, called a war of posts, was the preferred course, even though it defied every fiber of his being. His seminal strategic insight, which seems obvious in retrospect, was that he did not need to win the war. The British needed to win. He would win by not losing, which in practice meant keeping the Continental Army intact as the institutional embodiment of American independence. After the debacle in New

York in 1776, survival became his central mission, more important than besting the British army on the battlefield, where he was often outmaneuvered. (Indeed, no successful American general ever lost so many battles.) His greatest gift was resilience rather than brilliance, which just happened to be the quality of mind and heart that the American cause required.

All his energies and ambitions, both of which were bottomless, were fully invested in winning, or rather in not losing, the war, so that his iconic demeanor became a kind of personal signature about the inevitability of the eventual outcome. Within the Confederation Congress, then the state legislatures, then below them the county and town governments, there was a veritable cacophony of voices about what American independence, once achieved, would mean. And the further down you went, the more democratically you dove, the more diverse and dissonant the voices became. The only subject on which all those voices could agree was that, whatever the American Revolution meant, Washington epitomized it. He was, as the toasts in his honor put it, "the man who unites all hearts."[27]

Even though his commitment to civilian control of the military never wavered, Washington's deference to his civilian superiors did not deter him from lecturing them on the inadequacy of the confederation created by the Articles. The vantage point from which he viewed the pathetic powers of the Congress was, of course, distinctive, since he was always asking it for financial support that it was inherently incapable of providing. The disappointing direction of the dialogue became so predictable that Washington came to regard the ongoing conversations as a running joke: "The Army, as usual, is without pay; and a great part of the Soldiery without Shirts, and if one was to hazard for them [Congress] an opinion, it would be that the Army had contracted such a habit of encountering distress and difficulties, and of living without money, that it would be impolitic and injurious to introduce other customs to it."[28]

But he began to use his Circular Letters as occasions to lecture as well as joke. Even before the decisive victory at Yorktown, Washington was thinking about the postwar world. And his major concern was that the same structural problem that blocked support for the army—in effect, a confederation designed to be weak at the center—would have dire, indeed calamitous, consequences after independence. As he put it in a letter to the president of Congress:

> I am decided in my opinion, that if the powers of Congress are not enlarged, and made competent to all *general purposes,* that the Blood which has been spilt, the expense that has been incurred, and the distress that have been felt, will avail in nothing; and that the band, already too weak, which hold us together, will soon be broken; when anarchy and confusion must prevail.[29]

There is no question that Washington wanted the newly independent United States to become a republic in which consensus rather than coercion was the central political value. But he wanted that republic to cohere as a union rather than as a confederation of sovereign states. In his capacity as commander in chief, he could testify that the confederation model nearly lost the war. And if it persisted in its current form, he believed that it would lose the peace.

———⚌———

In June 1783 he sat down to compose his last Circular Letter to the States. Though a man of action more than words, on this occasion he offered a truly panoramic assessment of why the just-concluded war for independence could also be called the American Revolution, and why the consolidation of its revolutionary energies required a national government capable of orchestrating those energies. It was the most profound political statement he ever wrote.

In his visionary appraisal, the newly arrived American republic was the beneficiary of two extraordinary pieces of good fortune, the first a function of time and the second of space. On the time side, the United States came into existence during an era "when the rights of mankind were better understood and more clearly defined, than at any former period." Immanuel Kant had yet to coin the term *Enlightenment* to describe this chapter in Western history, but even without the convenient vocabulary, Washington clearly grasped the central idea: namely, that the American Revolution had happened at a truly providential moment. It occurred when a treasure trove of human knowledge about society and government had replaced the medieval assumptions—that "gloomy age of Ignorance and Superstition"—and thereby provided Americans with an unprecedented opportunity to construct a society according to political principles that maximized the prospects for personal freedom and happiness more fully than ever before. In effect, European thinkers over the past century had drafted the blueprint for a new political architecture, which was now readily available for Americans to implement. "At this period," he intoned, "the United States came into existence as a Nation, and if their Citizens should not be completely free and happy, the fault will be intirely their own."[30]

The problem with this prophecy was that its uplifting implications depended on the existence of a nation-state capable of enforcing a comprehensive version of political coherence. A confederation of sovereign states, the kind of league currently configured in the Articles, would not suffice. In that sense, Washington was implicitly arguing that the full potential of the American Revolution could be realized only if and when local, state, and regional alliances, which remained hegemonic, were subsumed within some larger purpose. Given the firmly lodged conviction—it was more a potent impulse than a mere idea—that any distant national government was, by definition, a hostile force, the potential of an American nation remained a utopian dream that few took seriously.

Washington was one of the few, and his expansive vision, which eventually came to be called Manifest Destiny, was continental in scale.

> The Citizens of America, placed in the most evitable conditions, as the Sole Lords and Proprietors of a vast tract of Continent, comprehending all the various Soils and climates of the World, and abounding with all the necessaries and conveniences of life, are now by the late satisfactory pacification, acknowledged to be possessed of absolute freedom and Independency. They are, from this period, to be considered as Actors on a most conspicuous Theatre, which seems to be peculiarly designed by Providence for the display of human greatness and felicity.[31]

By "the late . . . pacification," he was referring to the recently arrived Treaty of Paris (1783), officially ending the war and not so incidentally placing the western border of the United States at the Mississippi. The Americans had not only won their independence from the British Empire; they had also acquired an empire of their own.

No one quite knew what this enormous tract contained, apart from waves of impenetrable forests and clusters of virulently hostile Indian tribes, who had not been informed that, with a scratch of the pen in Paris, they had just lost the land they had been living on for several centuries. As a young man, Washington had explored and surveyed the eastern rim of this interior region, and as a reward for his service in the French and Indian War, he had been given nearly thirty thousand acres in what was called the Ohio Country. And like several other Virginians, including Thomas Jefferson, he was obsessed with the misguided idea that the Potomac provided the best access to the boundless riches on the far side of the Appalachian range, meaning that the town of Alexandria was destined to become the greatest port in North America.

More generally, over a century before Frederick Jackson Turner made western expansion the central theme in American history, Washington had realized that the occupation and settlement of the not-so-vacant land to the west would define America's domestic agenda for generations to come. When he was asked if he wished to do a grand tour of the European capitals—Paris, London, Rome, Vienna—he diplomatically declined, saying he preferred to visit Detroit, New Orleans, and the Floridas. Europe was the past. The American west was the future.[32]

And at least as Washington saw it, those western horizons fundamentally changed the chemistry of the political conversation by rendering the local and state perspectives of the current confederation pathetically provincial. To be sure, he was on record as a staunch advocate for a fully empowered federal government throughout the war, and he firmly believed that the failure to create such a government had severely handicapped the war effort, protracting the conflict and suffering unnecessarily. And he made no secret of his conviction that the Articles were a recipe for anarchy in postwar America, destined to dissolve his legacy of American independence into a confused constellation of at best regional sovereignties, vulnerable to the predatory plans of hovering European powers.

But now the almost inadvertent acquisition of a western empire created a collective interest that all the states shared. Throughout the war, the union of states had been held together, however tentatively, by the common goal of independence. Once that goal was achieved, the state governments were poised to go their separate ways, loosely confederated under the Articles. As Washington saw it, the west replaced the war as the common bond. How to manage this extraordinary asset was obviously the central question facing the next generation of American political leaders, and doing so required one to think nationally rather than locally.[33]

Washington was distinctive in his vision of a new nation, held together by a covenant to distribute the proceeds of a common trust that, truth be told, contained the most fertile land and some of the most untapped natural resources on earth. He was predicting that the imperatives of geography, which were apparently limitless, would overwhelm the imperatives of ideology, which were narrowly confined. Though history eventually proved him right, very few American statesmen agreed with him at the time, and the vast majority of American farmers, lacking the vision, were indisposed to look past the wooden fences enclosing their fields.

They were living in the moment, and that moment after the revolution imposed severe restrictions on the exercise of centralized political power that bore any similarity to the imperial power of the British rulers they had just vanquished. The state-based political architecture of the Articles accurately expressed the constricted convictions of that moment. Washington's vision was not about the moment but about the future. The great challenge was how to get there. For that would require replacing a political structure that was unequal to the task, a seismic step beyond the imagination of most Americans.

Chapter 2

THE FINANCIER AND THE PRODIGY

You are sure to be censured by malevolent Criticks and Bug Writers, who will abuse you while you are serving them, and wound your Character in nameless Pamphlets, thereby resembling those little dirty stinking Insects that attack us only in the dark, disturbing our Repose, molesting and wounding us while our Sweat and Blood is contributing to their Subsistence.

Benjamin Franklin to Robert Morris
JULY 26, 1781

$\mathcal{J}$f anyone harbored the hope that the recently ratified Articles would function as a viable American
government, that hope was exposed as an illusion in the first year of
its existence. The most glaring problem was attendance.

At the first session of the Confederation Congress, it was decided
that nine states constituted a quorum, with two delegates necessary
for a state to qualify as present. But on multiple occasions throughout the spring and summer of 1781, no official business could be done
because five or more state delegations were either absent altogether
or only partially represented. Part of the problem lay with the state
legislatures, which were often slow to select their delegates; part of
the problem was that the leading candidates refused to serve, preferring to perform their public duties at the state level. John Witherspoon of New Jersey became the most frequent and vocal critic of
this sorry situation, waiting around with nothing to do because his
erstwhile colleagues had failed to show up, but the attendance problem accurately reflected the political priorities of the most prominent
American leaders. In truth, it would be misleading to say that local
and state concerns trumped the national interest, because in most
minds no such thing as the national interest even existed.[1]

A second source of systemic malfunction was the coordination
of foreign policy. All business came before the full Congress, an
unwieldy arrangement at best, rendered more maddeningly chaotic
because the membership of state delegations kept changing. When
Arthur Lee joined the Virginia delegation, for example, his inveter-
ate suspicion of Benjamin Franklin's ties to the French court—Lee,

it soon became clear, was suspicious of everyone, especially non-Virginians—split the Virginia vote on almost every foreign policy issue, essentially negating the largest state's voice.[2]

In the late spring of 1781 word arrived in Philadelphia of some grand European conclave, led by France, Russia, and Austria, that purportedly intended to put an end to the war and impose a peace based on the current status of forces. Diplomats cited the venerable doctrine of *uti possidetis,* loosely translated as "keep what you currently control," which at the moment meant the British could claim parts of New York and Virginia as well as the Carolinas and Georgia, where, all in all, there were still twenty-five thousand British troops on the ground. Nothing came of this typically imperious European initiative, and the Confederation Congress ought not be blamed for the communication problem posed by the Atlantic Ocean, but the political reality was that there was no decisive American presence in the foreign policy conversation apart from the peace negotiators in Paris, who, at least officially, took their orders from Congress.[3]

A third problem that emerged early was the resolution of the western land disputes, which had been festering for several years. Although the states claiming land in the region west of the Alleghenies had been required to cede their claims to the Confederation Congress upon admission into the union, many of the landed states, most especially Virginia, insisted on their right to determine the borders of their cessions, and also on the revocation of all Indian treaties signed by land companies within the so-called domain. The question at issue was whether the states or the Congress possessed ultimate authority to resolve the disputes.[4]

The clearest argument for congressional authority came from John Witherspoon. He observed that Great Britain had acquired the vast tract from the Alleghenies to the Mississippi in 1763 by winning the French and Indian War. Then the United States acquired the same territory by winning the war against Great Britain: "This controversy [the war for independence] was begun and carried on by the united and joint efforts of the thirteen states. By their joint exertions and not by any one State the dominion of Great Britain was broken, and consequently the rights claimed and exercised by the Crown devolved on all, and not any individual state." This meant that the western lands were a national domain effectively held in trust by the union of states created under the Articles.[5]

This argument made logical and legal sense to almost everyone except the Virginians, who were accustomed to thinking of the Old Dominion as an empire of its own, with the Ohio Valley and Kentucky as extensions of "greater Virginia." Even James Madison, the most nonprovincial member of the Virginia delegation, felt obliged to defend his state's claim to Kentucky's borders, though he opposed the threat of the Virginia legislature to revoke its previous cession. (Intriguingly, he wrote to his new friend, Thomas Jefferson, that Virginia's recalcitrance on the Kentucky question had best end soon, since he presumed that "the present Union will but little survive the present war.") Although the western lands would eventually prove to be a treasure trove that helped to create a collective interest among the states, at the outset arguments over its management had just the opposite impact, exposing the fault lines still existing between landed and landless states, and the lack of any common history in thinking nationally rather than as sovereign states.[6]

Vermont was hardly a part of the western domain, but arguments over its petition for admission as a state dominated the deliberations of Congress throughout 1781. What was originally called the New Hampshire Grants included land that three states—New York, New Hampshire, and Massachusetts—claimed as their jurisdiction, producing interstate bickering that the Congress could not resolve. Meanwhile, Pierce Butler of South Carolina regarded Vermont's petition for statehood as a power play by the New England states to enhance their influence in the Congress, a malevolent move by the "Northern Interest" contrary to the "Southern Interest . . . by which the sectional balance will be quite destroyed." If the Confederation

Congress was intended to function as a political platform where all the states came together to address their common interests, the Vermont question seemed uniquely designed to expose their mutual jealousies and suspicions. Vermont statehood was held hostage to these state and sectional hostilities for the duration of the confederation.[7]

But the most serious problems facing the not-so-united states, more ominous than all the others put together, was the ballooning debt. Under the Continental Congress the main source of revenue was the printing press, meaning that Congress mass-produced paper money in the form of dollars, called continentals. It also issued what it called certificates, which were promissory notes given to merchants and farmers as payment for food and clothing needed by the Continental Army. In short, apart from French loans, the entire fiscal policy of the Continental Congress was based on a massive hoax, which resembled what today would be called a Ponzi scheme.[8]

There was nothing to back the continentals and certificates because the annual requests for money from the states, called requisitions, had become laughably plaintive pleas that the state legislatures, with debts of their own to pay, simply ignored. In 1781, for example, the Congress requested $3 million from the states and received $39,138 in return. A standing joke within Congress was that the "binding Requisitions are as binding as Religion is upon the Consciences of wicked Men."[9]

Unable to coerce the states to pay their annual tax bill, since coercion smacked of Parliament's infamous Stamp Act, which had started all the trouble, in 1780 the Congress proposed what was called an impost as an alternative source of revenue. The impost placed a 5 percent duty on all imports—in effect an indirect tax, or perhaps a tax by another name. But once again the ghosts of the American Revolution haunted the conversation, since the impost was a domestic version of the Townshend Acts (1767), which the colonists had opposed as an overly clever way to tax them without their consent. For obvious reasons, the impost was controversial, and when the

Articles went into effect, no vote on it had yet been taken. Because the Articles contained a clause prohibiting the Congress from raising revenue, passage of the impost required the equivalent of a constitutional amendment, which meant unanimous approval of all the states, a near impossibility.[10]

Somehow the full implications of the fiscal crisis facing the government had been conveniently obscured before the Articles were ratified. At least the correspondence of the delegates to the new Confederation Congress registered a genuine sense of shock upon realizing that the exchange rate for the continental had fallen to 500 to 1, meaning that it was essentially worthless. They had also inherited a federal debt of between $30 million and $40 million, swelling each month because of interest payments. The president of the Congress, Samuel Huntington, sent a circular letter to the states in May 1781, apprising them that "our Northern Army is starving," and there was no way for the Congress to raise funds for their relief unless the states paid their requisitions in full.[11]

That was not going to happen. The unimaginable and, until now, unspeakable implication was that all those ardent and heartfelt soliloquies to virtue and "The Cause" were in the process of evaporating before the sordid reality of American bankruptcy. It was entirely possible that the war for independence could be lost because the American government was broke and was configured in such a way that rendered any resolution of the problem impossible.

—⟨∞⟩—

If there was no structural solution to the fiscal problem—indeed, the state-based structure of the Articles was the core of the problem—the only possible answer was personal leadership. That is, find the right man, vest him with the requisite authority, then trust in his judgment to balance the books and rescue "The Cause" and the Continental Army from disintegration. There was only one man eligible for this desperate mission, who happened to be the wealthi-est man in America. His credentials were entirely financial, meaning that he was a latecomer to the movement for independence, but he was an acknowledged genius at reading account books, understand-ing markets, and winning the trust of his creditors. For all these conspicuous talents, he had acquired the nickname "The Financier." He was also shrewd enough to realize that rescuing American fiscal policy from insolvency was a thankless task that no sane man would ever assume, a reluctance that rendered him even more attractive. His name was Robert Morris.[12]

For several reasons, Morris did not want the job. As he wrote in his diary soon after receiving the offer: "A vigorous execution of the duties must inevitably expose me to the resentment of disappointed and designing Men and to the Calumny and Detraction of the Envious and Malicious. I am therefore absolutely determined not to engage in so arduous an undertaking." He was probably remember-ing his earlier service on what was called the Secret Committee of the Continental Congress, where he and Benjamin Franklin had orches-trated a series of covert negotiations with French suppliers to pro-vide arms, food, and equipment for the Continental Army. Because France was still a neutral nation at the time, all these dealings were clandestine and exposed Morris to the charge (groundless, it turned out) of profiteering at the public expense. He was a big man in all senses—physically, economically, and socially in Philadelphia—and so was a conspicuous target for newspaper editorials questioning his integrity as a merchant whose profits came at public expense.[13]

Benjamin Franklin knew firsthand that all the accusations were misguided, that in fact Morris had actually used his own credit to underwrite loans that rescued the Continental Army from starva-tion in the early years of the war, probably losing more money than he made in the process. Writing from Paris, Franklin urged Morris to assume the responsibility for directing American fiscal policy, all the while realizing that no matter how well Morris performed, his decisions would be criticized and his very character vilified: "You are sure to be censured by malevolent Criticks and Bug Writers, who will abuse you while you are serving them, and wound your Character in nameless Pamphlets, thereby resembling those little dirty stinking Insects that attack us only in the dark, disturbing our Repose, molesting and wounding us while our Sweat and Blood is contributing to their Subsistence." No good deed, in short, would go unpunished.[14]

Morris brooded for four months before accepting the job of superintendent of finance in May 1781. "Pressed by all my friends, acquaintances, and fellow citizens," he explained, "and still more by the *necessity*, the *absolute necessity* of a change in our moneyed system, I have yielded and taken a load to my shoulder." He knew what he was up against because he possessed a clear vision of what was needed to restore public credit, and an equally clear recognition that what needed to be done collided head-on with the state-based political structure of the Articles. The majority of delegates in the Congress initially welcomed Morris as the Messiah and granted him unprecedented powers to deliver them from the financial abyss. Morris realized from the start that he would need to lead them in a direction that most delegates, and most Americans, were unprepared to go.[15]

Much like Franklin's, Morris's biography has an opening scene in which a teenage boy arrives in Philadelphia with little more than his wits and the clothes on his back and twenty years later has become the most prominent—in Morris's case, the wealthiest—citizen of the city. A century before the Horatio Alger story of rag to riches took hold in American mythology, Morris lived that story to perfection.[16]

Unlike Franklin, Morris was an immigrant, born in Liverpool in 1734, the son of a merchant and a woman, Elizabeth Murphet, who disappeared from his life soon after delivering him into this world. His father migrated to the Eastern Shore of Maryland soon thereafter, pursuing his vocation as a tobacco merchant. In 1747 he brought his son over to join him, but parental duties apparently bored him, or conflicted with his mercantile aspirations, so the thirteen-year-old Morris was sent to Philadelphia to serve as an apprentice with the shipping firm headed by Charles Willing. Eight years later, in 1757, at the tender age of twenty-one, Morris was made a full partner in Willing, Morris and Company, the largest and most lucrative mercantile house in Philadelphia.

How that sudden surge happened is not fully recoverable, but young Morris, who had no formal education and showed little interest in books, apparently possessed an uncanny instinct for the way markets worked. For example, when Willing was away on business, Morris learned that a drought in Europe had created a market for flour, and on his own he purchased all the available wheat crop in eastern Pennsylvania, which when sold as flour in Paris and Madrid yielded huge profits. Under his canny eye the company tripled the size of its shipping fleet, established agents in all the European capitals and throughout the West Indies, and made Morris a very rich man.

He cut quite a figure in Philadelphia society in the 1760s: tall, slightly over six feet, with a Celtic complexion and pale blue eyes. In 1763 his sexual ramblings produced an illegitimate daughter, whom he supported financially until she married. He never forgot his impoverished origins. Walking the wharves, he knew most of the workers on a first-name basis, and he did much of his business with a wineglass in hand at City Tavern, where the bartenders and waiters relished his arrival and the huge tips that always followed. In 1769 he married Mary White, who came from a prominent Maryland family, and built a baronial estate called The Hills just outside the city for his family, which eventually included seven children.

Morris supported the protests against the Stamp Act but, much like Washington, left the political theorizing to others. Although it hurt his business, he supported the nonimportation agreements as a more effective form of protest than constitutional arguments. Appointed to the Continental Congress in 1775, he sided with the moderate faction led by John Dickinson, which sought, as Morris put it, "to procure Accommodation on terms consistent with our just claims." By the spring of 1776, as the prospects for reconciliation dissolved, he grudgingly embraced the inevitability of American independence. He absented himself from the vote for independence on July 2, explaining that the war would prove ruinous for both sides, but then he signed the Declaration on August 2, probably the most reluctant signer in the Congress.

He then threw his full energies and his matchless list of European and West Indian contacts into the procurement of arms and equipment for the Continental Army. He came under criticism for mixing his own private accounts with public trades, thereby making a profit on the war. But the awkward truth was that Morris's credit in the international marketplace was a kind of gold standard that enhanced the purchasing power of the American government. Most of the money his firm made during the war came from the fleet of privateers he outfitted that captured British cargoes in the Atlantic and Caribbean, which Morris regarded as a splendid example of patriotism and profit in one seamless package.

When he accepted the call to put America's financial house in order, he was forty-seven years old. The portrait painted by Charles Willson Peale about that time reveals a man comfortable with himself, with the customary accoutrements of middle age on display— a receding hairline and expanding girth. In addition to an enormous fortune, he brought two convictions to the task at hand: first, a firm belief that patriotism and its intellectual accomplice, virtue, were less effective motivating forces than interest; and second, an answer to the question everyone was asking—what will hold the states together once the war ends? Washington believed the answer was the western domain. Morris believed the answer was debt.

He also brought a way of thinking about money that did not yet have a name. (The term *capitalism* did not appear until 1850.) The key concept in this emerging mentality was *credit,* a word derived from the Latin *credere,* meaning "to believe." Credit refers not just to the money you possess but also to what others believe you will be able to pay. One economist has described credit as "money of the mind," which focuses attention on the psychological dimension of a capitalistic marketplace. When Morris gave his note to a customer in Madrid or Kingston, for example, he seldom had the cash on hand to pay for the purchase, but he could make the trade because the customer believed he would eventually make good on his promise, when one of his many ships delivered its cargo somewhere else in Europe or the West Indies.

Credit multiplies the amount of money in circulation, thereby giving a capitalistic economy greater productive potential, while making it vulnerable to endemic "bubbles," when projections prove illusory, credit collapses, and market adjustment takes the form of a depression. Morris was able to avoid that fate by adroitly juggling his expenses and his sales and by making Willing, Morris and Company into a de facto bank, with cash reserves that allowed him to survive the inevitable cargo lost at sea.[17]

All this became strikingly relevant when the Financier took command of the American economy. For Morris's way of thinking was terra incognita for most southern delegates in Congress, especially the Virginians, who still regarded land, not money, as the ultimate measure of wealth, and for whom the manipulation of numbers on a balance sheet came across as some sinister form of magic, eerily similar to the calculations their English and Scottish creditors were employing to drive them into bankruptcy.

At the public level, Morris's chief task was to restore the credit of the United States government. (Actually, *restore* is not right, since nothing had existed beforehand to be restored.) He faced some pressing problems that required immediate attention, chiefly the deplorable condition of the Continental Army. But his main task, as he saw it, was to establish the credit of the confederation as a whole, as if it were a unified fiscal entity. His initial impulse was to think about his goal in personal terms, bringing his own reputation to the rescue of the republic. "My personal Credit, which thank Heaven I have preserved through all the tempests of the War, has been substituted for that which the Country had lost," he wrote to the governor of Virginia. "I am now striving to transfer that Credit to the Public."[18]

There was also an implicit but deeply nationalistic motive in his mission: namely, to persuade the marketplace, meaning the European bankers and governments, that the United States was fully capable of honoring its foreign and domestic debts and becoming a reliable presence in the global economy. For a man who was on record as doubting the wisdom of the war for independence, it was a bold transition from reluctant patriot to ardent nationalist. But he had made his living, and an enormous fortune, anticipating before anyone else where the market was headed. And he brought the same confidence in his judgment about the marketplace into the political arena, where nothing less than America's destiny was the crucial question. He was accustomed to making all-or-nothing wagers in his business and almost always winning the bet. He carried that same confident mentality into his new role as custodian of the unforeseen implications of the American Revolution.[19]

Morris's first act as America's Financier was to announce the creation of the Bank of the United States. Since most Americans did not know what a bank was, Morris published an explanation in the *Pennsylvania Packet*. He described the bank—modestly capitalized at $400,000, with shares selling at $400—as a first step in the direction of national solvency: "I mean to render this [bank] a principal Pillar of American Credit so as to obtain the money of individuals for the benefit of the Union and thereby bind those individuals more strongly to the general cause by ties of private interest." Left unsaid was Morris's assumption that he was overseeing a national economy and that the bank was an institutional embodiment of that fiscal reality.[20]

He began sending a series of circular letters to the states in which he apprised the governors that the annual requisitions were mandatory obligations, not charitable requests. "As to the complaint made by the People of a want of money to pay their taxes," he observed, "it is nothing new to me, nor indeed to anybody. The Complaint is I believe quite as old as Taxation itself, and will last as long." All of a sudden there was a decisive presence in charge of fiscal policy, declaring that the days of mounting debt and routinized recalcitrance were over. "It is high time to relieve ourselves from the Infamy we have already sustained and to rescue and restore the public credit," he lectured. "This can only be done by solid revenue. . . . We may be as happy or miserable as we please."[21]

He also launched an all-out campaign for passage of the impost, the equivalent of a national tax, which, for substantive and symbolic reasons, was the acid test of the union's viability. He apprised the governors that all the European bankers were watching the vote on the impost, and if it failed, they would plausibly conclude "that we are unworthy of Confidence, that our Union is a Rope of Sand, that the People are weary of Congress and that the respective States are determined to reject its authority." The fact that the vote had to be unanimous was obviously a political challenge, all the more reason that the states had to speak with a single voice, since the impost was an essential instrument in paying off the debt they all shared together.[22]

Upon entering office, Morris had announced that his eye was

focused on the long-term health of the American economy, and that he therefore was not going to divert funds to pay the army. However sensible this decision was fiscally, it soon proved politically and even morally untenable. Letters from Nathanael Greene, who was commanding slightly more than a thousand troops in South Carolina, described men who were literally starving to death and walking around in loincloths.

And then Washington apprised Morris that a providential version of the perfect storm was occurring: that the French fleet had sailed up from the West Indies to the Chesapeake, just as the British army under General Cornwallis, 7,700 strong, had placed itself on the Yorktown peninsula. There was now an opportunity to trap and capture the largest British force on the continent, but Washington lacked the resources to move the Continental Army and its invaluable French allies from New York down to Virginia. Morris wrote personal checks to provide rations and clothing for Greene's troops and to cover the costs of Washington's Yorktown campaign, believing that he would recover his losses when a cargo of silver from France arrived in Boston the following month. This was the kind of juggling act that he had practiced and perfected as America's premier merchant, now deployed to assure success in what proved to be the culminating battle of the war.[23]

Within a few short months Morris had made himself the most powerful figure in the American government, second only to Washington as a national leader. In August 1781, at the same time he was signing the check to fund the Yorktown campaign, he drafted a comprehensive financial plan that synthesized his thinking about the reforms necessary to move the American economy from bankruptcy to solvency. The plan included the national bank, the impost, a land tax, a poll tax, and an excise tax on whiskey, plus the assumption of state debts by the Confederation Congress. It was a financial blueprint for a fully national economy almost identical to the plan that Alexander Hamilton would propose a decade later. Morris was at the peak of his power, and he felt it. "I can obtain whatever is wanted for the public service by a Script of the pen," he boasted. Benjamin Rush concurred, calling Morris "a new star in our America hemisphere."[24]

This could not last. For Morris was attempting, on his own, to impose a national economic architecture on a political foundation that vested sovereignty in the states. Arthur Lee, whose ideological antennae were poised to detect any stirrings in the political atmosphere that disrupted his keen sense of republican purity, regarded Morris's financial reforms as the second coming of George III. "The accumulation of offices in this man, the number of valuable appointments in his gift, the absolute control given him over all revenue officers, his money and his art," Lee lamented, "render him a most dangerous man to the Liberty of this Country."[25]

Lee's appetite for personal vendettas was voracious, and he now shifted his sights from Franklin to Morris, rising in Congress to question Morris's apparently limitless power, eventually publishing a series of articles in the *Freeman's Journal* attacking Morris's character. "In fine, sir, is not the disbursement of eight million annually in contracts," Lee asked rhetorically, "is not the profit and influence arising from this, is not the hourly offerings of incense and adulation from surrounding parasites . . . sufficient to satiate your vanity, pride, and avarice?" Even though Morris was spending substantial sums of his own money to subsidize the army, Lee accused him of profiteering at the expense of the public, casting a shadow over Morris's reputation that, no matter how misguided, never completely disappeared.[26]

Meanwhile, just as Morris's relentless campaign on behalf of the impost seemed successful—eleven of the necessary thirteen states had ratified—a change in the Rhode Island delegation created an impasse. The new member was David Howell, a former mathematics teacher at Rhode Island College (later Brown) who shared Lee's hostile attitude toward Morris and held some "pure Whig" political convictions of his own with theological fervor. Howell acknowledged that his opposition to the impost was partly economic, chiefly the fact that the duties proposed would fall disproportionately on maritime states like Rhode Island. But more menacingly, the impost violated a core revolutionary principle enshrined in the Articles—namely, the sovereignty of the states, making them instead "mere provinces of Congress and tending to the establishment of an aristocratical or monarchial government." Indeed, Howell described the Confederation Congress as "a foreign government" and the impost an updated version of the Townshend Acts.[27]

Rhode Island had a long-standing tradition of independence that sometimes verged on eccentricity. And following Howell's lead, the legislature voted unanimously to reject the impost in November 1782. Morris was stunned, insisting that he was acting in accord with Article XIII of the Articles of Confederation, which granted Congress the authority to raise revenue from the states and thereby create "a common treasury" to pay for the war. He dispatched a three-man delegation to make this point to the Rhode Island legislature, but before the delegation could reach Providence, word arrived that Virginia had changed its mind and revoked its ratification of the impost. How this happened never found its way into the historical record, though the murky shadow of Arthur Lee hovers behind the scenes.

The death of the impost marked the end of Morris's swashbuckling phase as Financier. Despite his relentless circulars to the states, the revenue acquired by requisition remained only a small fraction of what was required. "I am so habituated to receive apologies instead of Money," he explained to one governor, "that I am never surprised. If Complaints of Difficulties were equivalent to Cash, I should not complain. But that is not the Case." To make matters worse, his personal fortune suffered when the British navy, in reaction to the Yorktown disaster, decided to shut down American shipping all along the Atlantic coast, in the process scooping up the lion's share of Morris's fleet. "What I had afloat has all been lost," he explained to a friend requesting a loan, then adding with a touch of the Morris wit that "the amount of that loss I will forebear to mention as there might be in it an appearance of ostentation."[28]

While no treaty ending the war had yet been signed, and there was a firm consensus in the Congress as well as in the all-important mind of George Washington that one more campaign would be required to break the British will for good, out there in the countryside there was a conspicuous decline in support for a war that was all but over. And support for Morris's fiscal policies declined as a consequence, because the driving force for national unity had always been the war for independence, not any larger sense of the collective interest. In a confidential letter, Morris even acknowledged that he harbored a secret hope that the war would not end: "But was I to confine myself to the language of a Patriot, I should tell you that a continuance of the War is Necessary until our Confederation is more strongly knit, until a sense of the obligation to support it shall be more generally diffused among all Ranks of American Citizens."[29]

This might strike us as an odd argument, but it followed naturally from the widespread conviction that the primary motive for an American union had been winning the war, and once that motive was removed from the political equation, the union ended and only a loose confederation of states remained. What then happened to that confederation was anyone's guess. The youngest member of the Virginian delegation, who styled himself James Madison, Jr., believed it did not bode well. "If our voluminous & entangled acts be not put into some certain course of settlement before a foreign war is off our hands," he warned, "it is easy to see they must prove an exuberant & formidable source of intestine dissentions."[30]

Madison, almost preternaturally shy and the second-youngest delegate in the Congress, had become one of Morris's staunchest and most effective supporters. In some respects he remained a loyal Virginian—for instance, voting against the Bank of the United States, since Virginia regarded all banks as mysterious places where you sent your money to disappear. But Madison possessed a meticulous mind that liked to digest and assimilate evidence and experience in the deliberative style of a scholar or, once he made up his mind, like a lawyer defending his client. In 1782 he was still making up his mind, evolving toward his eventual role as, next to Washington, Virginia's preeminent nationalist.[31]

⸺ ⚬⚭⚬ ⸺

One man whose mind was already made up, who at twenty-seven was the youngest delegate in the Congress as well as Morris's most ardent supporter, was Alexander Hamilton. Soon after Morris's appointment as superintendent of finance was announced, Hamilton had written him a lengthy, unsolicited letter. It was, as it turned out, a typical Hamiltonian document, sweepingly self-confident in both message and style, brimming over with facts and figures describing the deplorable conditions of the American economy, with a comprehensive outline of the proper fiscal policy to fix it. The solution required a national bank capitalized at $3 million, mandatory tax requisitions on the states that yielded $20 million annually, and a tariff on imports, all of which should prove sufficient to supply the army and retire the national debt within thirty years.[32]

Morris had never before encountered such overflowing financial wisdom from anyone so young, all the more remarkable because—this was why Morris regarded it as wisdom—Hamilton's fiscal vision coincided perfectly with his own. Old enough to be Hamilton's father, Morris immediately recognized a precocious presence and took him under his wing, a pattern that fit perfectly into what had already become the dominant theme of Hamilton's young life.

The following year Morris asked Hamilton to serve as tax collector for New York, a thankless and ultimately hopeless task that Hamilton found frustrating. Morris consoled him by explaining that he was up against impossible odds and a state infrastructure that had perfected the art of avoiding taxes: "The several states and many of their public offices have so long been in the midst of boasting superior Assertions, that what was at first an Assumption has advanced along the Road to Belief, and then to perfect Conviction; And the Delusion is now kept up by the Darkness in which it is enveloped." Hamilton should learn from this experience, Morris advised, sustaining his vision of a larger public interest, all the while dealing on a daily basis "with those vulgar Souls whose narrow optics can see but the little Circle of their selfish concerns." As it turned out, it was a lesson that came naturally to Hamilton.[33]

Like Morris, Hamilton was an immigrant, though his origins were both more impoverished and more obscure. We know he was born out of wedlock in Nevis in the Caribbean to Rachel Faucette Lavien, a woman of French extraction. Historians disagree about his date of birth and his paternity. Hamilton claimed he was born in 1757, but several pieces of circumstantial evidence point to 1755. He also claimed that James Hamilton, a luckless Scottish merchant, was his father, though there is reason to believe that a well-to-do merchant in St. Croix named Thomas Stevens, who later took him in, was his real father. His early childhood was a grim catalog of disasters surrounded by broken, embittered people, topped off in 1768 when his mother came down with a mysterious fever, which Hamilton promptly caught. They lay in bed together, treated with the barbarous bloodletting and heavy laxatives that were the medical science of the day, until Rachel died next to him soaked in her own blood, vomit, and urine. Any attempt to imagine the young Hamilton of that horrific moment as a prominent statesman in a land he had never seen defies credibility.[34]

He was rescued from tropical obscurity by a combination of sheer talent, boundless ambition, and a series of powerful benefactors who all came to regard him as a prodigy. The talent was first put on display while he was working for the St. Croix shipping business of Beekman and Cruger, where he dazzled his employers with his deftness at manipulating account books and his conspicuous competence as a thirteen-year-old clerk. His ambition appears in the first surviving letter in his correspondence, which ends, "I wish there was a war." The benefactor was Hugh Knox, a Presbyterian minister of Scottish origins with American contacts, who recognized special qualities in the young man. These became visible in public circles for the first time in an especially dramatic account Hamilton wrote of a recent hurricane, which became a local sensation for its verbal flair. Other St. Croix merchants helped subsidize his passage to Boston, and once released from his Caribbean origins, he never looked back. It was a perfect match. The prodigy had come to the land of opportunity.[35]

Hamilton was supposed to attend the College of New Jersey (now Princeton), but the interview with President John Witherspoon did not go well because Hamilton, ever audacious, insisted on completing his degree at his own pace, preferably within a year, which Witherspoon rejected as ridiculous. King's College (now Columbia) accepted him without stipulation, a fateful decision that placed him in New York, where his education would benefit from the presence of a burgeoning mercantile elite and a hyperactive political climate vitalized by a roughly equal number of Whigs and Tories with fundamentally different views about America's proper place in the British Empire. There is a famous scene in which Hamilton rescued Myles Cooper, the Tory president of King's, from a mob—a scene rendered particularly poignant because Hamilton was already on record as supporting the cause of American independence.

The first occasion where he unveiled his political convictions was an impromptu speech delivered to a large crowd on the New York commons in July 1774, in which he endorsed the Boston Tea Party, the boycott of British goods, and preparation for war. He followed up the following year with two essays, *A Full Vindication* and *The Farmer Refuted*, both of which were bravura performances demonstrating what became the trademark Hamilton style: an assurance bordering on arrogance; a slashing mode of attack that would one day make him the most feared polemicist in America; the capacity to control and incisively convey a large body of information; and a keen sense of where history was headed, in this case a prediction that war with Great Britain was coming and, even more prophetic, that the Americans would win it by unconventional tactics that eventually eroded the British will to fight. No one could believe that all this was coming from a nineteen-year-old college student recently arrived from the West Indies.

Physical descriptions of the young man begin to appear in the historical record about this time, depicting a five-foot-seven lad of fair complexion, auburn hair, and flashing eyes, deep blue or purple in color. Commentators tended to notice his conspicuous sense of self-possession, his unique combination of serenity and energy, and his ability to focus with such intensity on a text or piece of writing that he was oblivious to others in the room, often pacing back and forth muttering semi-silently to himself as if in a trance.

But his defining characteristic was the ability to mesmerize everyone in his presence with the speed and flow of his conversation, which was simultaneously dazzling and yet never theatrical in an overly ostentatious fashion. He came across as a man's man and a woman's man, meaning that he could dominate a brandy-and-cigars discussion of politics, then move across the room and flirtatiously commend the ladies on their dress or jewelry. Men found him admirable, clubby, and disarmingly potent. Women found him irresistible. All these contemporary accounts suggest a man to the manor born, when in fact Hamilton was a penniless immigrant of questionable origins, whose resources were completely within himself. The only conclusion to reach is that those resources were truly massive and that Hamilton was the poster child for the kind of merit-based natural aristocrat uniquely possible in America. He clearly came from further behind than any prominent member of the revolutionary generation.

The war that he had been looking for as a young adolescent found him as a young man. He joined the Continental Army in March 1776 as captain of an artillery company. Henry Knox, head of artillery, soon identified him as the finest officer under his command. Hamilton maintained discipline in his company during the catastrophic New York campaign, when it was breaking down all around him. (In the headlong retreat up Manhattan, Hamilton and Aaron Burr, future duelists on the plains of Weehawken, bonded in a narrow escape from death or capture.) Then the familiar Hamilton pattern repeated itself in March 1777, when Washington plucked him from the ranks to serve as an aide-de-camp at the rank of lieutenant colonel. He was twenty or twenty-two at the time, depending on which of his birthdays is used to calculate his age.

This was an auspicious but awkward promotion for Hamilton. All of a sudden, it placed him in the center of the wind tunnel, drafting general orders for Washington's signature and participating in the conferences among the general staff and in the nightly conversations within Washington's official "family" about military strategy and tactics. There is no way of knowing for sure, but the bulk of the evidence makes it probable that this was the time when Hamilton developed a pronounced sense of disdain for the competence of the Continental Congress, which was sustaining the Continental Army on life support. During the last four years of the war—a roller-coaster ride when the Continental Army nearly evaporated on several occasions—Hamilton reached the conclusion that a state-based confederation was inadequate for the conduct of the war and even more inadequate for the postwar peace.

But Hamilton also bristled under the duties of aide-de-camp, which forced his instinctive sense of superiority into a subordinate status within Washington's huge shadow. Starting in 1779, Hamilton began to badger Washington for an independent command in which he could lead troops in battle. There was a potent psychological impulse at work here, for Hamilton harbored a quasi-chivalric sense of war as a ritualistic test of his own manhood. He needed to risk death in order to prove to the world, and himself, that he was worthy. For two years Washington dismissed these requests as misguided, arguing that Hamilton was an invaluable member of his staff whose aspirations for personal glory needed to be subordinated to the larger purposes of the war.

Hamilton began his correspondence with Morris in April 1781, when he was on furlough from the army to marry Elizabeth Schuyler, daughter of Philip Schuyler, patriarch of one of New York's most prominent families. The fact that Hamilton was acceptable within that privileged circle is a testament to his mounting reputation but also to the more open-minded American society. Such a marriage would have been unimaginable in England or Europe. Orders then came for him to rejoin the army on its race toward Yorktown, along with Washington's reluctant agreement to give him a combat command during the battle. On the evening of October 14, Hamilton led a bayonet charge across a pockmarked landscape to seize a well-defended British redoubt. Among the first over the breastworks, Hamilton subdued a British officer, bayonet against sword. It was all over in ten minutes. He had finally gotten his piece of glory, and newspaper accounts embellished the story to make Hamilton the hero of Yorktown. The young immigrant had made himself one of the most famous men in America.

In between his marriage to Betsy Schuyler and his dramatic, almost scripted act of heroism at Yorktown, Hamilton had somehow found the time to dash off six essays purporting to describe the proper course for postwar America, a typically Hamiltonian act of presumption, since the outcome of the war at that stage was undecided. He announced its central message in his title, *The Continentalist*.

"When the war began," Hamilton acknowledged, "we possessed ideas adapted to the narrow colonial sphere, in which we had been accustomed to move, not of that enlarged kind suited to the government of an INDEPENDENT NATION." As he saw it, too many Americans had learned the wrong lesson from the American Revolution: namely, to avoid establishing any political institutions that even remotely resembled the British government against which they were rebelling. By overcorrecting out of fear of despotism, they had carried the country in the opposite direction, which now verged on anarchy. This fear of political power per se had reached epidemic proportions: "It is to this Source that we are to trace many of the fatal mistakes which have so deeply endangered the common cause." Here Hamilton mentioned the failure to provide for the Continental Army, which "had prolonged the war by several years."[36]

These errors were clear for all to see, as were the political and economic problems they were producing. Unless corrected, Hamilton wrote, they would haunt the infant republic, leading to "a number of petty states with the appearance only of union, jarring, jealous and perverse, without any determined direction, fluctuating and unhappy at home, weak and insignificant by their dissensions in the eyes of the nation." The core mistake was to vest sovereignty in the states rather than in a federal government empowered to oversee the economy, including collecting taxes and regulating commerce, and to manage the inevitable expansion of a continental empire. As Hamilton put it, "Americans needed to think continentally."[37]

That core mistake, currently embodied in the Articles, obviously had to be corrected, which should be the work of "those with the enlightened and liberal views necessary to make a great and flourishing people"—in other words, men like himself. But beyond the specific political reforms that would be necessary, there was also a grand illusion that had to be dispelled, which was another unfortunate by-product of the movement for independence: namely, the belief that political power itself was inherently evil and ultimately unnecessary, because virtuous citizens would internalize such a high level of sacrifice to the collective good that all forms of political coercion would prove superfluous. Hamilton unleashed all his political energy against what he regarded as the most seductive delusion generated by the patriotic rhetoric of the American Revolution:

> We may preach till we are tired of the theme, the necessity of disinterestedness in republics without making a single proselyte. . . . We might as well reconcile ourselves to the Spartan community of goods and wives, to their iron coin, their long beards, or their black broth; for it is as ridiculous to seek for models in the simple ages of Greece and Rome as it would be to go in quest of them among the Hottentots and Laplanders.[38]

A full year before he was elected to the Confederation Congress, then, Hamilton had developed a full-blooded vision of a truly national government to replace the Articles and the basic framework for the argument to justify that change. While Madison was still evolving in a national direction, Hamilton was already there. Part of the reason was his wartime experience, where the inadequacies of the state-based confederation were experienced on a daily basis in the form of periodic starvation and troops without shoes. Part of the reason was that as a recent immigrant with no long-standing loyalty to a particular state, Hamilton had no local or regional allegiance that needed to be overcome. (This was Madison's problem.) And part of the reason was Hamilton's distinctive personality, which instinctively regarded halfway measures as mere bromides, incremental acts that defied the aggressive core of his character. Whether Hamilton was charging a British redoubt or arguing about the full meaning of the American Revolution, he had to be out front. Nothing less was psychologically tolerable.

This all-or-nothing audacity posed problems, as he quickly learned when taking his seat in the Congress in July 1782. Upon arrival, he submitted a resolution, announcing that "the situation of these states is in a peculiar manner critical." The main problem was the mounting debt and, despite heroic efforts by the Financier, the obvious inability of the current government to restore public credit. There was but one answer, the resolution concluded, and that was to call a constitutional convention "to revise and amend the confederation." The delegates in the Congress promptly and without debate sent the resolution to a committee, which just as promptly buried it in a pile of papers, never to be seen again. Political combat, it turned out, was not like charging a redoubt, because a leader could get too far ahead of his constituents. This was a problem that would haunt Hamilton throughout the decade, for he was so far ahead of public opinion that his views were often discounted or ignored altogether.[39]

Hindsight allows us to see that Yorktown was the culminating battle of the war, but few if any political or military leaders at the time recognized that reality. Washington was especially outspoken on the need to maintain the Continental Army at full strength in order to meet a new British offensive. "The king will push the War as long as the Nation would find men or Money," he warned, because all members of the British ministry believed that "the Sun of Great Britain will set the moment American Independence is acknowledged." As a result, a full year after Yorktown the soldiers of the Continental Army—about ten thousand officers and men—were drilling every day at the main cantonment on the Hudson outside Newburgh, New York, waiting for the climactic battle that had, in fact, already happened.[40]

Long-standing grievances had been festering in the army for many months, and in January 1783 a delegation of officers headed by Alexander McDougall delivered a petition to Congress demanding their back pay, which was over a year in arrears; assurance that their promised pensions of half pay for life would be honored; and more generous rations and clothing allocations. McDougall's petition, which was signed by thirteen generals, painted a pathetic picture of the Continental Army—half-starved, poorly clothed, and apprehensive that, when the war ended, they would be disbanded and sent home as beggars. Then McDougall ended on an ominous note: "The uneasiness of the soldiers, for want of pay, is great and dangerous; any further experiments on their patience must have fatal effects." Congress needed to know that unless these grievances were addressed, the army might decide to mutiny.[41]

What happened next, called the Newburgh Conspiracy, has all the elements of a classic mystery novel, rendered more intriguing because of the multiple behind-the-scenes conversations that, for obvious reasons, never found their way into the historical record. The essence of the story, as best we can recover it, goes like this: the army was prepared to threaten mutiny in order to pressure Congress for its promised pay and pensions; Hamilton and Morris decided to use the crisis to generate support for reform of the Articles to permit passage of the impost and more vigorous tax collection; meanwhile, a faction in the army, led by Horatio Gates, Washington's chief bête noire, was prepared not just to threaten mutiny but to act on the threat. For our purposes, however, the significance of the Newburgh Conspiracy goes beyond the layered plotting and clandestine scheming that gives the story its seductive allure. The episode is also an airburst in the night that exposed the fault lines running through any projections of American nationhood as the war ended.[42]

The idea to manipulate the army's grievances to effect fiscal reform probably originated with Morris's assistant and best friend, Gouverneur Morris (no relation), a towering peg-legged raconteur whose reputation as a wit and ladies' man endeared him to both Morris and Hamilton. But the key player, once the scheme was hatched, was Hamilton, currently serving in the Confederation Congress, whose connections with the officers in the army and with Washington himself were impeccable. The chief problem was to maximize the threat posed by the army while controlling the explosive energies such a threat created. Hamilton explained to Washington that he was, once again, the indispensable man:

> It appears to be a prevailing opinion in the army that . . . if they once lay down their arms, they will part with the means of obtaining Justice. It is to be lamented that appearances afford too much ground for their distrust. . . . The claims of the army, assigned with moderations and firmness, may operate on those weak minds which are influenced by their apprehensions more than their judgments. . . . But the difficulty will be to keep a complaining and suffering army within the bounds of moderation. . . . This Your Excellency must effect.[43]

There was no doubt in Hamilton's mind that Washington was up to the task. Having spent four years working at his side, Hamilton could attest that "his virtue, his patriotism, and his firmness would never yield to any dishonorable or disloyal plans, that he would sooner suffer himself to be cut to pieces."[44]

Washington's massive probity precluded any possibility of making himself complicitous in any Morris-Hamilton plot. He sensed that, as he put it, "there is something very mysterious in this business." And later, when the full contours of Hamilton's scheme became clear, he lectured his former aide-de-camp on the impropriety of manipulating soldiers "as mere Puppets to establish Continental funds" and finally scolded, "The Army is a dangerous instrument to play with."[45]

But in response to Hamilton's initial solicitation, he expressed agreement on the two most substantive issues. First, the army deserved better treatment than it had received, and "the prevailing sentiment in the Army is that the prospect of compensation for past Services will terminate with the War." And second, the government under the Articles had to be revised: "For it is clearly my opinion that unless Congress possess powers competent to all general purposes, that the distresses we have incurred, and the blood we have spilt in the course of an eight year war, will avail us nothing."[46]

Washington played his role to perfection. He canceled a meeting of officers that had been called by the radical faction loyal to Horatio Gates, who were intending to vote on a proposal to mutiny by refusing to throw down their arms when peace was declared, or if the war continued, by refusing to fight. Instead, Washington scheduled his own meeting on March 16, and all five hundred officers showed up at a large auditorium called the Temple to hear him deliver what has come to be regarded as the most important speech of his life. Here is the most salient passage:

> But as I was among the first who embarked in the Cause of our common Country. As I have never left your side for one moment. . . . As I have been the constant companion and witness of your distress, and not among the last to feel and acknowledge your Merits. As I have ever considered my own Military regulation as inseparably connected with that of the army . . . it can be *scarcely be supposed* at this stage of the War that I am indifferent to its interests. And let me conjure you, in the name of our Common Country, as you value your own sacred honor—and as you regard the Military and National Character of America, to express your utmost horror and detestation of the Man who wishes, under any pretences, to overturn the liberties of our Country, and who wickedly attempts to open the flood Gates of civil discord, and deluge our rising Empire in Blood.[47]

The audience sat in frozen silence for several seconds after Washington had finished, momentarily obscuring their reaction to his words. Then Washington pulled out of his waistcoat a recently acquired pair of spectacles and said: "Gentlemen, you will permit me to put on my spectacles, for I have not only grown grey, but almost blind in service to my country." Several officers began to sob, then came a smattering of applause, then resounding applause, then a standing ovation. All prospects for a military coup died at that moment.

Within the long arc of American history, Washington's speech is significant because it prevented the American Revolution from descending the path taken by previous and future revolutionary movements, from republican ideals to military dictatorships. Which is to say that Washington did not do what Julius Caesar and Oliver Cromwell had done before him and Napoleon would do after him. In the crucible of that moment, however, the more immediate significance was that the army ceased to be a pawn in a plot to expand the powers of the Congress. The failure of the Newburgh Conspiracy meant that whatever dim prospects for a revision of the Articles it had created were now dead.

Henry Knox, trying to sound an upbeat note, proposed an elegantly simple solution. "As the present constitution [the Articles] is so defective," he observed, "why do not you great men call the people together and tell them so. That is, to have a convention of the states to form a better constitution." This suggestion must have generated a bemused smile from Hamilton, who viewed the political prospects from his cockpit in Philadelphia. He had reached the conclusion that even holding the current confederation together would prove "arduous work, for to borrow a figure from mechanics, the centrifugal is much stronger than the centripetal force in these states—the seeds of disunion much more numerous than those of union." He told Washington that the prospects for reform were bleak: "I fear we have been contending for a shadow."[48]

Washington wanted it to be known that he had done his level best to get the army what it justly deserved, and to register his rather conspicuous opinion that only a radical change in the Articles could permit that to happen. "No man in the United States is, or can be, more deeply impressed with the present necessity of a reform in the present Confederation than myself," he explained, "for to the defects thereof, and want of powers in the Congress may justly be ascribed the prolongation of the War and the current plight of the Army."[49]

The unattractive truth was that the arrival of the provisional treaty ending the war in April 1783 made the Continental Army superfluous, and the sooner it disappeared, the better. Congress eventually voted to provide full pay for five years for officers in lieu of half pay for life, but doing so was a purely rhetorical exercise, since there was no money in the federal coffers to pay anyone. Even that meaningless commitment generated widespread criticism, especially in New England, where returning officers were greeted with newspaper editorials describing them as blood-beaked vultures feeding at the public trough. At least in retrospect, the dissolution of the Continental Army in the spring of 1783 was one of the most poignant scenes in American history, as the men who had stayed the course and won the war were ushered off without pay, with paper pensions and only grudging recognition of their service. Washington could only weep: "To be disbanded . . . like a set of beggars, needy, distressed, and without prospect . . . will drive every man of Honor and Sensibility to the extreme Horrors of Despair."[50]

Morris could not tolerate the injustice of it all. So he agreed to pay all members of the army for three months, and since there were no federal funds to cover that expense, he spent his last days in office writing personal checks, called Morris notes, to the tune of $750,000 in today's dollars. This nearly bankrupted him, but it constituted a dramatic statement to his critics that he had never been in it for the money.[51]

Morris had already announced his decision to step down, declaring that "I will never be the Minister of Injustice," presumably referring to the shabby treatment of the army. More broadly, he had been overseeing an inherently dysfunctional fiscal policy. "To increase our debts while the Prospect of paying them diminishes," he caustically noted, "does not consist with my Ideas of integrity." Throughout his tenure as superintendent of finance, Morris had acted on the assumption that the United States were in fact bound together by a common debt incurred in the war for independence, and that bond created a common obligation to support a national fiscal policy. But it was now clear beyond any doubt that very few Americans shared that assumption. "I hope my successor will be more fortunate than I have been," Morris explained to Washington upon resigning, "and that our glorious Revolution may be crowned by those Acts of Justice, without which the greatest human Glory is but the Shadow of Shade."[52]

—❧—

As if to underline the growing sense of dissolution, when the provisional treaty arrived in Congress, a quorum did not exist to approve it, and no one was sure who had the authority to sign it as that body's official representative.

A dramatic sequel to this silliness then occurred in June, when three hundred soldiers from the Lancaster and Philadelphia barracks, dissatisfied with the Morris notes and demanding their back pay, refused to stack their weapons and instead marched on the Pennsylvania State House, where the Congress was sitting. Enjoying the support of the local residents, who dispensed free alcohol to the troops as they surrounded the statehouse, for several hours they peered into the windows at the delegates, shouted obscenities, and aimed their muskets at any delegate who protested the demonstration.[53]

Though rowdy, the troops remained nonviolent and eventually marched back to their barracks to the cheers of the assembled crowd. Hamilton was especially incensed at being the target of intimidation—in his highly refined code of honor, the troops had challenged his manhood. He wrote a blistering letter to John Dickinson, currently serving as president of the Pennsylvania Council, inquiring in belligerent fashion why the Pennsylvania militia had not been called out to disperse the mutinous troops. Dickinson explained that the militia might very well have joined the mutiny. This was probably true, but it did not satisfy Hamilton, who drafted a resolution, endorsed by the full Congress, that the inability of the Pennsylvania government to provide security for the delegates meant that the seat of the American government should move to New Jersey.[54]

That decision initiated a long odyssey for the Congress, first to Princeton, then to Trenton, then to Annapolis, and finally to New York, creating the impression of an itinerant traveler moving from boardinghouse to boardinghouse with no real home of his own. Hamilton bemoaned the appearance of such a transitory body, especially in the eyes of European powers already convinced that the infant American republic was likely to die in the cradle.[55]

But by midsummer 1783 Hamilton himself had given up the ghost. "There is so little disposition either in or out of Congress to give solidity to our national system," he explained to Nathanael Greene, "that there is no motive for a man to lose his time in the public service. . . . Experience must convince us that our present establishments are Utopian before we shall be ready to part with them for better." Not the kind of man to waste his time in noble but futile causes, Hamilton believed that he had done his best, just as Morris had done his best, but America was not yet ready for what they wanted. He was going back to New York, to his beloved Betsy and their infant son, where he could "begin the business of making my future."[56]

Once he had settled in with Betsy outside Albany, Hamilton conjured up his vision of an American people that seemed determined to repudiate its national destiny, no matter how hard he, Morris, and Washington had tried to persuade them otherwise:

We have now happily concluded the great work of independence, but much remains to be done to reach the fruits of it. Our prospects are not flattering. Every day proves the inefficacy of the present confederation, yet the common danger being removed, we are receding instead of advancing in a disposition to amend its defects. The road to popularity in each state is to inspire jealousies of the power of Congress, though nothing can be more apparent than that they have no power; and that for the want of it the resources of the country during the war could not be drawn out, and we at the moment experience all the mischiefs of a bankrupted and ruined credit. It is hoped when prejudice and folly have run themselves out of breath, we may embrace reason and correct our errors.[57]

One of the reasons Hamilton found the word *democracy* so offensive was because he realized that the vast majority of American citizens had not the dimmest understanding of what he was talking about.

Chapter 3

THE DOMAIN

There is as much intrigue in this State House as in the Vatican, but as little secrecy as in a boarding school.

John Jay to Lafayette
JANUARY 3, 1779

*T*here is a consensus among historians that the Treaty of Paris, though coming at the very start, can be regarded as the greatest triumph in the annals of American diplomacy. Its two cardinal achievements were the recognition of American independence and the acquisition of the eastern third of the North American continent—all the land south of Canada and north of Florida. If independence was the all-important principle, the western domain was the invaluable prize, for it immediately made the United States larger geographically than any European nation, with natural resources that defied comprehension.[1]

At a celebratory dinner in Paris for the negotiators of the definitive treaty, a French delegate proposed a toast to "the growing greatness of America," now poised to become "the greatest empire in the world." The British negotiating team seconded the toast, then with a wink added, "And they will speak English, every one of 'em." There was a shared sense among all the participants that the Americans had just won a lopsided victory, topped off by the acquisition of a landmass larger than England, France, and Spain put together. When Benjamin West, the American-born artist and a favorite of George III's, accepted a commission to paint the negotiators of the peace, the entire British delegation refused to show up, fearful of being memorialized for posterity as the losers of Britain's North American empire to an upstart American empire of its own.[2]

The man most responsible for this rather extraordinary achievement was John Jay. In part, Jay's influence was a function of chance and circumstance. Thomas Jefferson had declined the offer to serve on the American negotiating committee, citing the recent death of his wife. His replacement, Henry Laurens of South Carolina, was captured at sea and thrown into the Tower of London. John Adams was moving between Leyden, The Hague, and Amsterdam, trying to negotiate a loan from the notoriously tightfisted Dutch bankers. That left Jay and Benjamin Franklin to handle what Jay called "the skirmishing business." And a flare-up of gout caused Franklin to delegate most of the backroom diplomacy to Jay.

The most important meeting occurred on August 3, 1782, when Jay met with the Spanish minister, Count Aranda. It was diplomatically necessary to consult with Aranda because France was bound to Spain by treaty, and the American negotiators were under strict orders from the Confederation Congress "to undertake nothing in the negotiations for peace or truce without their [French] knowledge and concurrence." As Jay and Aranda bent over a map of North America, Aranda drew a line from what is now Lake Erie, south through central Ohio, and down to the Florida panhandle, near modern-day Tallahassee. Everything east of that line, Orlando declared, belonged to the United States, and everything west belonged to Spain. Jay did not need to draw a line. He simply pointed his finger at the Mississippi River.[3]

Jay immediately roused Franklin from his sickbed and declared that it had become clear that the long-term interest of America required that they disregard their instructions—he tossed his clay pipe into the fireplace for emphasis—and negotiate a separate treaty with Great Britain without any consultations with France. Franklin resisted, but Jay insisted. At stake was nothing less than the continental destiny of the American republic. Jay then proceeded to lead the American negotiations with the British delegation, making recognition of American independence and the Mississippi as the western border the two nonnegotiable items.[4]

When Adams came down from Holland, Jay had already composed a first draft of the treaty. After meeting with Jay for several hours, Adams recorded his stunned sense of agreement with everything Jay had done. "Nothing has ever struck me more forcibly or affected me more instinctively," Adams wrote in his diary, "than our entire coincidence of principles and opinions." Adams was most pleased with Jay's decision to bypass the French, despite the instructions from the Congress. "It is glorious to have broken such infamous orders," Adams declared, "or so it will appear to all posterity." Humility was not a natural act for Adams, but he went to his grave acknowledging that in the Paris peace negotiations, Jay was "of more importance than any of the rest of us, indeed of almost as much weight as all the rest of us together."[5]

Unlike Morris and Hamilton, Jay did not have to leap from impoverished oblivion to center stage. He was born into comfortable circumstances, the son of Peter Jay, a prosperous New York merchant, and Mary Van Cortlandt, a member of the city's Dutch aristocracy. Raised on a handsome estate in Rye on the coast of Long Island Sound, surrounded by books and enveloped in love, he enjoyed a privileged childhood. His older brother, James, who turned out a bothersome scoundrel, was sent to Edinburgh to study medicine, while Jay went to King's College. There he befriended Robert Livingston, brother of his future wife, the famously beautiful Sarah Livingston. After graduation Jay decided to pursue a career in the law and joined the circle of aspiring young New Yorkers destined to be divided over the issue of American independence.[6]

In the 1760s Jay endorsed the American protest of Parliament's right to tax the colonies, though he was uncomfortable with the mob demonstrations against the Stamp Act, regarding them as a disquieting threat to the established social order of which he was a part. As a delegate in the Continental Congress, he sided with the moderates, supporting American grievances while searching for a road to reconciliation. "This is an unnatural quarrel," he observed as late as January 1776, "and God only knows why the British Empire should be torn to pieces by unjust attempts to subjugate us." By April 1776, once it was clear that George III was committed to a military resolution that would take the form of an invasion of New York, Jay stepped over the line and never looked back. Like Franklin, he was late to the cause but all the more ardent once committed.

He became a leader in the provisional government of New York, drafting the resolution that made that colony the last to endorse the Declaration of Independence. The British occupation of New York in the fall of 1776 forced him to move his family to Fishkill. In this tense and dangerous time—British patrols and Tory gangs were roaming the countryside—his letters exhibited the otherworldly serenity for which he would become famous: "I am in a hot little room [in Poughkeepsie]," he wrote to Sarah, "and in defiance of the god of sleep, whom the bugs and fleas banished from my pillow last night, I sit down to write a few lines to my good wife." He simply presumed that he would never be captured or killed, just as he presumed that the British military triumph in New York was only a temporary setback and that American independence was inevitable.[7]

Early in 1777 he almost singlehandedly wrote the New York constitution, which vested more power in the executive branch than any other state constitution. The presence of the British army on New York's soil, he explained, demanded a government that could respond decisively and quickly to any sudden military threat. But Jay was also showing his true colors as a conservative revolutionary, a rare hybrid that simultaneously embraced American independence and endorsed political structures that filtered popular opinion through several layers of institutionalized deliberation before it became the law of the land.[8]

Elected to the Continental Congress in 1778, he was almost immediately chosen to serve as president. This kept happening to Jay, in large part because his peers viewed him as a man of principle who could be trusted even by those who disagreed with his principles. His massive probity, combined with his persistent geniality, made him impossible to hate. He lacked Washington's gravitas, Hamilton's charisma, and Madison's cerebral power, but he more than compensated with a conspicuous cogency in both his conversation and his prose that suggested a deep reservoir of learning he could tap at will. Permanently poised, always the calm center of the storm, when a controversial issue arose, he always seemed to have thought it through more clearly and deeply than anyone else, so that his opinion had a matter-of-fact quality that made dissent seem impolite.

In 1778 he was appointed to the Continental Congress to defend New York's claim against Vermont's petition for statehood. But Jay decided, upon reflection, that New York's case was petty and partisan, and that the larger interest of the confederation would be best served by accepting Vermont into the union. Despite pressure from the New York legislature, he would not budge from his conviction that the whole needed to take precedence over the parts, the first clear expression of his national orientation. Despite his best efforts, the Vermont question became a victim of gridlock in the Congress. As he put it with obvious disdain, "the issue was 'bitched' in its last as well as its first stages."[9]

His ten-month term as president of the Continental Congress convinced him that any coherent national policy was impossible within the confederation format. "There is as much intrigue in this State House as in the Vatican," he complained to Lafayette, "but as little secrecy as in a boarding school." Even before Hamilton had gone public with his criticism of the government under the Articles, Jay had concluded, on the basis of his experience in the Congress, that no state-based confederation could harness the full energies of the American Revolution once the war ended. As he saw it, there were really only two courses of action available: stay on the current path and witness "the Diminution of our Respectability, Power, and Felicity"; or create a government with sufficient powers to manage an ascendant American nation. That was the real choice, as Jay saw it, and all the petty squabbles within the Congress—over Vermont's status, Virginia's territorial prerogatives, the disproportionate impact of the impost on different states, even the payment of the federal debt—were just distractions, or perhaps symptoms of the deeper malaise. "I hope that the wheel turns round," Jay observed, meaning that the choice would be faced rather than finessed, "for I am persuaded that America possesses too much wisdom and virtue to permit her brilliant Prospects to fade away."[10]

Jay was also one of the first to recognize that America's prospects were inextricably linked to possession of the huge landmass between the Alleghenies and the Mississippi. During his presidency of the Congress, he had the audacity to apprise the unofficial Spanish minister, Don Juan de Miralles, that he regarded Spain as a hollowed-out European power destined to be overwhelmed demographically by the wave of American settlers sweeping across the North American continent. As for the Mississippi, any discussion of Spanish control was superfluous. "The Americans, almost to a man," he declared, "believe that God Almighty had made that river a highway for the people of the upper country to go to the sea." The clarity of his thinking about the nonnegotiable status of the Mississippi border during the peace negotiations was a product of his long-standing conviction about the significance of the western domain for American destiny.[11]

In 1779, four years before Washington declared his vision of a continental American empire, Jay had a vision of his own: "Extensive wildernesses, now scarcely known or exposed, remain yet to be cultivated, and vast lakes and rivers, whose waters have for ages rolled in silence and obscurity to the ocean, are yet to hear the din of industry, become subservient to commerce, and boast villas, gilded spires, and spacious cities rising on their banks." Just as Morris had made a career, and a fortune, betting on the way markets would move, Jay had made a reputation predicting the future course of American history, and he shared Washington's keen sense that all arrows pointed west.[12]

Although Jay had earned his diplomatic reputation in Europe, he shared Washington's belief that the western lands acquired in the Treaty of Paris made Europe a sideshow. The chief task for the foreseeable future was to manage westward expansion across the North American continent. And the very act of performing that task would require the members of the confederation to abandon their provincial perspectives in favor of a common goal that bound them together as an emerging nation with prospects as unlimited as the western horizon.

Such was Jay's state of mind when he and Sarah returned to New York in July 1784. The glow of his diplomatic triumph in Paris still burned brightly, so only five days after his arrival the delegates of the Confederation Congress requested his service as secretary of foreign affairs. It is doubtful that the delegates recognized that they were courting an unalloyed nationalist with the courage of his convictions and a track record of fiercely independent behavior. On the other hand, it is also doubtful that Jay recognized the political cloud bank that he was being asked to enter. In the year since the war had ended, a majority of candidates elected to serve in the Congress had declined, or just failed to show up, and on fourteen occasions no business could be conducted for lack of a quorum. More dispiriting than any clash of opinions was the pervasive indifference that rendered argument itself impossible. There was not even a quorum available to ratify the definitive version of the Treaty of Paris or to accept Washington's highly symbolic resignation as commander in chief at Annapolis.

The delegates were essentially asking Jay to do for American foreign policy what they had asked Robert Morris to do for fiscal policy. Morris's heroic efforts, as we have seen, eventually fell victim to the political provincialism they were intended to correct. But there was some reason to believe that the Jay appointment would not meet the same fate, for while the states could and did remain sovereign when it came to taxes, they could not plausibly claim to exercise the same control over foreign policy, which almost by definition needed to speak with one voice. (Abigail Adams, writing from London, somewhat caustically observed that British diplomats loved to ridicule her husband for allegedly representing a government that in fact did not exist.) Jay was being asked to convert the American cacophony on foreign policy into a chorus.

It is a measure of Jay's prestige, and also of the delegates' desperation, that all the conditions he proposed were found acceptable. He could appoint his own staff, presume to speak as a representative of the confederation as a collective, and—this was a rather audacious demand—the Congress would move from its current location in Trenton to New York in order to facilitate his family obligations. With Morris now retired, Jay became the most powerful person in the Confederation Congress.

———— ∞≋∞ ————

All thinking about development of the western domain had been delayed until agreement was reached on Virginia's cession of its claims to the Ohio Country. Congress never agreed to all the terms Virginia insisted upon, chiefly the voiding of all treaties between Indian tribes and land speculators. But in an act of uncharacteristic generosity, Virginia went ahead with the cession in February 1784, albeit under pressure from other states to end the impasse in order to start earning revenue from land sales. "It is said by good judges that the tract acquired comprehends five hundred thousand square miles," one delegate observed, "and some men who are acquainted with that country assert that the value of it is sufficient to discharge the public debt." David Howell of Rhode Island, who had been the most outspoken opponent of the impost, took great satisfaction in calculating that the sale of 320 million acres at a dollar an acre would easily retire the national debt without recourse to an impost. Most of the initial thinking about what to do with the domain, then, focused less on its boundless borders than on its equally boundless prospects as a providential solution to America's debt crisis.[13]

A distinctively different voice then entered the conversation, less interested in the revenue to be acquired than in the values that should guide American western expansion. In the deed ceding its claims to land northwest of the Ohio River, the Virginia delegation proposed the following principles: "The Territory so ceded shall be laid out and formed into states containing a suitable extent of Territory not less than one hundred or more than one hundred and fifty square miles . . . and that the states so formed shall be distinctive Republican States and admitted members of the Federal Union, having the same rights of Sovereignty, Freedom, and Independence as the other states." These words were written by Thomas Jefferson, and it is possible to argue that, apart from his more famous phrases in the Declaration of Independence, they are the most historically consequential words he ever wrote, since they defined the political and legal framework that would shape American expansion across the entire North American continent for the next century.[14]

It was only by accident, really a series of accidents, that Jefferson was present at this propitious moment. As noted earlier, he was supposed to be in Paris as part of the American negotiating team, but he had declined the appointment, citing the recent death of his wife in childbirth. Once recovered, he reluctantly agreed to brave the Atlantic voyage to join the ongoing peace negotiations, only to discover that the British navy had imposed a more stringent blockade of American ports, making his capture on the high seas extremely likely. (Indeed, that is what happened to Henry Laurens, sent as Jefferson's replacement.) Though he preferred to remain in splendid isolation at Monticello, the Virginia legislature decided that a man of his proven talents should not be allowed to retire from public life, so it elected him as a delegate to the Confederation Congress. He took his seat in November 1783, just in time to guide the Virginia cession through Congress and then be appointed chair of the committee that would prepare a plan for developing and governing the western lands. The result was the Ordinance of 1784, in all respects save one a thoroughly Jeffersonian document.

There was no need to encourage migration. The flow of settlers over the Alleghenies already threatened to become a flood. The challenge was to channel it in accord with republican principles. For Jefferson, that meant westward expansion should benefit settlers rather than speculators; that each new territory, once sufficiently populated at twenty thousand souls, should decide on what form of republican government it wanted; and then, when its population matched that of the smallest state, it could apply for admission into the confederation. There would be no permanent colonies in the expanding American republic. If you decided to carry your family west, you would know that there was a plan in place to ensure that you and your descendants would be folded into the United States as equal citizens.

In order to underline the presumption that the core principles of the American Revolution would prevail in the steady march across the continent, Jefferson insisted that all hereditary titles and privileges would be repudiated and that slavery would end no later than 1800. Though it is mere speculation, the entire course of American history might have been different if the stipulation on slavery had won acceptance by the Congress, but it lost by one vote.[15]

Jefferson attempted to provide some semblance of geographic coherence to this visionary plan by sketching the borders of fourteen prospective states. Several generations of historians have enjoyed a field day ridiculing Jefferson's attempt to impose a geometric grid over the mountains and rivers of the early northwest, and they have made even greater fun of the names he suggested for the states—for example, Sylvania, Chersonesus, Metropotania, Polypotamia. This is not quite fair, since Jefferson was only attempting to provide the first draft of a territorial scheme that, in fact, did become quite geometric once westward expansion crossed the Mississippi. And the names he suggested, no matter how silly they might seem now, were driven by the desire to combine classical and Native American vocabularies, a thoughtful if, in the end, futile effort.[16]

All in all, the Ordinance of 1784 benefited from Jefferson's fortuitous presence in two enduring ways. First, he brought his impeccable revolutionary credentials to the task and insisted that the settlement of the western domain occur within a framework true to the principles on which the American republic was founded. Second, although he never traveled farther west than the Natural Bridge in the foothills of the Blue Ridge Mountains, Jefferson owned the finest collection of North American maps extant at the time. When a self-proclaimed geographer named Thomas Hutchins published a pamphlet purporting to show that the Ohio Valley was a vast tract of one million square miles, Jefferson corrected him. The Ohio Valley was truly vast, Jefferson observed, but only one-quarter the size that Hutchins described. Hutchins quickly apologized for his error. In terms of maps, Jefferson was the reigning expert on all the land east of the Mississippi.[17]

In one respect, however, Jefferson saw fit to modify his vision, not so much on how the new states would be configured as on how they would be settled. His original formulation gave no role to the federal government in managing westward migration, which he thought would occur naturally and freely—two primal Jeffersonian values—as individuals and families moved over the mountains, found the land they liked, and put down stakes. Initially, he even thought the land should be free. But conversations within the Congress, and especially in the Virginia delegation, convinced Jefferson that this laissez-faire approach would produce multiple problems that he had not foreseen.

None other than George Washington was the first to sound the warning. "To suffer a wide extended country to be over run with Land Jobbers, Speculators, Monopolizers, or even with scatter'd settlers," Washington declared, "is, in my opinion inconsistent with the wisdom and policy which our true interest dictates." A policy of unregulated "diffusion" would be sure to generate Indian wars up and down the frontier, the kind of legal confusion over land patents that had already produced vigilante violence in Kentucky, and the likelihood that some settlers would move so far west that they would repudiate their American citizenship and set up independent states or seek support from foreign powers like Spain or Great Britain.[18]

The vastly preferable alternative was called "compact" or "progressive seating," meaning a more managed and monitored approach to westward migration that ensured a steadier and more staged march of more densely populated settlements across the continent. There would always be free spirits—Washington usually described them as "banditti"—who refused to comply and were prepared to take their chances with the Indians. But the westward flow of population should assume the shape of a concentrated wave rather than a free-floating gush.

The full implications of "progressive seating" required the Ordinance of 1785. (By that time Jefferson was in Paris, not so much replacing Franklin, as he put it, since no one could do that, but succeeding him as American minister to France.) The new ordinance organized the western border into townships of thirty-six square miles that would be surveyed, sold for no less than a dollar an acre, then settled as the surveyors moved on to the next range. It was presumed, correctly it turned out, that the bulk of the settlers would come from New England, drawn from that rocky region to the more lush and fertile soil of the Ohio Valley, so the townships resembled a parade of New England communities marching at a stately pace into the wilderness.

By controlling the demographic flow of western migration and ensuring its density, the Ordinance of 1785 minimized the likelihood of Indian wars, the idea being to sign treaties with the resident tribes in advance of the surveyors. The treaties signed with the Six Nations at Fort Stanwix, the Cherokees at Hopewell, and the Ohio tribes at Fort McIntosh were all one-sided affairs in which American negotiators claimed ownership of all the land east of the Mississippi, citing the Treaty of Paris, which rendered the Native American population "a conquered people" who should be grateful to be consulted at all.[19]

But the conquest theory had the distinct appearance of imperialism in the European mode, making it awkwardly clear that the republican principles that were supposed to govern westward expansion did not apply to Native Americans. Although there was an unspoken understanding that Indian removal east of the Mississippi was inevitable, how that removal was to occur did matter, meaning that outright coercion needed to be replaced with some semblance of mutual consent.

Philip Schuyler, a former general in the Continental Army who had extensive experience dealing with the Six Nations during the war (and who, it so happened, was Alexander Hamilton's father-in-law), came up with an alternative way of thinking about Native Americans other than as "a conquered people." "As our settlements approach their country," Schuyler explained, "they [Indians] must, from scarcity of game, retire further back, and dispose of their lands, until they dwindle comparatively to nothing, as all savages have done . . . when compelled to live in the vicinity of civilized people." In effect, demography would do the work of armies.[20]

What Schuyler attributed to a cultural collision that would cause Native American societies to disintegrate upon contact with white civilization was most probably as much biological as cultural. Settlers of European ancestry carried diseases, chiefly smallpox and measles, to which most Native Americans had never been exposed, making them vulnerable to epidemics that on occasion generated mortality rates of 90 percent or higher. The real weapons of mass destruction in the eighteenth century were viruses, and the major reason the Native American population would recede upon contact with the front edge of white settlements was that they were defenseless against such biological weapons. What Schuyler liked to think of as the march of civilization was in fact a policy of genocide in slow motion, in which the march of white migration was accompanied by an artillery barrage of microbes that cleared the way.[21]

Both the cultural and biological versions of westward expansion led to the same inevitable conclusion: Indian removal east of the Mississippi—achieved in a way that avoided any explicit embrace of imperialistic assumptions that defied America's republican principles. The less attractive features of the western story were thereby conveniently obscured, allowing the conversation to focus on the white beneficiaries rather than the Indian victims.

The Ordinances of 1784 and 1785 defined the western domain as a sacred trust, requiring management by a federal government that was prepared to deliver the full promise of its boundless bounty into the coffers of the United States. The management of western expansion thus became a domestic version of foreign policy, demanding a unified response that spoke with one voice. Unfortunately, the Confederation Congress had never been designed to function in that fashion, and the end of the war had removed its primary motive for political cooperation. Whether management of the domain would replace the war as a collective responsibility was not at all clear.

To the extent that the correspondence of the delegates at the Confederation Congress is an accurate barometer of the political pressures of the moment, nothing could replace the war as a unifying force. The absenteeism and inability to muster a quorum did not just impede any semblance of competence or coherence; more ominously, it suggested a prevailing indifference to any national project at all, perhaps the most palpable manifestation of the quite simple conviction that no one cared. When the delegates realized that they could not decide between two locations for a permanent capital, one on the Delaware (presumably Trenton) and one on the Potomac, an editorial in the *Freeman's Journal* proposed constructing an "imperial city on wheels" and rolling it from place to place.[22]

Before he departed for Paris, Jefferson was interviewed by a visiting Dutch nobleman, who asked his opinion of the current American government. Comparing the Confederation Congress to those heady days of 1775–76 in the Continental Congress, Jefferson saw a precipitous decline. "The members of Congress are no longer, generally speaking, men of worth or distinction," he lamented. "For Congress is not, as formally, held in respect; there is indeed dread of its power, though it has none." Benjamin Harrison, the governor of Virginia, concurred, observing that the very survival of the Congress "seems to be problematical." Like Jefferson, Harrison looked back to better days, "when the eyes of the world were upon us, and we were the wonder and envy of all," whereas now "we are sinking faster in esteem than we rose," and European nations were waiting "like buzzards to feast on the spoils of our demise." "Let the Blame fall where it ought," wrote one delegate to Washington, "on those Whose attachment to State Views, State Interests, & State prejudices is so great as to render them eternally opposed to every Measure that can be devised for the public good."[23]

All the news Washington was getting followed the same dispiriting script. "We have no politics excepting those creeping principles of self and local interest," wrote Henry Knox, his old artillery commander, "which are the reverse of what ought to actuate us in the present moment, and which can neither form the dignity nor strengths of a great nation." For both private and public reasons, Washington worried most about the inherent inability of the Congress to supervise the integration of the western domain into the confederation, which he regarded as the great project that would decide whether such a thing as a union would endure. After returning from a trip to visit his own western lands—over thirty thousand acres on the borders of what is now Ohio, Pennsylvania, and West

Virginia—he let it be known that the fate of his own fortune and the future of the American experience in republican government were inextricably bound together.[24]

It was the political version of the decisive moment in a great battle, he claimed, that could go either way, depending on how western expansion was managed. "The western settlers stand as if it were upon a pivot," he warned, "and the touch of a feather would turn them any way." Unless there was a viable American nation-state to join, Washington worried that the western territories would drift into the orbit of lurking European powers or go off on their own to form independent states. Washington's great fear was that North America would become a version of Europe, a collection of coexistent sovereignties rather than a coherent nation of its own. All the evidence seemed to support the conclusion that the very term *United States* was becoming a preposterous illusion.[25]

The one group expressing unrelieved optimism about the domain was the tiny tribe of bards and poets, who almost by definition felt free to levitate out of the messy particularities of westward expansion in favor of more visionary vistas. David Humphreys saw a quasi-paradise where the skies were always bright:

> Then let us go where happier climes invite,
> To midland seas and regions of delight;
> With all that's ours, together let us rise,
> Seek brighter plains and more indulgent skies.[26]

Philip Freneau had a more practical vision, emphasizing the commercial potential of the underdeveloped land:

> No longer shall they useless prove,
> Nor idly through the forest rove. . . .
> For other ends the fates decree,
> And commerce plans new freights for thee.[27]

Perhaps the most uplifting interpretation of all came from David Howell. As a Rhode Island delegate, Howell was on record as regarding the western lands as a source of revenue. But as a true believer in the semi-sacred character of republican values, his view of the west assumed a spiritual aura that Jefferson himself would later embrace in the wake of the Louisiana Purchase:

The Western World opens an amazing prospect. As a national fund, in my opinion, it is equal to our debt. As a source of future population & strength, it is a guarantee of our Independence. As its Inhabitants will be mostly cultivators of the soil, republicanism looks to them as its Guardians. When the States on the eastern shore, or Atlantic shall have become populous, rich, & luxurious & ready to yield their Liberties into the hands of a tyrant—*The Gods of the Mountains will save us.*[28]

This kind of political redemption of the east by the west could occur, of course, only if the two sections remained politically connected. The pessimistic prophets harbored serious doubts, envisioning a series of independent republics or, worse yet, autocratic states just as jealous of their sovereignty as the thirteen original states were jealous of theirs. After all, why should one expect the western territories to join a union that was on the verge of dissolution?

Both the optimists and the pessimists were just guessing, but the increasingly dysfunctional character of the Confederation Congress seemed to tilt the argument toward the pessimists, since the emergence of a gigantic American nation required the existence of a national government that did not exist. Washington regarded this as a failure of will, a fundamental misreading of what the American Revolution intended, and perhaps the greatest lost opportunity in recorded history. In 1785 Washington's nightmare scenario grew even darker as a sectional split emerged within Congress over what came to be called the Mississippi Question.[29]

On the North American continent, the Mississippi was the Nile, the Amazon, and the Danube all rolled into one. Even though the front edge of American settlements remained over five hundred miles to the east, and the Ordinance of 1785 decreed that westward expansion would proceed only in a compacted fashion at a stately pace, meaning that it would not reach the Mississippi until early in the next century, for palpably geographic and more elusively mythic reasons, the Mississippi loomed large both as a destination and as the futuristic focus for American destiny. All talk about the emergence of America as a continental empire recognized the Mississippi as the centerpiece in the conversation.

Jay's Mississippi credentials were impeccable, so when he assumed office as secretary of foreign affairs in December 1784, there was little reason to expect that he would become the center of a controversy over the role of that great river in shaping American expansion. After all, Jay had been the dominant voice at the Paris peace negotiations, insisting on the Mississippi as the western border of the domain and American navigation rights as nonnegotiable. He had also served for two frustrating years as American envoy to Spain, where he had concluded that the once-great Spanish Empire was in a state of steady and irreversible decline, so that despite the presumptive posture of the courtiers in Madrid, Spain was the ideal European power to claim control over the vast region west of the Mississippi. In effect, Spain was like a cowbird that occupied the nest until the American eagle, in the form of a relentless demographic wave of settlers, arrived to replace her as the dominant power on the North American continent.[30]

From the very start of his tenure, Jay assumed that he possessed sweeping powers over American foreign policy, much as Robert Morris had assumed over fiscal policy. And lurking beneath that assumption was an even grander presumption that his role as de facto secretary of state would contribute to an inevitable evolution from an American confederation to an American nation. "Our federal government is incompetent to its objects," he explained to Adams, "and so as it is in the Interest of our Country, so it is the Duty of our leading Characters to Cooperate in measures for enlarging and navigating it." Jay believed that the incoherent course of the current confederation was suicidal: "It will unless checked Scatter our Resources and in every View enfeeble the Union." As he saw it, his role was to avoid that fate by deploying the imperatives of a coherent American foreign policy to galvanize support for a singular sense of a truly United States.[31]

Most critics of the Confederation Congress wanted specific reforms, chiefly the authority to make its tax requisitions mandatory rather than voluntary, and equivalent federal authority over foreign and interstate commerce. Jay, however, did not just want the Articles reformed. He wanted them replaced:

It is my first wish to see the United States assume and merit the character of one great nation, whose territory is divided into different states merely for more convenient government, and the more easy and prompt administration of justice, just as our several States are divided into countries and townships for like purposes. Until this be done, the chain which holds us together will be too feeble to bear much opposition or exertion and we shall be daily mortified by seeing the links of it give way.[32]

Jay assumed that Spain was doomed as an imperial power in North America, and he also assumed that the current confederation was a mere way station on the road to full-blooded American nationhood. These were heady prophecies, both of which proved correct in the long run but were highly problematic at the time. This was made painfully obvious at the outset, when Jay sent a

letter to all the governors, requesting the states to forward all correspondence relating to foreign policy to him so that he might consolidate diplomatic affairs in his office. Few of the governors responded,
none complied, and none of the delegates in Congress found that
objectionable. "I have some Reason, Sir, to apprehend," he complained to Richard Henry Lee, then serving as president, "that I have
come into the Office of Secretary for foreign affairs with Ideas of its
Duties and Rights somewhat different from those which seemed to
be entertained by Congress."[33]

That bracing—and depressing—insight was only reinforced
when Jay objected to the presence of British troops garrisoned in
several forts just south of the Canadian border on the Great Lakes,
a clear violation of the Treaty of Paris. But the British justified this
violation as a response to the American violation of Article IV of
the treaty, which required payment of all prewar debts to the British
creditors, nearly £4 million, more than half of it owed by Virginia
planters. The British also objected to the violation of Article VI of
the treaty, which forbade punitive action against American loyalists
who had not borne arms on the British side during the war. In effect,
the British would remove their troops, who were hovering in anticipation of an expected collapse of the American confederation, only
if and when the Americans honored their own treaty obligations.[34]

No one knew the provisions of the Treaty of Paris better than Jay,
who therefore acknowledged that the British had a legitimate point,
and he ordered Adams, now American minister in London, not to
press the issue of British garrisons until he could put the American
house in order. In a lengthy report to Congress, Jay argued that all
treaties were laws of the land, an early anticipation of what became
the Supremacy Clause in the Constitution, meaning that the states
were legally obliged to comply with all provisions of the Treaty of
Paris. The Virginians would have to pay their back debts, and New
Yorkers would have to stop confiscating loyalist estates.[35]

A majority of delegates in the Confederation Congress supported

Jay's recommendations, but they were powerless to enforce compliance by the state legislatures. So the British troops remained on American soil, Virginia found ways to avoid paying its British creditors, and New York continued to confiscate loyalist estates. Every Jay initiative based on the assumption that foreign policy would force the confederation to recognize a collective responsibility that cemented the union had become an unmitigated failure. On the contrary, all of Jay's nationalistic convictions disintegrated once they encountered controversial questions requiring consensus among the states. As Jay succinctly put it to Adams, "I accept that our posterity will read the history of our last four years with much regret."[36]

Jay's final failure ironically involved the Mississippi, which drew all the dreams of American destiny into its currents. The arrival of a new Spanish ambassador, Don Diego María de Gardoqui, in June 1785 launched a debate over the Mississippi Question, when Gardoqui declared that Spain was closing the southern Mississippi to American traffic. As it soon became clear, there were conflicting dreams about America's westward destiny that quickly assumed a decidedly sectional shape, not so much east versus west as north versus south.[37]

Congress had provided Jay with strict instructions to regard American navigation rights on the Mississippi as nonnegotiable. Jay himself had taken that same position in Paris three years earlier, but the Gardoqui announcement altered the political context. As Jay explained to Congress, the United States was not prepared to go to war with Spain, at least at present: "For, unblessed with an efficient government, destitute of funds, without Public Credit either at home or abroad, war is beyond our reach."[38]

Some kind of negotiated settlement, then, was vastly preferable. And Jay had, in fact, been negotiating privately with Gardoqui for several weeks. (Spanish officials, upon learning of Jay's well-known affection for his wife, attempted to send Sarah several presents, including a prize horse, but Jay had them returned.) During the negotiations, Jay operated on the assumption that surrendering control of the Mississippi for a limited time would not be a major concession: "As that Navigation is not *at present* important nor will probably become much so in less than twenty-five years, so a forbearance to use it while we do not *want it* is no great sacrifice." And when the advancing wave of American settlements eventually reached the Mississippi Valley, Spanish control of navigation rights would die a natural death, much in the manner of any Native American presence east of the Mississippi.[39]

In return for the temporary surrender of navigation rights, Jay obtained a significant concession from Gardoqui: namely, the granting of "favored nation" status with Spain for all American commodities except tobacco. Jay had violated his instructions in Paris and achieved stunning success. Now he was doing it again—striking a bargain with Spain that averted war and expanded American trade to boot. And there was even a collateral benefit that Jay noticed only near the end of the negotiations. In effect, by temporarily closing American access to the Mississippi, the proposed treaty would discourage settlers from venturing beyond the gradually advancing line envisioned in the Ordinance of 1785, thereby helping to ensure "compact seating."[40]

When Jay presented the proposed treaty to Congress in the summer of 1786, there was a thoroughly sectional split in the reaction. Northern states, which stood to gain the most from the new commercial agreement with Spain, were wholly supportive and praised Jay's diplomatic savvy. Southern states, with little to gain, conjured up nightmare scenarios of western land values dropping precipitously because of the uncertainty generated by Spanish control of the Mississippi. In a long speech, Charles Pinckney of South Carolina foresaw western settlers throwing themselves into the arms of Spain and severing their connection with the United States. According to Pinckney, surrendering control of the Mississippi, even for a short time, placed American control of the entire domain at risk.[41]

This was rather far-fetched, especially given Spain's waning power, but mere mention of the Mississippi touched a raw nerve for most southern delegates, who regarded Jay's pragmatic approach to the Mississippi Question as an unprincipled abandonment of America's singular role as master of the eastern third of the continent. And speaking of singular roles, Jay's insistence on conducting the negotiations privately and in total secrecy almost invited questions about a northern conspiracy. James Monroe, a Virginia delegate who had initially supported the treaty, had a political version of the conversion experience, concluding that Jay was complicitous in a plot to shift American policy toward the west in a way that sacrificed southern interests to some ill-defined northern plan for domination. "This is one of the most extraordinary transactions I have ever known," Monroe wrote to Patrick Henry, "a minister negotiating expressly for the purpose of defeating the object of his instructions, and by a long train of intrigue and management seducing the representatives of the [northern] states to concur in it."[42]

Conspiracy theories usually look rather bizarre in retrospect, when the issues at stake have lost their relevance and the political temperatures have cooled down. In order to comprehend the irrational edge of the southern argument against Jay's proposed treaty, one needs to recover the following forgotten facts: first, that the Virginians were accustomed to regarding themselves as the proprietors of the Ohio Country and therefore deeply resented any policy toward western expansion that spoke with a northern rather than a southern accent; second, any discussion of the Mississippi generated a kind of electromagnetic field in which alternative visions of America's future hovered like mirages over the western horizon; and third, Jay's previous diplomatic posts in Madrid and Paris had allowed him considerable independence from Congress—a discretion that came with distance—but what worked so well abroad generated resentment at home. It also did not help that he was the person who officially apprised all the southern states that they were obliged by treaty to pay back debts owed to British creditors, a price tag that Monroe estimated at £2.8 million for Virginia.[43]

In the end, the Mississippi Question was never answered. All seven northern states voted to ratify Jay's treaty. All five southern states voted to reject it. (The Delaware delegation lacked a quorum.) Then the southern states, led by Virginia and South Carolina, invoked the provision in the Articles requiring a nine-vote majority for approval of all treaties. Pinckney wrote Jay, warning that "if you proceed we shall consider you as proceeding upon powers incompetent and unconstitutional."[44]

Jay was gracious in defeat, thanking the delegates of Congress for their obviously difficult deliberations. Then he paid a call on Gardoqui, informing him that the treaty was dead, but that he could privately assure the Spanish king that the United States would not contest Spain's control of navigation of the Mississippi for the foreseeable future. Americans would have to forfeit the benefits of expanded trade with Spain, but there would be no war.

Watching all this from Mount Vernon, Washington regarded this inconclusive outcome as wholly satisfactory. With his preternatural sense of where history was headed, he observed that demography would trump diplomacy. The delegates in Philadelphia were merely quibbling over problems that would be settled by those families streaming over the Alleghenies by the thousands: "Once the white population becomes sufficient in western lands, there is no power that can deprive them of the use of the Mississippi. Why then should we prematurely urge a matter . . . if it is our interest to let it sleep?"[45]

⎯⎯⎯⎯∞⎯⎯⎯⎯

While Jay agreed with Washington's strategic assessment, his experience with the sectional politics surrounding the Mississippi Question deepened his despondency about the fate of the Confederation Congress, which he now regarded as a political arena in which the states came together to display their mutual jealousies, almost a laboratory for the triumph of parochialism and provincialism. To say that something snapped in Jay would not be accurate; he was temperamentally incapable of losing his composure. But something shook his faith that providence had plans for America, that the current confederation of states was destined to cohere into a single nation-state if one waited patiently for the providential forces to align themselves.

In that somber mood, he unburdened himself to Washington: "Our affairs seem to lead to some Crisis, some Revolution, something that I cannot foresee or Conjecture. I am uneasy and apprehensive, more so than during the war. Then we had a fixed Object, and though the Means and Time of attaining it were often problematical, yet I did firmly believe we would ultimately succeed because I was convinced that Justice was with us. The case is now altered, we are going and doing wrong, and I therefore look forward to Evils and Calamities." Achieving nationhood, he now believed, was a more challenging task than winning independence.[46]

During more optimistic moments, Jay had expressed his belief that the inadequacies of the government under the Articles would prove so obvious over time that they would be corrected incrementally, from within, without recourse to dramatic interventions. Now he reached the conclusion that the very structure of the Articles of Confederation was fatally flawed, inherently incapable of self-correction. He shared this diagnosis with Adams, his former colleague in Paris, who he knew would agree with him:

> I have long thought and become daily more convinced that the Construction of our federal Government is fundamentally wrong. To vest legislative, judicial, and executive Powers in one and the same Body of Men, and that too in a Body daily changing its members, can never be wise. In my opinion these three great Departments of Sovereignty should be forever separated, and so distributed as to serve as checks on each

other. But these are Subjects that have long been familiar to you and on which you are so well informed to anticipate every thing that I might say on them.[47]

Jay was referring to Adams's *Thoughts on Government* (1776), which had proposed the basic framework subsequently embodied in the state constitutions, now suggesting that the same three-branch framework should be established at the federal level. Given the current political context in the Confederation Congress, there was not the slightest possibility that such a fundamental reform would occur from within; indeed, any proposal to establish a more energetic federal government would be eviscerated by the state and sectional voting blocs it sought to replace.

It followed logically, then, that root-and-branch reform was necessary, and that the leadership for such a movement must come from outside the currently gridlocked Congress. In a separate letter, Jay shared these same strategic thoughts with Washington, then concluded: "The Plan is not matured; if it should be well concerted and take Effect, I am fervent in my wishes that it may conform with the Line of Life you have marked out for yourself, to favor your Country with our Counsels on such an important and single occasion. I suggest this merely as a Hint for your Consideration." This was a diplomatic way of alerting Washington that the looming crisis might require his reappearance on the public stage.[48]

There were almost surely other unrecorded conversations about reform of the Articles going on in the corridors and taverns of New York. But with all the advantages of hindsight, if one was looking for the moment when the first glimmering of a campaign to replace and not just reform the Articles enlisted the enormous prestige of America's singular figure, this was it.

Washington, for his part, agreed wholeheartedly with Jay's analysis of the problem, but not with his solution. "I coincide perfectly in sentiment with you," he wrote, "that there are errors in our National

Government which call for correcting, loudly I will add . . . but my fear is that the people are not yet sufficiently misled to retract from error." His major task in the recent war had been deciding when to engage the British army and when to defer in favor of better terrain or superior numbers. In this case, deferral was probably the wise choice, he advised, since a convention called to reform or replace the Articles at present would most probably produce an embarrassing defeat that would set back the cause indefinitely. In short, though things were bad, they had to get worse before they became better. On the matter of his own role in Jay's prospective political campaign, Washington remained enigmatically silent. Meanwhile, things proceeded to get worse.[49]

Chapter 4

THE COURTING

I have had my day.

George Washington to Lafayette
DECEMBER 8, 1784

$\mathscr{S}$oon after receiving Jay's proposal, Washington summed up his sense of the political situation in a letter to Lafayette. "A General Convention is talked of by many for the purpose of revising & correcting the defects of the federal Government," he observed, "but whilst this is the wish of some, it is the dread of others from an opinion that matters are not yet sufficiently ripe for such an event." Left unsaid was the intractable fact that the majority of state legislators opposed any effort at political reform, not because they believed it would fail but because they feared it might succeed. Any energetic projection of power at the federal level defied their understanding of revolutionary principles, making the very weakness of the Confederation Congress its most attractive feature. Meanwhile, beyond the halls of Congress and the corridors of the state legislators, ordinary Americans were getting on with their lives, relieved that the war was over, blissfully indifferent to any political debate that ranged beyond the borders of their towns or counties.[1]

Nevertheless, Washington's description of the dilemma facing prospective reformers of the Articles was quite accurate, and it was just the latest installment in a long-standing pattern of frustration almost as old as the Articles themselves.

As we have seen, the first reform proposal to find its way into the historical record came from Alexander Hamilton in July 1783, when he was serving as a delegate in the Confederation Congress. A few weeks later, with time on his hands while waiting for a quorum to arrive at Princeton, Hamilton decided to draft a resolution calling for a convention to amend the Articles. Characteristically, it was the political equivalent of a cavalry charge against impossible odds in which even assessing the risk was regarded as a form of cowardice.

Hamilton's list of defects in the Articles began with the basic flaw: namely, that they were less a government than a league of nations lacking even a mandate to govern. (The fact that you had to use the plural rather than the singular to describe the Articles provided a grammatical clue to the deeper problem.) There needed to be stronger executive and judicial branches; the legislature should be empowered to tax and not just request money from the states; and foreign policy, especially the treaty-making power, must become a federal responsibility immune to meddling by the states. Finally, the nine-vote requirement for principal legislation was a recipe for stalemate and had to be scaled back.

Early on, then, Hamilton had created a generic blueprint for what would eventually, four years later, become the Constitution. But in the current context, Hamilton's version of political leadership was so far ahead of both public and political opinion that it was never even debated by the Congress. "Resolutions intended to be submitted to the Congress at Princeton," he scribbled at the end of his draft, "but abandoned for want of support."[2]

Over the course of the next two years, several proposals calling for a convention to revise the Articles floated through the Congress, one by Madison emphasizing the need for federal control over commerce, another by Charles Pinckney of South Carolina prompted by the sectional split over the Mississippi Question. None of these proposals were as specific or sweeping as Hamilton's, but all met the same fatal fate. It was an eighteenth-century version of *Catch-22*. The moribund character of the Confederation Congress required reform by a separate and independent body, but such an effort could not muster support within the Congress unless or until it was reformed.[3]

Finally, a breakthrough of sorts came in January 1786, when Congress approved a convention at Annapolis to discuss the rules governing interstate commerce. This was hardly a mandate for sweeping reform in the Hamiltonian mode, but rather an effort at incremental improvement by establishing federal authority over the commerce of the states, which were currently in the process of passing tariffs restricting trade with one another. Madison saw it as a small-scale experiment in political reform. "If it succeeds," he wrote Monroe, "it can be repeated as other defects force themselves on the public attention, and as the public mind becomes prepared for further remedies." Then he added: ". . . I am not in general an advocate of temporizing or partial remedies. But rigor in this respect, if pushed too far, may hazard everything."[4]

In effect, since all previous efforts at a more comprehensive reform of the Articles had failed miserably, perhaps a more limited approach focusing only on commercial reform was worth trying. "To speak the truth," Madison confessed to Jefferson, "I almost despair that if it [Annapolis] should come to nothing, it will I fear confirm Great Britain and all the world in the belief that we are not to be respected, nor apprehended as a nation in matters of commerce."[5]

The Annapolis convention justified Madison's worst fears. Both he and Hamilton were appointed as delegates to the convention, but only five states showed up (Virginia, New York, Pennsylvania, Delaware, and New Jersey). All the delegates could do was meet and then adjourn. "Your co-missioners," explained Hamilton, "did not conceive it advisable to proceed on the business of their Mission, under Circumstances of so partial and defective a recommendation."[6]

It was now clear that even modest attempts at political reform were impossible in the current context. The state legislatures were staunch opponents of any federal government that challenged their sovereignty, and that inchoate congregation called "the people" were indifferent to any political project that required them to think outside their own local orbits.

At this dispiriting moment, Hamilton rose to the occasion in a display of almost preposterous audacity. Before the delegates at Annapolis dispersed, they gathered for one final conversation and reached the conclusion that, as Hamilton put it, "the Situation of the United States [is] delicate and critical, calling for an exertion . . . of all the members of the Confederacy." There was, Hamilton intoned, a prevailing sense that the confederation was on the verge of dissolution, and reforms were necessary "to render the constitution of the Federal Government adequate to the exigencies of the Union." In order to address and resolve these outstanding issues, Hamilton claimed there was unanimous support within the Annapolis delegation for "a future Convention" with a roving mandate to address all the most salient issues, scheduled to meet in Philadelphia on the second Sunday in May 1787.[7]

This was Hamilton's out-front brand of leadership in its most flamboyant form. A convention called to address the modest matter of commercial reform had just failed to attract even a quorum, and now Hamilton was using this grim occasion to announce the date for another convention that would tackle all the problems affecting the confederation at once. It was as if a prizefighter, having just been knocked out by a journeyman boxer, declared his intention to challenge the heavyweight champion of the world. Given the overwhelming indifference that had suffocated all previous attempts at comprehensive reform of the Articles, no one with any semblance of sanity could possibly believe that Hamilton's proposal enjoyed even the slightest chance of success.

───── ❦ ─────

This resounding verdict became somewhat less clear because of a discernible shift in the political atmosphere in the fall of 1786. The cause was an insurrection by farmers in western Massachusetts protesting mortgage foreclosures and tax increases by the state legislature aimed at retiring the war debt. Dubbed Shays' Rebellion after Daniel Shays, one of its leaders, it is best understood not as a fore-runner of the Populist movement, as some historians have argued, but rather as an epilogue to the American Revolution. Shays, for ex-ample, was a veteran of Bunker Hill and Saratoga who regarded the taxes imposed by the Massachusetts legislature as the second coming of the taxes imposed by Parliament. About two thousand farmers rallied to the cause, which reached its crescendo during an ill-fated attempt to seize the federal arsenal at Springfield.[8]

The insurrection was quickly put down by the Massachusetts militia under the command of Benjamin Lincoln, and the state leg-islature then saw fit to pardon most of the ringleaders and even meet many of their demands. Shays' Rebellion really was, as Jefferson (safely ensconced in Paris) so famously put it, "a little rebellion" of minor significance.

But initial press reports vastly exaggerated the size of the rebel force and the scale of its political agenda. Instead of two thousand insurgents, the gossip mills in the Confederation Congress imag-ined a force of twenty to forty thousand, with plans to secede from Massachusetts or even march on Boston. Madison and several other delegates believed that the rebellion was instigated by British agents in Canada who were plotting to bring western Massachusetts and Vermont back into the British Empire. "There is good reason to believe that the rebels are secretly stimulated by British influence," Madison speculated, a development that "furnished new proofs of the necessity of such a vigour in the Genl. Govt. as will be able to restore health to any diseased part of the federal body." Then he added: "An attempt to bring about such an amendment of the federal Constitution is on the Anvil," referring to the proposed convention at Philadelphia in May.[9]

Madison's frenzied response to Shays' Rebellion, however mis-guided, was apparently authentic, meaning that he truly believed this minor incident was in fact a major threat to the survival of the American republic. So, for that matter, did Washington, whose stolid serenity customarily made him immune to such wild overreactions:

> The accounts which are published, of the commotions . . . in the Eastern States, are equally to be lamented and deprecated. They exhibit a melancholy proof of what our trans Atlantic foes have predicted; and of another thing perhaps, which is still more to be regretted, and is yet more unaccountable; that mankind left to themselves are unfit for their own government. I am mortified beyond expression whenever I view the clouds which have spread over the brightest morn that ever dawned upon my Country. . . . For it is hardly to be imagined that the great body of the people can be so enveloped in darkness, or short sighted as not to see the rays of distant sun through all this mist of intoxication and folly.[10]

Perhaps the best explanation for all this melodramatic excess is that both Madison and Washington had been warning that the confederation was on the verge of collapse for so long that they were poised to impose that verdict on whatever crisis appeared. Alongside their sincere misperception of Shays' Rebellion, the correspondence of some delegates in the Confederation Congress suggests more manipulative motives, urging that the political turmoil it created "must be used as a Stock upon which the best Fruits are to be engrafted." Most advocates for reform of the Articles still embraced some version of the "ripened fruit" metaphor, counseling patience until some providential event made the time appropriate for such an effort. In the wake of Shays' Rebellion, that time seemed more imminent.[11]

The watchword for those predisposed toward apocalyptic scenarios was *anarchy*, the complete collapse of the confederation leading to civil wars between the states and predatory intrusions by

European powers, chiefly Great Britain and Spain, eager to carve up the North American continent in the conventional imperialistic European mode. The more realistic scenario was dissolution into two or three regional confederacies that created an American version of Europe. New England would become like Scandinavia, the middle states like western Europe, the states south of the Potomac like the Mediterranean countries. The New England press enhanced the credibility of such prophecies, observing that the attempt at a national union was obviously a failure because regional differences made political consensus impossible. The only option was a union of the five New England states, "leaving the rest of the continent to pursue their own imbecilic and disjointed plans." The prevailing assumption was that the attempt to sustain some semblance of a national union after the war had failed because allegiances remained local and, at best, regional, and no government could convincingly represent this diversity of interests once common cause against Great Britain was removed from the political equation.[12]

Jay had alerted Washington that he had a crucial role to play if and when some crisis forced a choice between political dissolution and some new version of national union. Madison had insisted that Shays' Rebellion constituted just that crisis, interpreting the insurrection as symptomatic of looming anarchy or dissolution of the current confederation into a series of smaller sovereignties. Hamilton had, quite boldly and unilaterally, proposed a date in May 1787 for a convention to consider a major overhaul of the Articles. All these efforts had happened separately, without collusion or cooperation. In a substantive sense, they all shared a common conviction that the full promise of the American Revolution was being betrayed. But that conviction was controversial, since resistance to any coercive version of government power could claim to be the central impulse of the American Revolution. What brought them together in the last months of 1786 was the common recognition that one man possessed the potential to transform the improbable into the inevitable.

If the attempt to reform—or better yet, replace—the Articles was to levitate above the lethal combination of entrenched parochialism and studied indifference, it had to be led by the same man who, against all odds, had won the war for independence. Thus began the courting of George Washington.

∞∞∞

The specific event that launched the campaign was the announcement by the Confederation Congress of a resolution authorizing the state legislators to appoint delegates to attend a convention in Philadelphia, in effect endorsing the proposal Hamilton had made at the Annapolis convention.

While most of the state governments regarded the status quo as wholly acceptable, and any enhanced authority at the federal level as both threatening and unnecessary, within the Confederation Congress there was an emerging sense that reform of the Articles was probably necessary in order to ensure the survival of the confederation. Correspondence among delegates mentioned enhanced control over commerce, greater federal authority over taxes—though that would be hard—and some kind of mechanism to provide a single voice in foreign policy, Jay's hobbyhorse. In what was obviously a very fluid situation, the delegates seemed to recognize that something had to be done, and they seized upon Hamilton's proposal for a convention to reform the Articles on the assumption that some kind of modest reform defined the parameters of the possible.

The lack of a quorum delayed a vote on the bill for two months, an ominous sign, but Madison wrote Washington on November 8, 1786, while the bill was pending, to inform him that history was about to happen:

We can no longer doubt that the crisis is arrived at which the good people of America are to decide the solemn question, whether they will reap the fruits of that Independence . . . and of that Union which they have cemented with so much of their common blood, or whether by giving way to unmanly jealousies and prejudices, or to partial and transitory interests, they will renounce the auspicious blessings prepared for them by the Revolution, and furnish its enemies an eventual triumph.[13]

This was an ingenious way to frame the issue, essentially describing the looming convention in Philadelphia as the ultimate arbiter of Washington's legacy. Nor was that all. Madison claimed to know on good authority that the Virginia legislature fully intended to take the convention seriously and, as the largest state, to name a seven-man delegation with Washington's name at the head of the list. Washington had deflected Jay's earlier probe the previous spring by agreeing that the issues were huge but firmly refusing to abandon his role as the American Cincinnatus, permanently retired at his beloved Mount Vernon. "Yet having happily assisted in bringing the ship into port," he explained to Jay, "and having been fairly discharged, it is not my business to embark again on a Sea of troubles." The Virginia legislature could do as it pleased, and Washington acknowledged that he would be honored by the nomination. But the script for this play had already been written by the ancients. Cincinnatus could never come back.[14]

Even a glance at Washington's postwar correspondence reveals that there was more to his reticence than a desire to stay on script. The phrase that keeps recurring in his letters is "gliding down the stream of life," his way of realizing that, to shift the metaphor, the sands in his hourglass were running out. He was profoundly aware that no male in the Washington line had lived beyond his fifties, so he was much closer to the end than the beginning. After an extended visit by Lafayette, whom he regarded as an adopted son, he waxed eloquent, almost elegiac, on the likelihood that they would ever meet again:

I called to mind the days of my youth, & found they had long
since fled to return no more, that I was descending the hill I
had been 52 years climbing—& that tho' I was blessed with a
good Constitution, I was of a short lived family—and might
soon expect to be entombed in the dreary mansion of my
fathers—These things darkened the shades & gave a gloom
to the picture . . . but I will not repine—I have had my day.[15]

He regarded these intimations of mortality less as morose moods
than as realistic recognitions of his limited time. When he learned
that Nathanael Greene had died of sunstroke outside Savannah in
1786, he lamented the loss of his ablest lieutenant during the war,
and the passing of an era in which he was an aging survivor. He was,
so he thought, living out the last chapter of his own story, posing
for painters "whilst they are delineating the lines of my face." His
time had come and gone, or so he firmly believed, and any attempt
to lure him back into public life ran against the grain of his deepest
emotional convictions.[16]

These were not the kind of personal concerns that he felt comfortable talking about with Madison, whom he had met and come
to admire only a year earlier during a conference at Mount Vernon about improving navigation routes on the Potomac. Instead
of unburdening himself in ways that required personal confessions
that he regarded as inappropriate, Washington took refuge behind
a scheduling conflict. A meeting of the Society of the Cincinnati
had been scheduled in Philadelphia in early May 1787, and he had
already apprised the members of that venerable, if controversial,
organization that he was unable to attend. "I could not appear at the
same time & place on any other occasion," he explained to Madison
"without giving offence to a very respecting & deserving part of the
Community—the late officers of the American Army."[17]

Madison claimed to understand Washington's awkward predica-
ment but urged him not to decline the Virginia nomination, so that

"at least a door could be kept open for your acceptance hereafter, in case the gathering clouds should become so dark and menacing as to supersede every consideration but that of our national existence and safety." His sense of loyalty to the Society of the Cincinnati was understandable, Madison explained, but Washington needed to weigh that loyalty against the survival of the republic. Left unsaid, but obvious to all, was that Washington's inclusion instantly transformed a highly problematic cause into something suddenly serious. With Washington on board, the embarrassment at Annapolis would not be repeated at Philadelphia. And if the assembled delegates decided not just to revise the Articles but to replace them altogether with a new government, Washington's presence would provide an invaluable veneer of legitimacy for extensive reform that was, strictly speaking, a violation of the mandate soon to be issued by the Confederation Congress.[18]

Jay rejoined the campaign to lure Washington out of retirement in January 1787 with a long letter arguing that nothing less than root-and-branch reform would do. "Would the giving any further degree of power to congress do the Business?" he asked rhetorically. "I am much inclined to think it would not." The structure of government provided by the Articles was inherently inadequate, almost designed to be so. There were, to be sure, occasions that required caution and prudence, but this was not one of them. As in 1776, this was the time for leaders to step forward.[19]

This message harmonized with the patriotic notes Washington was hearing from several quarters. "From the gloomy prospect still admits one ray of hope," wrote Edmund Randolph from Richmond, "that those who began, carried on & consummated the revolution, can yet rescue America from impending ruin." Madison chimed in, adding that "having your name at the front of the appointments [serves] as a mark on the earnestness of Virginia." Even if he eventually decided to withdraw his name, allowing it to stand for the present had immeasurable political advantages, virtually ensuring robust attendance at the convention in May. Meanwhile, behind the scenes, Madison was spreading the word that Washington was on board, and at the same time he was conferring privately to have Benjamin Franklin appointed as chair of the convention if Washington backed out.[20]

As Washington saw it, he was not backing out because he had never backed in. His name was included on the list of the Virginia delegation without his permission, and he was on record, in a quite public fashion, as forever forbidden to step back onto the stage. The Cincinnatus role became his chief line of defense well into the spring of 1787. As he explained to Randolph, his presence at Philadelphia "would be considered as inconsistent with my public declaration delivered in a solemn manner at an interesting Aera of my life, never more to meddle in public matters. This declaration not only stands in the files of Congress, but is I believe registered in almost all the Gazettes and magazines that are published." This sacred vow was perfectly aligned with his private preference, indeed deeply personal urge, "to see this Country happy whilst I am gliding down the stream of life in tranquil retirement," an urge that was "so much the wish of my Soul, that nothing on this side of Elysium can be placed in competition with it."[21]

⎯⎯⎯∞∞∞⎯⎯⎯

Despite what had become a multilayered series of defense mechanisms, Washington was vulnerable to entreaties from Jay and Madison because he was also on record, at least privately, advocating precisely the political agenda they were now proposing. In fact, as he himself acknowledged, "No Man in the United States is, or can be, more deeply impressed with the necessity of reform in our present Confederation than myself." By disposition given to some combinations of prudence and reticence on most controversial issues, when it came to the postwar government, he was slashing in his criticism. "In a word," he declared, "the Confederation appears to me to be little more than an empty sound and Congress a nugatory body." During the war the Continental Congress had barely kept the Continental Army on life support, routinely rejecting requests for money and troops. As he saw it, the Confederation Congress had sustained that ignoble tradition after the war in its deliberate embrace of indifference and inadequacy. "We are either a United people or we are not," he observed. "If the former, let us, in all matters of general concern act as a nation. . . . If we are not, let us no longer act a farce by pretending to it." There is a certain irony to the political situation in the winter of 1786–87, since Washington was resisting attempts by Jay and Madison to recruit him to a cause that he cared about as much or more than they did.[22]

Washington's mind, then, was completely clear on the substantive question: the Articles needed to be replaced, not just revised, by a federal government empowered to act as a representative of the American people as a whole. He was, in truth, the most nationalistic of the nationalists, because he had invested more than anyone else in making the American Revolution succeed, and he had concluded during the course of the war that success entailed a consolidated national government capable of managing the states.

The crucial question was whether now was the time to invest his enormous prestige in a cause that, at least as he saw it, might very well repeat the fiasco at Annapolis. He consulted Henry Knox, his old artillery commander, framing the issue along the lines of a military decision: Should we risk a battle, or avoid a fight until the strategic situation improved? Knox and Washington had made countless decisions of that sort during the war, and Knox argued that in this case the political terrain was too treacherous, the gamble too great. The state delegations to the Philadelphia convention, as Knox saw it, were likely to be divided into three factions: conservatives, who wished no change at all; moderates, who wished only modest revisions in the Articles; and radicals, who wished a major transforma-

tion into an energetic national government. Only if the latter group
was likely to triumph should Washington join the battle, and that
outcome was currently unpredictable. Best, therefore, to resist all
overtures to attend the convention. Knox's analysis struck Washington as the kind of cautious wisdom that echoed battlefield decisions
in days of yore. "In confidence, I inform you," he apprised Knox in
March 1787, "that it is not, at this time, my purpose to attend."[23]

This conclusion, while avowedly tentative, received reinforce-
ment in a lengthy memorandum from David Humphreys—like
Knox, a fellow veteran who had served on Washington's staff as an
aide-de-camp. A Yale graduate, an aspiring poet, and the kind of
bright young man Washington liked to fold into his official family,
Humphreys had recently arrived at Mount Vernon to serve as Washington's private secretary. He saw himself as guardian of Washington's reputation and prepared a list of reasons why attendance at the
convention would be a huge mistake.

The old arguments were trotted out: the Society of the Cincinnati, meeting in Philadelphia at the same time, would feel betrayed;
and Washington would be violating his solemn vow never to reenter
public life, the Cincinnatus argument. He then confirmed Knox's
assessment that the political context was highly problematic, going
further to predict failure to reach consensus on any new political
framework, making Washington's presence a massive embarrassment
("Your opinions & your eloquence regarded as 'trifles-light as air'"),
thereby burdening his legacy with a dramatic failure. Humphreys
then added one new ingredient to the political equation: even if by
some miracle the convention succeeded, Washington would almost
surely be asked to head the new government, sweeping him back
into the public arena and the inevitable vicissitudes of domestic politics, ending forever the bucolic splendor of his retirement years at
Mount Vernon, most probably staining his heretofore spotless reputation as a heroic figure who levitated above such political infighting.

In Humphreys's calculation, Washington had nothing to gain and much to lose by going to Philadelphia.[24]

There is no written record of Washington's response to Humphreys's memorandum—their proximity at Mount Vernon precluded correspondence. But indirect evidence suggests that Washington was wavering, though still leaning toward remaining retired, groping for personal reasons to justify his absence from Philadelphia. He wrote Knox to explain that his arm was in a sling due to rheumatism, making travel difficult. In addition, his brother had just died, "the most affectionate friend of my ripened age," and his mother, Mary Ball Washington, was dying of breast cancer in Fredericksburg, and though he and she had been estranged for many years, now was not the time to leave her alone.[25]

But these domestic considerations, it turns out, were final flings of resistance against the persuasive powers of Madison, who was providing updated reports on a state-by-state basis of the delegates chosen to attend the convention. Madison's tallies revealed that, unlike at Annapolis, a quorum would be present in Philadelphia; only Rhode Island would fail to show up. Even more significant, most of the opponents of reform had decided to boycott the convention, thereby confining the debate to advocates of moderate and radical reform. If Washington's major reservation was that he should not risk his reputation in a political contest that was doomed to fail, Madison's analysis of the delegate count indicated that abject failure was highly unlikely. And with Washington on board, the prospect for thoroughgoing reform of the Articles became realistic, if not assured.

Though he lacked Madison's mastery of the state-by-state numbers, Knox altered his advice in mid-March on the basis of information indicating that attendance at the convention would be more robust than he had expected. Along with Humphreys, he had earlier urged caution on the grounds that Washington's prestige was too precious to risk in such a questionable venture. Now, however,

he reversed his view of the risk. "But were an energetic and judi-
cious system to be proposed with Your Signature," Knox predicted,
"it would be a circumstance highly honorable to your fame, in the
judgment of present and future ages; and doubly entitle you to the
glorious republican epithet—the Father of Your Country." In this
formulation, Washington had much to lose if he refused to show up
at Philadelphia and the convention succeeded in creating the kind of
national government that he had always advocated. The legacy question, then, was double-edged.[26]

Madison's canvass of the state delegations altered Washington's
sense of the odds, and Knox's new formulation of the legacy question
pushed him over the edge. Though he retained his reservations about
"again appearing on a public theatre after a public declaration of the
contrary," by late March he had decided to join the Virginia delegation in Philadelphia. He wanted and received a final commitment
from Madison that the convention would "adopt no temporizing
expedient, but probe the defects of the Constitution to the bottom,
and provide radical cures, whether they are agreed to or not." The
goal must be replacing the Articles, not just revising them.[27]

<hr />

Once they had captured the great prize, Jay and Madison, soon
joined by Hamilton and Knox, formed an informal council of advis-
ers to give Washington a tutorial in political theory. Washington
had a firm grasp of the big picture—the new government needed
to possess expanded powers sufficient to make laws for the nation
as a whole—but its political architecture had never attracted his
full attention. Since it was a foregone conclusion that he would be
chosen president of the convention, he needed an education in the
basic vocabulary of republican government. Jay and Madison were
both sophisticated political thinkers eager to provide Washington
with an intellectual road map to reach the destination that all of

them already agreed upon. For his part, Washington was accustomed to leading by listening, having chaired countless councils of war in which junior officers presented options to the commander in chief. He spent much of April taking notes on the letters from Jay and Madison.

Jay believed that the core debate at the convention would be between those who wished to reform the Articles and those who wished to replace them. Washington did not need to be coached on this issue, having long since declared himself a radical rather than a reformer. The preferred framework for the new government, as Jay saw it, was the tripartite model embodied in most of the state governments: executive, legislative, and judicial branches. The executive branch would generate the greatest opposition, because critics would claim that any energetic exercise of executive power was monarchical. This debate would be fierce, because "the spirit of '76" stigmatized a potent executive as the second coming of George III, but it was a battle that had to be won.

In order to ensure federal sovereignty over the states, Jay believed that the national government should have a veto over all state laws, much like the British king's veto over colonial legislation, another crucial principle that would prove extremely controversial but could not be compromised. The knotty question of sovereignty—did it reside in the states or in the federal government?—was the central issue requiring a clear resolution. If the federal veto proved impossible, an alternative argument, an artful finesse, might be that sovereignty was located in "the people," a somewhat ambiguous formulation that bent the shape of the new constitution in a national direction.[28]

Madison predicted that the big fight would come on the question of representation in the legislature, which would be bicameral. Would it be by state or by population? A successful outcome depended on the rejection of the state-based system in the Articles, because only a Congress that accurately reflected the population as a whole could claim to be a national government. Like Jay, Madison wanted a federal veto over state laws, and he also thought that this would be a hard-fought battle in which defeat would mean failure of the entire enterprise.

On the sovereignty question, Madison suggested a subtler and in the end more ingenious solution, which was to abandon the belief that it must be singular and indivisible: "I have sought for some middle ground, which may at once support a due supremacy of the national authority, and not exclude the local authorities when they can be subordinately useful." Instead of arguing about the ultimate location of sovereignty, Madison was suggesting that no such place existed. In purely rhetorical terms, Jay's resort to "the people" worked well, but in practical terms it might prove preferable to embrace some version of shared sovereignty that blurred the line between federal and state authority. Madison was inventing what came to be called "federalism," a government in which sovereignty was a matter of ongoing negotiations between the state and federal governments on a case-by-case basis. The genius of Madison's formulation was that it imposed a national grid in lieu of the state-based Articles but left room for local, state, and regional loyalties to remain relevant.[29]

This was actually Madison's "fallback" position, a compromise on the all-important sovereignty question that he was prepared to share, in confidence with Washington in the spring of 1787, but then vigorously oppose during the deliberations in Philadelphia. He would embrace it again during the ratification debates of 1787–88, once the delegates at the Constitutional Convention had rejected his more radical insistence that the sovereignty question be clearly resolved. Since it turned out to be a defining principle of federalism and perhaps Madison's central contribution to American political thought, it is interesting to note that the germ of the idea was there from the start.

While Washington remained the central prize in the spring of 1787, Madison had become the central player. Although Jay had initiated the seduction of Washington, Madison had consummated his capture by demonstrating, on the basis of state-by-state assessments of the delegates, that the prospects for success in Philadelphia were plausible. He had also demonstrated the intellectual agility to move comfortably between the nitty-gritty world of practical politics and the more rarified world of political theory.

Currently serving his second term as a member of the Virginia delegation in the Confederation Congress, Madison was also perfectly positioned to orchestrate the political strategy that would maximize the prospects for success at the looming convention in Philadelphia. And as it turned out, he was thoroughly prepared for that task both intellectually and emotionally. Though he still signed all his letters "James Madison, Jr.," at thirty-six years of age he was a veteran political operative at both the state and national levels, already famous for his ability to count noses, keep a confidence, cultivate colleagues, and let others take credit for political victories that he had actually managed.

Both experience and temperament, then, had prepared him to play a leadership role at a most propitious moment in American history. In retrospect, Madison was about to enter the most productive and consequential chapter of what turned out to be a fifty-year career in public service.

⚭

Madison's emerging political stature defied his physical appearance, since "little Jemmy Madison" was, at five foot four and 120 pounds, a diminutive young man, forever lingering on the edge of some fatal ailment. Born into a prominent Virginia family with a sizable plantation in the foothills of the Blue Ridge Mountains, he enjoyed a sheltered childhood before being sent off to the College at New Jersey (later Princeton) in 1769. Classmates described him as brilliant but paralyzingly shy, perhaps best suited for a career as a schoolmaster or librarian. Madison himself, somewhat morbidly, predicted that whatever career he pursued would be short-lived, given his frailty. As it turned out, he outlived all his classmates and most of his contemporaries, observing near the end that "I ought not to forget that I may be thought to have outlived myself."[30]

Like most members of Virginia's planter class, Madison was an early advocate of American independence. Though he served briefly in the Virginia militia, the very idea of Madison as a soldier was ridiculous. His natural environment was the political rather than the military battlefield, and his version of leadership, so different from Hamilton's, was very much a product of his experience in the Virginia legislature, which put a premium on building consensus rather than dashing out in front of the troops in a headlong charge.

The collaborative context also fit nicely with Madison's deep-rooted reticence. For example, while serving with George Mason on a committee to draft a Declaration of Rights for Virginia's new constitution in the spring of 1776, Madison expanded Mason's language on religious freedom, going beyond mere toleration to insist that "all men are equally entitled to the full and free exercise of religion." But he did so silently, allowing Mason, his senior and Virginia's leading student of political theory, to claim all the credit. Then, eight years later, it was Madison who ushered Jefferson's draft of a bill for religious freedom through the Virginia legislature, while Jefferson received all the recognition for the landmark law, even putting it on his tombstone as one of his proudest achievements.

Madison's trademark talent was superior preparation. While serving on the Governor's Council (1778–79), then again in the Virginia legislature (1779–80), he seldom missed a session and always seemed to have more facts at his fingertips than anyone else. Amid the flamboyant orators of the Virginia dynasty he was almost invisible and wholly unthreatening, but the acknowledged master of the inoffensive argument that so often proved decisive. He seemed so innocuous, even gentle, that it was impossible to unleash one's full fury against him without seeming a belligerent fool. His style, in effect, was not to have one. As a result, a Madisonian argument lacked all the emotional affectations but struck with the force of pure thought, embedded in often overwhelming amounts of evidence. As one commentator put it later, "Never have I seen *so much mind in so little matter*."[31]

It is difficult to identify the time, much less the moment, when Madison became a full-blooded nationalist. Unlike Washington and Hamilton, he lacked the experience of serving in the Continental Army, which was the political and psychological foundation of their disgust with the confederation framework. And unlike Jay, he never served abroad, so he was denied Jay's experience of representing a government purporting to be the United States that, in fact, did not exist.

Madison was born and raised a Virginian. And he never completely shed his Virginia identity in the same way that Washington did. For instance, while he supported most of Robert Morris's program to establish public credit, he opposed Morris's proposal for the Bank of the United States. Like most Virginians, he regarded banks as places where "papermen" manipulated numbers to drive the planter class into bankruptcy. Again, he was a Virginian in thinking about wealth in terms of land rather than money. And his endorsement of fiscal reform was driven by the desire to pay off the wartime debt in responsible fashion, not—like Morris and Hamilton—to create the foundation of a truly national economy. Temperamentally the exact opposite of Hamilton in his preference for caution over daring, Madison, also unlike Hamilton, thought politically rather than economically. And it was his experience of the inherently dysfunctional Articles as a political framework that made him an advocate of radical reform.

Madison's disenchantment with the confederation model was an evolutionary process that began during his time in the Virginia legislature, then accelerated when he served in the Confederation Congress. Two nearly simultaneous events in 1783 seemed to persuade him that any voluntary alliance of sovereign states was inherently unworkable and doomed to dissolution. The first was the Newburgh Crisis, which he regarded as a dramatic demonstration of the quite shameful treatment of the Continental Army that almost provoked a mutiny and was rescued from catastrophe only by Washington's elegiac intervention. The second was the failure to pass the impost, an essential source of revenue blocked by Rhode Island's indulgent sense of its inflated significance. "If the substance of it [the impost] is rejected," Madison observed, "and nothing better introduced in its place, I shall consider it as a melancholy proof that narrow and local views prevail over that liberal policy & those mutual concessions which our future tranquility and present reputation call for."[32]

To say that Madison became a full-blooded nationalist in that moment would be an exaggeration. His Virginian roots were deep and never really died. But from that time onward he concluded that the current arrangement under the Articles was obviously and desperately in need of reform, though he was unsure how and when that should occur: "The question therefore is, in what mode & at what moment the experiment for supplying the defects [of the Articles] are to be made. The answer to that question cannot be given without a knowledge greater than I possess." At this stage of his evolution, in late 1783 and early 1784, Madison seemed to believe that the Articles needed to be revised, not replaced.[33]

His evolution continued apace in a more radical direction over the next three years. Hamilton, Jay, and Washington had reached that conclusion by an earlier and faster route. Madison arrived at the same destination more gradually and grudgingly, because a national perspective did not come to him naturally.

Though obvious in retrospect, it came as a revelation to him that a state-based confederation could not regulate interstate commerce because each state had its own economic agenda. "They can no more exercise this power separately," Madison now recognized, "than they could separately carry on war, or separately form treaties." And yet cooperation on the economic front was unlikely, because it would appear "unpalatable on minds unaccustomed to consider the interests of their state as interwoven with those of the Confederacy." The great strength of the confederation model was its flexible accommodation of multiple and diverse interests under one canopy. The great weakness, now being embarrassingly exposed, was its inherent incoherence. The center could not hold because it did not exist. And it did not exist because local, state, and at best regional allegiances remained more potent than any larger sense of national unity. Madison understood that problem viscerally because up until then he had thought of himself as a Virginian rather than an American.[34]

While Washington tended to emphasize the great opportunity that was being lost by the failure to function as a coherent collective, Madison stressed the horrific consequences that would ensue if and when the confederation imploded. "The question whether it is possible and worthwhile [to preserve] the union of the States must be speedily decided some way or other," he wrote to Monroe. "Those who are indifferent to the preservation would do well to look forward to the consequences of its extinction."[35]

But indifference continued to haunt the halls of Congress, which failed to muster a quorum in January and February 1787. Madison customarily kept extensive notes on the deliberations of the delegates but stopped doing so, scribbling "nothing worth noting" in his journal.

In the course of his campaign to recruit Washington to the cause, he had promised that the upcoming convention in Philadelphia would not be satisfied with temporary solutions, an implicit commitment to replace rather than merely revise the Articles. That, in turn, meant an entirely new political framework would be required to replace the current confederation. Like an assiduous student preparing for a final exam, Madison focused his formidable energies on designing the political architecture for a truly national government that would set the agenda in Philadelphia. His duties as a delegate

in the Confederation Congress became abiding irrelevancies. Everything now depended on what happened in Philadelphia.[36]

And that, in turn, depended to a great degree on the presence
of America's most indispensable character. After some last-minute
second thoughts about the wisdom of it all, Washington rode out
of Mount Vernon in early May. His very presence certified the significance of the occasion, as did his willingness to risk his reputation
in order to rescue the American Revolution from its own excesses.
As for what he referred to as a "remedy," that was Madison's department. And one would be hard pressed to find anyone else on the
planet with his unique combination of political savvy, psychological
intensity, and cerebral power. This would be his finest hour.[37]

Chapter 5

MADISON'S MOMENT

I am afraid you will think this project, if not extravagant, absolutely unattainable and unworthy of being attempted.

James Madison to Edmund Randolph
APRIL 8, 1787

*M*adison had a bimodal mind that was capable of functioning with great agility in a complicated political context, then ascending above the fray to a higher level of political theory, the latter a talent that has earned him a reputation as one of America's preeminent political philosophers. Both sides of the Madisonian mind were operating at full speed in the spring of 1787, though the tactical side dictated the agenda for the theoretical side, meaning that Madison thought less like a philosopher than a lawyer preparing his case.[1]

His client, in this instance, was a fully empowered federal government operating directly on the citizenry of the United States rather than indirectly through the states. His opponent was the state-based confederation embodied in the Articles, which had to be exposed under cross-examination as an ineffectual body that must be displaced rather than merely reformed. Unlike a detached philosopher, Madison drew conclusions that were politically preordained, and as he sifted through the piles of evidence, he was not searching for truth so much as building his case in preparation for the looming debate in Philadelphia. The only acceptable verdict was a clear shift in sovereignty from the state to the national level.

Many observers at the time regarded such a goal as preposterously unrealistic, the eighteenth-century equivalent of hitting the lottery. But Madison had promised Washington, as a condition of his participation, that nothing short of radical change was worth their effort, and in April he reassured Washington that he remembered that pledge. "Radical attempts, although unsuccessful," he promised, "will at least justify the authors of them." Better to fail in a noble cause, in short, than to succeed in a more limited effort that would only postpone the inevitable descent into political dissolution.[2]

He reiterated his commitment to a radical agenda in a lengthy letter to Edmund Randolph, the current governor and a member of the Virginia delegation with long bloodlines that placed him in the upper echelon of the Tidewater aristocracy. Randolph had expressed his belief that modest reform of the Articles was the best one could hope for. But Madison would have none of it. "In truth my ideas of a reform strike so deeply at the old Confederation," he explained, "and lead to such a systematic change, that they will scarcely admit of an expedient." He was going to Philadelphia prepared to defend fundamental reform, he insisted, "on a take it or leave it basis."[3]

But then a small crack appeared in Madison's otherwise non-negotiable agenda. Once the all-important principle of federal sovereignty over the states was accepted, but only then, he was prepared to be gracious in victory, endorsing a "middle ground" that allowed the state governments, which he called "the local authorities," to remain in force "as far as they can be subordinately useful." Madison did not know it at the time, but he was describing a version of the core political compromise that would shape the willfully ambiguous framework of the Constitution.[4]

There were two principles, Madison explained to Randolph, that he was prepared to defend to the death because both were essential for the survival of a viable national government. The first was proportional representation by population in both branches of the legislature, since nothing else would permit the Congress to speak for the American people as a whole. The second was an executive veto over all state laws, "much like the K. of G.B. had heretofore." This was asking a lot, because it conjured up the arbitrary power of George III, against which the American colonists had rebelled. But Madison believed that nothing less than this executive veto power could ensure the supremacy of the federal government over the states.

"I am afraid you will think this project, if not extravagant, absolutely unattainable and unworthy of being attempted," he confessed to Randolph. But on the other hand—he was thinking out loud—perhaps his radical goals were not as impossible as they might appear. On the issue of proportional representation in both houses of Congress, for example, Madison speculated that "northern states will like popular representation because of the actual superiority of their populousness, and the southern by their *expected* superiority on this point." He was only guessing, of course, and largely because of slavery the population of the southern states fell even further behind that of their northern counterparts. But he was expressing a common misconception of the moment. And however misguided, it exposed the tactical level at which his mind was working.[5]

Madison's cautious confidence was also buoyed by his ongoing analysis of the state delegations to the convention. His calculations, like those of Jay and Knox, grouped the delegates into three categories: first, those who wished to replace the Articles, the radical faction he favored; second, those who wished to revise the Articles, the moderates; and third, those who wished no change at all, the conservatives. His big discovery was that the last group had chosen to boycott the convention. The only exception was the New York delegation, where Hamilton's efforts to have Jay selected were blocked by Governor George Clinton's upstate supporters, despite Jay's status as New York's most prominent statesman. This meant that Hamilton, the ultranationalist, would be outvoted by two conservative colleagues opposed to any and all changes in the Articles. Apart from New York, however, the delegates seemed to be evenly divided between radicals and moderates.[6]

How Madison managed to gather this valuable information remains a bit of a mystery. Obviously, modern technology was not available to communicate with his network of contacts in the different states. And while his correspondence reveals the conclusions he reached about each of the state delegations, it does not provide the evidence on which those conclusions were based. He was in New York, serving in the moribund Confederation Congress, which could do no business because it lacked a quorum. Most likely Madison used the time to interrogate his colleagues about political developments in their respective states in conversations that, for obvious reasons, never found their way into the historical record.

This was backroom politics in the nose-counting tradition that most Virginian gentlemen would have found distasteful and slightly offensive. But it came to Madison naturally, and he was very good at it. Like a poker player counting cards, he was deciding how to play his hand in Philadelphia. According to his calculations, the odds for radical change seemed about even, much better than most observers believed.

The theoretical side of Madison's mind began operating at full power in April 1787. Jefferson had recently sent him several crates of books by English, Scottish, and French writers, a "literary cargo" that represented the most up-to-date European wisdom in the intellectual tradition soon to be called the Enlightenment. Historians interested in undermining the Beardian interpretation of the Constitution have relished the opportunity to point out that, on the eve of the Constitutional Convention, Madison was not studying his financial portfolio in order to assess the economic consequences of the looming deliberations in Philadelphia on his investments, but rather reading Voltaire and David Hume in order to refine his thinking about the historical fate of confederacies and the challenges faced by previous efforts to establish a republican form of government on a national scale.[7]

This is true enough and worthy of notice. But it is also necessary to notice, once again, that Madison's mind was more political than philosophical. Which is to say that his reading was driven by a clear sense of the arguments he anticipated from confederationists and the arguments he needed to make for a nation-size republic. He knew what he was looking for as he read, and chose accordingly. There were, it turned out, three areas of inquiry of sufficient significance to merit his full attention.

The first was the history of confederacies. Madison's "Notes on Ancient and Modern Confederacies" seems, at first glance, a tedious and pedantic review of Greek, Italian, Dutch, and Germanic confederations over a thousand years of European history. All the stories were boringly similar, tales of temporary stability, usually based on a political alliance against a common enemy that eventually dissolved into civil war, anarchy, and political oblivion. But the boringly similar pattern was actually Madison's main point. The kind of confederation the Americans had created in the Articles was an inherently transitory political configuration destined to self-destruct because there was no overarching source of sovereignty larger than the narrow interests of the states. The vast majority of confederations degenerated into smaller political units that then went to war against one another.[8]

The implications of this long-standing historical pattern for the current American context were obvious. The upcoming convention in Philadelphia offered the opportunity to avoid the customary fate of confederacies by shifting sovereignty from the state to the federal level. Madison intended his somewhat arcane research into the history of European confederations as an opening argument designed to catch defenders of the confederation framework by surprise and place them on the defensive in a debate where his mastery of the evidence gave him an overwhelming tactical advantage.

His second research project followed logically from the first: a catalog of the political failures under the Articles, entitled "Vices of the Political System of the United States," designed to demonstrate that the inherent inadequacies that afflicted all European confederations in the past were infecting the American confederation in the present. "Vices" read like a prosecuting attorney's brief against the Articles as a viable government.[9]

The litany of failures went on for thirteen pages: the states had refused to honor their tax obligations during the war and their promises to fund veterans' pensions after the war; they had also refused to cooperate on internal improvements like roads and canals and had even imposed domestic tariffs on trade among themselves; they had encroached on federal authority by signing separate treaties with various Indian tribes, essentially stealing Native American land to line the pockets of local land speculators; they had violated provisions of the Treaty of Paris that required payment of prewar debts to British creditors and that forbade persecution of loyalists who had never borne arms on behalf of the Crown; their obsession with local and state interests had prevented any coherent foreign policy and also created a bewildering variety of county and state laws that rendered any uniform system of justice impossible. Taken together, the multiple failures of the Confederation Congress had demonstrated that any state-based confederation was an inherently inadequate political arrangement, incapable of fulfilling the full promise of the American Revolution. Any delegates coming to Philadelphia intending to defend the political record under the Articles could now expect to be buried under an avalanche of informed Madisonian arguments.[10]

Third, based on his analysis of the state delegations, Madison realized that the central debate at the convention would pit confederationists against nationalists. And he also anticipated that the chief weapon in the arsenal of the confederationists would be the claim, articulated in *The Spirit of the Laws* (1748) by the great Montesquieu, that republican governments could function only in small geographic areas like Greek city-states and Swiss cantons, where representatives remained close to the interests of the citizenry who elected them. Madison knew he needed an answer to this argument, which had achieved the status of a self-evident truth during the American Revolution, when the colonists insisted that only their colonial legislatures could comprehend their interests, and that parliamentary authority was too distant and disconnected to represent them. The most potent implication of this size-based argument was that any national government was inherently incompatible with the political principles and the more proximate version of representation on which the American Revolution was based.[11]

The size argument, then, was obviously going to be a key ingredient in the agenda of those opposing any kind of national government, so Madison knew that he needed to have a rebuttal prepared, designed to disarm the opposition of one of its most potent weapons. Believing that the best defense was a strong offense, he decided to attack on two fronts.

His first assault was aimed at the assumption that small republics, like the state governments created during the war, were inherently superior to large ones. But the historical record, as Madison read it, contradicted that assumption. The state governments had failed to meet their troop quotas and financial obligations throughout the war, thereby prolonging the conflict by several years, and in several desperate moments putting the eventual outcome at risk. (One could almost see Washington nodding with approval in the background.) Smallness in size, in effect, facilitated the smallness in thinking that had almost proved fatal to the cause of independence.

Another long catalog of failures at the state level then ensued, suggesting that the previously described inadequacies of the Confederation Congress were in great part a consequence of the prevalent provincialism and localism within the states. The much-vaunted intimacy between elected representatives and their constituents, it turned out, had a quite deplorable downside, as representatives, in order to appease the voters, told them that they did not have to pay taxes, could settle on land promised to the Native Americans, could confiscate loyalist estates regardless of legal prohibitions against doing so, and were perfectly justified in accepting vastly inflated currency, since it permitted debtors to pay their creditors with money that was nearly worthless.[12]

There was in Madison's critical assessment of the state governments a discernible antidemocratic ethos rooted in the conviction that political popularity generated a toxic chemistry of appeasement and demagoguery that privileged popular whim and short-term interests at the expense of the long-term public interest. Fifty years later such a posture would be regarded as unacceptably elitist. But at the time, Madison felt no need to apologize for his critique, which derived its credibility not from some theoretical aversion to the will of the majority, but from a critical assessment of the popularly elected state governments during and after the war. He harbored an eighteenth-century sense that unbridled democracy was incompatible with the political health of a republic.[13]

His second assault was a counterintuitive companion to the first, an argument that large republics were actually more stable and politically accountable than small ones. The core of this claim was that a larger republic increased the number of factions beyond the merely local sphere to create a new kind of political chemistry that generated its own discipline. As he put it in "Vices," a large republic produced "a greater variety of interests, of pursuits, of passions, which check each other. . . . So an extensive Republic meliorates the administration of a small Republic." This also meant that the central fear of the confederationists—namely, that a consolidated national government would tend toward tyranny—was misguided, because the interaction of interest groups in a large republic would prove self-regulating, making a coercive federal government unnecessary.[14]

Where did the inspiration for this novel idea come from? Because political scientists have identified Madison's argument, most fully expressed later in Federalist 10, as one of the earliest expressions of a pluralistic version of modern politics, the answer to that question has attracted considerable scholarly attention. Some of the histories of

David Hume, which were included in the "literary cargo" Madison
received from Jefferson, contained an embryonic version of the idea.
Madison had also read Adam Smith's *The Wealth of Nations* (1776),
which provided an economic argument—the self-regulating character of a laissez-faire marketplace—that he might have transported
to the political arena. And Madison's battle for religious freedom in
Virginia had exposed him to the argument that the sheer prolifera-
tion of religious sects and denominations made toleration politically
preferable because no single creed could achieve dominance. All
these intellectual influences are eminently plausible.[15]

But they all assume that Madison was functioning as a philosopher most interested in exploring the frontiers of political thought.
Instead, in the spring of 1787 he was behaving as a highly sophisticated political partisan, mobilizing his considerable resources to
defend the prospects for a truly national government. He knew he
needed to counter Montesquieu's classic condemnation of large
republics because the confederationists were sure to deploy it as a
centerpiece of their agenda in Philadelphia. So his research that
spring was highly selective. He harbored no desire to make a contribution to modern political science. His primary goal was to win the
argument for a new constitution.

That said, Madison's tactical motivations ought not obscure his
courage in taking on the dominant assumptions about the limitations of republican governments. Montesquieu's case against large
republics was not just a theoretical argument. During two thousand
years of European history, no republic of the scale and size of the
United States had ever survived for long. And the political arguments
that American patriots had thrown at Parliament and George III
stigmatized any political power that was not proximate to its constituents. So Madison was implicitly arguing that the meaning of the
American Revolution had to be revised. He did not put it that way
explicitly, since such a statement would have alienated delegates still
basking in the afterglow of those revolutionary embers. But that was

the inescapable thrust of his argument. Once you moved from a local and state to a national scale, the definition of political representation would have to change.

The "spirit of '76" had served its purpose in justifying American independence, he thought, but it was now an anachronism because it stigmatized any energetic projection of political power as inherently tyrannical. There needed to be a second founding in which the "spirit of '87" replaced the "spirit of '76," establishing and institutionalizing a national political framework capable of functioning on a much larger scale, yet doing so without threatening the hard-won liberties of the first founding. Madison realized that he was asking his fellow Americans to abandon their local and state-based orientation, to regard themselves as fellow citizens in a much larger enterprise, and to modify their view of government as an alien force. The federal government must become "us" rather than "them." One might credibly call this change a second American Revolution.[16]

Madison's third area of thinking and reading in preparation for the Philadelphia convention is more difficult to categorize. It was not driven by the need to anticipate and counter the arguments of the confederationists. It was more a question of language or vocabulary, how to talk about the principle of representation in a large republic.

For there were no precedents. The state governments, to be sure, were mini-republics, but their limited size sustained the sense of proximity between representatives and voters that obviously did not translate to a nation-size republic. And the current Confederation Congress did not work as the model for a republican government, since it had never been designed to be a representative government or even a government at all.

Moreover, Madison did not believe that the orthodox answer to the problem was tenable. Once they had rejected the authority of George III, so the story went, sovereignty had shifted from a monarchy claiming to derive its authority from God to a legislature claiming to derive its authority from "the people." Political power flowed not downward from the heavens but upward from the citizenry. Indeed, this was the fundamental change that had made the war for independence a revolution.

But experience during and after the war had demonstrated beyond any doubt that romantic descriptions of "the people" were delusional fabrications, just as far-fetched as the divine right of kings. Madison's experience at both the state and the federal level had convinced him that "the people" was not some benevolent, harmonious collective but rather a smoldering and ever-shifting gathering of factions or interest groups committed to provincial perspectives and vulnerable to demagogues with partisan agendas. The question, then, was how to reconcile the creedal conviction about popular sovereignty with the highly combustible, inherently swoonish character of democracy. Perhaps the most succinct way to put the question was this: How could a republic bottomed on the principle of popular sovereignty be structured in such a way to manage the inevitable excesses of democracy and best serve the long-term public interest?[17]

Madison's one-word answer was "filtration." He probably got the idea from David Hume's *Idea of a Perfect Commonwealth* (1754), an uncharacteristically utopian essay in which Hume imagined how to construct the ideal republican government from scratch. Ordinary voters would elect local representatives, who would elect the next tier of representatives, and so on up the political ladder in a process of refinement that left the leaders at the top connected only distantly with the original electorate and therefore free to make decisions that might be unpopular. A republic under this filtration scheme was a political framework with a democratic base and a hierarchical superstructure that allowed what Madison described as "the purest and noblest characters" to function as public servants rather than popular politicians.[18]

Some semblance of the filtration idea was already embodied in several of the state constitutions, where the upper house was elected by the lower house, and in a few instances the governor was chosen by the upper house. Even Jefferson, perhaps the most democratically inclined member of the founding generation, implicitly accepted the filtration principle, acknowledging "a choice by the people themselves is not generally distinguished for its wisdom, that the first secretion from them is usually crude and heterogeneous."[19]

Madison's aversion to unfettered (or unfiltered) democracy was less theoretical than practical. The state governments created during and after the war for independence were the closest thing to laboratories for democracy ever established beyond the local level in recorded history. And there was little doubt in his mind that these political experiments, Virginia's included, were demonstrable failures, clear examples of how easily demagogues could manipulate popular opinion and provincial prejudices, thereby rendering any considerations of the larger public interest impossible.

His argument about the inherent advantages of a large republic represented his way to bring demography and geography to the rescue by enlarging the political arena. His argument for filtration represented his attempt to achieve a similar goal—that is, to harness the raw energies of that semi-sacred thing called "the people" while simultaneously controlling and refining its inevitable excesses. A large and properly layered republican government, therefore, would have a popular foundation and a meritocratic infrastructure, which was the political equivalent to having your cake and eating it too.

These were Madison's major goals, key ideas, and core convictions on the eve of the Constitutional Convention. It is difficult to imagine a lawyer more fully prepared to prosecute a defendant, which in this case was the moribund Articles, or to defend a client, which here was a fully sovereign government of the United States.

—∞∞∞—

Bad weather up and down the Eastern Seaboard, especially in New England, delayed many delegates, but the obsessively prepared and prompt Madison managed to arrive in Philadelphia more than a week early, on May 3. The seven-man Virginia delegation trickled in over the next two weeks, the all-important Washington on May 13, as they waited for a quorum to arrive. That left eight days for the Virginians to caucus over food and drink at the City Tavern and the Indian Queen. Madison seized the opportunity to lobby his Virginia colleagues, some of whom, like George Mason and Edmund Randolph, needed convincing, to assume a united front in support of a radical rather than a moderate agenda.

For obvious reasons, no record of these conversations has survived. But we know, based on his comments beforehand, that Washington strongly supported Madison's radical strategy; indeed, his reluctant decision to attend the convention was prompted by Madison's assurance that halfway measures would not be attempted because they were not worth the effort and therefore not worth his presence. We also know, based on their comments during the debates over the following months, that Mason and Randolph had serious reservations about any fully empowered federal government that put Virginia's primacy at risk. And so while we are only guessing, it seems quite possible that the Virginia delegation eventually endorsed Madison's radical strategy, not so much because of his argumentative skills as because Washington made his continued presence in Philadelphia contingent upon its adoption. And without Washington the entire enterprise was almost surely doomed.[20]

During these preconvention sessions, the Virginians were joined by two members of the Pennsylvania delegation, Gouverneur Morris and James Wilson. Both were committed nationalists destined to play crucial roles during the ensuing months. Morris rose to speak, peg leg and all, more often than any other delegate, and he had a greater influence on the final wording of the document than anyone else. Wilson was a bespectacled former Scotsman with a degree from St. Andrews who combined a Madisonian command of the issues with an impressive presence on his feet that Madison lacked. With the exception of Hamilton, who arrived late, all the prominent advocates for replacing the Articles with a fully empowered federal government spent a week together, planning how to set the agenda of the convention.[21]

The fruit of their clandestine labors was the fifteen-point Virginia Plan. It proposed the creation of a tripartite government modeled on the state constitutions with an executive branch, a bicameral legislature, and a judiciary. Unlike the Articles, it was designed and intended to function as a government representing the American citizenry rather than the states. Madison got all that he wanted on the all-important representation issue, since both branches of the legislature would be allocated by population. He got most of what he wanted on the highly controversial issue of an executive veto over state legislations. Borrowing from Jay's language in the New York constitution, the Virginia Plan vested veto power over state legislation in an executive council that included federal judges. But the crucial principle was uncompromisingly clear: sovereignty was to be shifted from the state to the federal level.[22]

For all defenders of the status quo, the Virginia Plan represented a second coup. The first coup, as they saw it, was the calling of the Constitutional Convention itself, which represented a hijacking of the ongoing debate about the Articles by an organized minority of alarmists, who had somehow recruited Washington to lend legitimacy to their dubious cause. Now the Virginia Plan represented a capture of the convention itself by imposing a national agenda as the basis for the looming debates. No one on the moderate side of the argument had come up with equivalently clear alternatives, so the Virginia Plan commanded the field by default. This tactical victory was sealed on May 30, when a majority of the delegates endorsed the resolution, proposed by Gouverneur Morris, "for a national government . . . consisting of a supreme legislature, executive, and judiciary." The national agenda was now firmly in the saddle, and Washington, as everyone expected, after a pro forma nomination by Robert Morris—his only public utterance at the convention—stepped forward to chair the convention. Madison could hardly have hoped for more.[23]

Indeed, the majority vote on the core plank of the Virginia Plan was really another coup of sorts, since only seven states were present for the vote—none of the New England states had yet arrived—and based on subsequent voting patterns of the absent delegations, it seems unlikely that the Morris resolution would have garnered a majority if all the delegates had been in attendance. For that matter, there was never a moment during the entire summer when all fifty-five delegates were present. Given our sense that this was almost assuredly the most consequential conclave in American history, it strains credibility to realize that the Constitutional Convention was an ever-shifting, highly transitory body of men with different degrees of commitment to the enterprise. One of the intangible advantages the nationalists enjoyed in this swirling context was that, thanks largely to Madison, they were better organized and—though this is impossible to prove—more invested in the outcome.[24]

But neither superior organization nor greater commitment was likely to translate into an assured victory for the nationalists. On the second day of the convention a procedural motion was made, without fanfare or opposition, that the one-state-one-vote principle enshrined in the Articles would continue to apply in the convention. This was a huge decision, for it meant that Delaware, with only 60,000 residents, enjoyed equal political status with Virginia, at 750,000. As a result, the small states, which depending on how you counted enjoyed a roughly two-to-one advantage over the large states, could block any national initiative.

And this in turn meant that any robust national agenda on the model of the Virginia Plan was going to be forced to run a very challenging gauntlet in order to win acceptance. For the same state-based principle that Madison and his fellow nationalists sought to replace remained the operative mode of proceeding in the convention. And the small states, which were sure to oppose proportional representation in both branches of the legislature, had the votes to do it.[25]

Before the convention had barely begun, then, some combination of gridlock or compromise between nationalists and confederationists was virtually inevitable. Under Madison's leadership the radicals had seized control of the agenda. But given the powers of the small states under the one-state-one-vote policy, the proponents of the radical agenda would have to make concessions to win their way, thereby creating a document in which the salient question of federal versus state sovereignty could not be resolved, only conveniently obscured. While hindsight makes that conclusion almost unavoidable, the delegates lacked access to hindsight, so they spent the summer arguing their respective convictions in the belief that their arguments, not the inherent structure of the debate, would decide the outcome. In fact, the parameters of the possible were predetermined.

Finally, two other procedural decisions made at the start would turn out to have an abiding influence on the deliberations in Philadelphia and the ways they would be regarded by posterity. The first was the decision that absolute secrecy must prevail, that "nothing spoken in the House be printed, or otherwise published, or communicated without leave." There would be no journalists or spectators in attendance, sentries would be posted at the doors, and delegates were prohibited from discussing the debates in public or in correspondence.[26]

These restrictions were designed to ensure confidentiality and thereby promote the freer exchange of ideas during the debates. And based on the subsequent testimony of the delegates, there is good reason to believe that they did just that. But they ever after made the Constitutional Convention vulnerable to charges of conspiracy, corruption, and skullduggery. And since it is unimaginable in any modern context for such restricted conditions to exist for any political gathering charged with significant responsibility over matters of such consequence, the specter of conspiracy has understandably haunted all histories of the convention. Ironically, to the extent that the delegates at Philadelphia succeeded, their success was dependent on violating all of our contemporary convictions about transparency and diversity, which is one reason why their success could never be duplicated in our time.

The second decision was merely symbolic, but this is an instance when the word *merely* is not helpful. The venue chosen for the convention was the East Room of the redbrick Pennsylvania State House. Modern tourists are often surprised at the small size of the room, with its Windsor chairs arranged in arcs facing Washington's high backed semi-throne, the tall windows with green drapes and small tables with green coverings. More a seminar room than an amphitheater, it created an atmosphere of intimacy that interacted nicely with the preferred policy of confidentiality and secrecy.[27]

Most significantly, it was the same room in which the Declaration of Independence had been debated and signed. No one at the time commented on the implications of that coincidence, but it is too glaringly obvious to be overlooked. Opponents of any new political framework to replace or significantly revise the Articles believed that doing so would constitute a repudiation of the core values of the American Revolution. By choosing the same city, the same building, even the same room where those values were first discovered and declared, the delegates were making a statement—whether they knew it or not—that whatever they produced should be regarded as a continuation rather than a rejection of "the spirit of '76." This made the convention a new chapter in a continuing story—not a break with the past but an expression of its full meaning. And no less a figure than Washington himself seemed to be nodding in agreement with this story line as he sat in that high-backed wooden chair.

All efforts to impose a monolithic set of motives on the assembled delegates at Philadelphia, whether economic or ideological, have been discredited. And the very effort to do so misses the most salient point, which is that the vast majority of delegates came as representatives of their respective states, so that no single interpretive category could do justice to their bafflingly complex angles of vision. What needs to be remembered and recovered is that no collective sense of an American identity yet existed in the populace at large. Even outright nationalists like Madison, Washington, and Hamilton recognized that they were arguing for a political framework that would consolidate the states into a union in which a truly national sense of allegiance would develop gradually over time. In effect, the national government they sought to establish would provide a political structure for a nation-in-the-making, thereby facilitating and accelerating the "making" process, much like an incubator for a newborn child.

Looked upon as a collective, the fifty-five delegates to the Constitutional Convention were surprisingly young—average age forty-four—and disproportionately well educated. Twenty-nine had college degrees, and the same number had studied law. Their educational backgrounds were more conspicuous than their wealth, making them more an intellectual than an economic elite. Thirty-five had served as officers in the Continental Army, and forty-two had served in the Continental or Confederation Congress.[28]

This was the most important political indicator of all, for it meant that a sizable majority of the delegates had had intimate experience with the inadequacy of the Articles as a makeshift government during and after the war. Army veterans could testify more poignantly than anyone else that the very structure of the state-based government under the Articles had relegated their sacrifices to oblivion. Whether you served in the Continental Congress or the Continental Army, you tended to understand more palpably how the current arrangement under the Articles was not working.

For the next fifteen weeks, from May 25 to September 17, an ever-shifting collection of delegates from twelve states met in general sessions, on appointed committees, and in informal gatherings at City Tavern. Important if unrecorded conversations also occurred at Robert Morris's mansion on Market and Sixth Streets, where Washington was staying. An important procedural decision was made early on to conduct most debates in a committee-of-the-whole format, which enhanced the seminar-like atmosphere in which delegates could try out arguments, then change their minds after listening to different opinions, without being forced to register a formal vote.

Since it proved to be the most consequential political gathering in American history, historians, political scientists, and constitutional scholars have gravitated to this moment in great numbers, generating a massive body of scholarship almost designed to discourage the faint of heart. The earliest historians, elegantly synthesized by George Bancroft in the late nineteenth century, tended to cast a spiritual haze over the proceedings, describing the delegates under "divine guidance," and the Constitution itself as a product of "the divine power which gives unity to the universe, and order and connection to events." This supernatural emphasis was probably inevitable given the tendency of most new nations to shroud their origins beneath a mystical veil of elevated omniscience.[29]

The potency of the Progressive interpretive tradition in the first half of the twentieth century derived in great part from the easy exposure of such a mythical and hagiographic depiction as patriotic nonsense. What the Progressives proposed as an alternative perspective might be described as quasi-Marxist nonsense, but it at least had the advantage of demolishing the mystical haze surrounding the Constitutional Convention.[30]

Our current twenty-first-century perspective demands that we regard the convention as a secular rather than a spiritual occasion, but also recognize that any purely, or even primarily, economic understanding of the founders' behavior does a gross injustice to their political motives and to the larger ideological issues at stake as they understood them. For if you go back to the correspondence of the most prominent nationalists on the eve of the Constitutional Convention, it becomes abundantly clear that Madison, Washington, Hamilton, and Jay, as well as Gouverneur Morris and James Wilson, had their eyes on something larger than their own balance sheets.

That something was the future of the United States as the world's largest republic, poised to become an emerging nation rather than a tottering and disintegrating confederation. For six years the loose arrangement of sovereign states under the Articles had claimed to embody the core principles of the American Revolution, which were incompatible with a national government empowered to make domestic and foreign policy for all its citizens. The nationalists were making an argument that American independence had been the mere start of a political process that now had to continue if its full potential was ever to be realized. No less a figure than Washington fervently believed that the failure to create a sovereign national government would represent a repudiation of everything he had fought for. What was at stake, then, was nothing less than what the American Revolution meant, or had come to mean, and that was how all the most prominent nationalists thought about it.

There were two ghosts at the banquet, though they haunted the deliberations in decidedly different ways. The first, monarchy, was an ever-present evil, a word on everyone's lips, a specter so sinister that both nationalists and confederationists felt obliged to register their dread of its reappearance in America in even the faintest form. Any robust expression of executive power was, therefore, forced to fight a constant rearguard action against accusations of monarchy. Madison's proposal for an executive veto over state legislation was dead on arrival at the convention because it seemed almost designed to conjure up the ghastly image of George III imposing his presumptive power in arbitrary and capricious fashion. Since the American Revolution had supposedly ended forever such monarchical travesties, all discussions of executive power lived under a shadow of suspicion as a species of monarchy, the rough equivalent of a Trojan horse in the republican fortress.[31]

The debate over the executive took up more time and energy than any other issue at the convention, largely because the delegates could not agree on how much authority to place in the office; whether it should be a single person or a troika representing the northern, middle, and southern states; how long he should serve (a woman was unimaginable); and how he should be elected and impeached. The resolution in the Virginia Plan was elliptical on all those details, saying only that "a National Executive be instituted, to be chosen by the National Legislature for the term of _____ years." If some form of that vague proposal had been accepted, the United States would have had a parliamentary system of government.[32]

But it was not. Instead, late in their deliberations the delegates invented that strange thing that continues to befuddle foreign observers called the Electoral College. Trying to follow the flow of the argument about executive authority over the course of the summer is an inherently impossible task, because there was no flow, just a series of erratic waves. Several delegates obviously wanted the office to be largely symbolic, noting that the title of president implied that his chief duty was merely to preside. The only moment of utter clarity came on June 18, when Hamilton rose to deliver a six-hour speech that his best biographer has called "brilliant, courageous, and completely daft." In it he used the dreaded word, calling for "an elected monarch" who would serve for life. For the remainder of Hamilton's career that speech was used against him as evidence of his danger-ously monarchical instincts. Although it was becoming increasingly clear that the central goal of the convention was to reach a sensible accommodation between nationalists and confederationists, Hamil-ton's six-hour harangue demonstrated that he was unwilling to play that political game.[33]

The other ghost at the banquet was slavery, which was simul-taneously omnipresent and unmentionable. Lincoln subsequently claimed that the decision to avoid the word *slavery* in the founding document accurately reflected the widespread recognition that the "peculiar institution" was fundamentally incompatible with the val-ues on which the American Revolution was based, so that the bulk of the delegates realized that any explicit mention of the offensive term would, over time, prove embarrassing.[34]

This was true enough, but the more palpable and pressing truth in the summer of 1787 was that slavery was deeply embedded in the economies of all states south of the Potomac and that no political plan that questioned that reality had any prospect of winning approval. Much like the big-state-small-state conflict, then, a sectional split was, from the beginning, built into the very structure of the conven-tion, and some kind of political compromise was inevitable if the Constitution were to stand any chance of passage and ratification. Madison himself believed that slavery was the most elemental source of conflict. "The states were divided into different interests not by their difference in size," he recalled later, "but principally from their having or not having slaves. . . . It did not lie between the large and small states, it lay between the Northern and Southern."[35]

The crucial compromise was an agreement to avoid any direct discussion of the divisive issue and to use euphemisms like "that species of property" when the forbidden topic forced itself onto the agenda. The two most explicit decisions implicitly endorsing slavery were the agreement to count slaves as three-fifths of a person for purposes of representation in the House and a prohibition against ending the slave trade for twenty years, concessions to the Deep South, especially South Carolina, that appear horrific to our eyes but without which the Constitution almost certainly could never have come into existence.[36]

There were, to be sure, flashes of emotional honesty that exposed the depth of the sectional divide. Luther Martin of Maryland denounced slavery as "an odious bargain with sin, inconsistent with the principles of the revolution and dishonorable to the American character." Gouverneur Morris pronounced slavery "a curse," an anachronistic "vestige of feudalism" that would actually retard the economic development of the South, and "the most prominent feature in the aristocratic countenance of the proposed Constitution." On the pro-slavery side, the most succinct statement came from Charles Cotesworth Pinckney of South Carolina: "South Carolina and Georgia cannot do without slaves."[37]

Such statements accurately expressed the broadly shared recognition that slavery was, on the one hand, a cancerous tumor in the American body politic and, on the other, a malignancy so deeply embedded that it could not be removed without killing the patient, which in this case was a newly created American nation. As a result, the most salient piece of evidence is silence. No one proposed any provision condemning slavery and insisting that it be put on the road to extinction. And no one proposed that the Constitution contain language explicitly justifying or protecting slavery or defending its permanent place in American society.

The euphemisms and circumlocutions in the language of the Constitution accurately reflected the ambiguous and ambivalent mentality of the delegates. If there was one explosive device that could blow up the entire national enterprise, this was it, and the delegates knew it. Leadership, as they saw it, meant evading rather than facing the moral implications of the slavery question. Whether this was a failure of moral leadership or a realistic recognition of the politically possible can be debated until the end of time.

By transforming slavery from a moral to a political problem, the delegates made it susceptible to compromise, but this achievement came at a cost. Writing in his notebook on July 9, John Dickinson of Delaware expressed his personal disappointment that the moral question posed by slavery was being conveniently obscured: "Acting before the World, what will be said of this new principle of founding a Right to govern Freemen on a power derived from Slaves. . . . The omitting of the WORD will be regarded as an Endeavor to conceal a principle of which we are ashamed."[38]

From the perspective of abolitionists fifty years later, the conscious decision to bury the slavery issue was a moral travesty that rendered the Constitution "a covenant with death." It is clear that several delegates, like Dickinson, shared their moral concerns. But they chose to subordinate those concerns to the political priority of creating a national government that included the South. Hamilton, for example, who was a charter member of the Manumission Society in New York, never rose in debate to express his antislavery convictions because he knew the political consequences. Moral purity on this score would come at the cost of American nationhood. And if you lost that, all moral concerns would become irrelevant, because there would be no political framework to enforce them. Historians who have embraced a neoabolitionist critique of the Constitution need to come to terms with the intractability of that dilemma.

At an even deeper psychological level, the circumlocutions deployed for evasive purposes in the Constitution accurately captured the denial mechanisms that many of the southern delegates had developed in their daily lives as slave owners: ways of talking and even thinking designed to obscure the moral implications of their livelihoods and lifestyles. Twenty-five of the delegates owned slaves, including George Mason, who oversaw three hundred slaves at Gunston Hall and never freed them but incongruously delivered several passionate critiques of slavery at the convention.

George Washington arrived in Philadelphia accompanied by

three slaves, including his personal valet, Billy Lee, who stood behind his master's chair throughout the convention, tending to his personal needs. One can only wonder what Billy Lee thought about the tortured debate over slavery. Or whether Washington wondered what Billy Lee was thinking. On the latter score, the likely answer is that Washington gave the matter no thought at all. And if he did, it would be the last thing he would ever talk about or record in his diary. The unofficial policy of silence at the convention on the all-important question of slavery was, to be sure, a political decision driven by a collective awareness of its explosive implications, but silence and willful obliviousness came naturally to most southern slave owners. It was the way they had learned to live their lives.

The crescendo moment in the convention occurred in mid-July. Madison had by then given up any hope for his federal veto of state laws, and it was now clear that the small states had the votes to block his other nonnegotiable principle, proportional representation in both branches of the legislature. Because Madison and the bloc of nationalists he was leading refused to budge on this core principle, the convention was gridlocked. A grim and somber mood began to settle in as the impasse seemed to suggest that the Philadelphia convention would go the way of Annapolis, meaning total and abject failure.[39]

Washington sensed the emerging pessimism, and in a letter to Hamilton, who had left the convention on June 30 to attend a meeting of the Manumission Society in New York, he confessed his doubts about lending his prestige to such a problematic venture: "I almost despair of seeing a favourable issue to the proceedings of the Convention, and do therefore regret at having any urgency in the business." Franklin, also sensing that this was the critical moment, proposed that the delegates invite a chaplain to read a prayer before their deliberations. This seems strange coming from America's most prominent deist, but it happened. Legend has it that Hamilton rose to oppose the proposal, saying he "saw no reason to call in foreign aid." But this clever retort is surely apocryphal, since Hamilton was not present in Philadelphia at the time. It was now clear that the convention was on the verge of dissolution unless some compromise could be hammered out on the question of representation in both houses of the new Congress.[40]

The crucial vote came on July 16. Madison and Gouverneur Morris each delivered a passionate plea for proportional representation in both branches of Congress, Morris somewhat melodramatically predicting civil war if the new government did not accurately represent the will of all its citizens. The nationalists were destined to lose this debate because voting in the convention followed the state-based model under the Articles that they were rejecting for the new Constitution. The so-called Great Compromise, also called the Connecticut Compromise because its chief sponsor came from that state, was a classic split-the-difference solution, making representation proportional in the House and state-based in the Senate, with two representatives for each state.[41]

Both Madison and Washington interpreted the compromise as a devastating defeat, because the principle of state sovereignty had been qualified but not killed. Writing in code to Jefferson in Paris, Madison shared his deep disappointment at the outcome, which blasted his hopes for a fully empowered national government. "I hazard an opinion," he lamented, "that the plan should it be adopted will neither effectively answer the national object nor prevent the local mischiefs which everywhere excite disgust agst the state governments." The new political framework was going to be partly national and partly federal, thereby leaving the all-important sovereignty question inherently ambiguous. He had not been able to keep his promise to Washington that only a radical, wholly national solution would be acceptable.[42]

Washington was slightly more sanguine. In a letter to his beloved Lafayette, he viewed the hybrid character of the proposed constitution as an inherently equivocal document that almost invited contradictory interpretations: "It is now a child of fortune to be fostered by some and buffeted by others. What will be the General opinion on, or reception of it, is not for me to decide, nor shall I say anything for or against it." Given the diversity of opinions at the convention, however, Washington believed that "it was probably the best that could be obtained at this time."[43]

The optimistic way to see it was that a consolidated American nation was still very much a work in progress, and the willfully ambiguous political architecture that the delegates in Philadelphia had constructed reflected not just the voting blocs at the convention, but also the still-embryonic status of American nationalism. The vast bulk of the citizenry was not ready for a fully empowered federal government. What the delegates in Philadelphia were giving them was a halfway house on the road to the promised land.

For our purposes, looking back at the way in which the political campaign to create the Constitutional Convention proceeded, a small group of uncompromising believers in America's national potential—Washington, Madison, Hamilton, and Jay—had orchestrated the strategy that produced the convention. And then Madison, taking the lead, had set the agenda for the convention with the Virginia Plan and drawn other nationalists like Gouverneur Morris and Wilson into his camp.

But in Philadelphia during the summer of 1787, Madison and his nationalist colleagues lost control of the debate. Their national aspirations had always been far ahead of popular opinion. They were forced to learn a political lesson that leaders in any truly representative government, itself a new thing under the sun, had to learn: namely, that leadership sometimes means slowing down to allow stragglers to catch up. (Hamilton regarded this lesson as cowardice.) A small elite of like-minded souls could and did force a political debate that would otherwise not have happened. But once that debate moved to a larger arena that contained actors who did not share their radical assumptions, the definition of leadership changed. Compromise, the old enemy, became the new friend.

Better a confederated nation than a mere confederation. Better still a constitution that created the framework in which the question of federal versus state sovereignty was left ambiguous and therefore provided the political arena for an ongoing argument that would get clarified incrementally over a comfortable stretch of time, though never completely resolved.

———⚌———

Madison is customarily recognized as "Father of the Constitution," and there are sound reasons why he merits that recognition, the chief ones being that he set the political agenda for the convention with his Virginia Plan, and he performed his Madisonian magic in behind-the-scenes strategy sessions with his fellow nationalists. But as the convention concluded, Madison would most probably have regarded such recognition as excessive and perplexing. He had, after all, lost all the major battles. And there is good reason to believe that, when he unfurled his most original idea about the political chemistry in a large republic, most delegates did not know what he was talking about.

There are also sound reasons why Madison should share the title with Gouverneur Morris. He was the only delegate to speak more frequently than Madison, and because of his massive ego, flamboyant style, and utter disregard for giving offense to his political enemies, the most forceful advocate for the national vision. He also delivered some of the most eloquent harangues against slavery, a topic on which Madison was mostly mute.

More important, while the Constitution was clearly the creation of many hands, Morris was the man who actually wrote it. Both

Hamilton and Madison served with him on the Committee on Style and Arrangement in mid-September, but Madison later testified that it was Morris who gave the final draft of the document its "finish," adding that "a better choice could not have been made, as the performance of the task proves."[44]

Morris took the earlier draft prepared by the Committee on Detail and compressed the twenty-three articles in that somewhat legalistic and tangled version to seven, giving the final draft of the Constitution a clarity and accessibility that it had not previously possessed. Morris's Constitution does not quite sing like Jefferson's Declaration, which had the rhetorical advantage of being about founding principles rather than about the political structure to implement those principles. But Morris's language cast the Constitution into an elevated format that rose above the nettlesome details of its content.

Finally, Morris revised the preamble of the previous draft in a fashion that has continued to echo through the ages. The Committee on Detail had written "We the people of the states of New Hampshire, Massachusetts, Rhode Island . . ." and then down the Atlantic coast on a state-by-state basis. Morris single-handedly chose to change that to "We the People of the United States." This was not just a stylistic revision, for it imposed, at least verbally, a crucial and clear presumption that the rest of the document was designed to finesse: namely, that the newly created government operated directly on the whole American citizenry, not indirectly through the states. Just as Jefferson had smuggled an expansive liberal mandate into the Declaration, Morris smuggled the national agenda into the preamble of the Constitution. In retrospect, this was probably the most consequential editorial act in American history, the political equivalent at the end of the convention of Madison's bold decision to impose a national agenda at the start.[45]

But the last word must go to the oldest and most venerable delegate at the convention, who captured with perfect pitch and homespun wisdom the mood of the moment. Benjamin Franklin was eighty-one, afflicted with kidney stones and gout, but he was one of the few delegates to attend every session, carried in on an elaborate sedan by four husky prisoners from the local jail. Most of his comments during the debates needed to be read by James Wilson, his Pennsylvania colleague, and they were often off-point or politically eccentric. He remained enamored, for example, with a single-house legislature in the mode of the Pennsylvania constitution, and he expressed his conviction that all government officials at the federal level should serve without pay. But his reputation as second only to Washington in stature meant that other delegates humored his suggestions, never questioned his judgment, and allowed his proposals to die respectfully and silently without a vote. There was an unspoken consensus that he was the wisest man in the room.

He lived up to that reputation on the last day of the convention with remarks, again delivered by Wilson, that were both elegantly pragmatic and politically profound:

> I confess that I do not entirely approve this Constitution at present, but Sir, I am not sure I shall never approve it: For having lived long, I have experienced many Instances of being oblig'd, by better Information or fuller Consideration, to change opinions on important Subjects, which I once thought Right, but found to be otherwise. It is therefore that the older I grow the more apt I am to doubt my own Judgment, and to pay more respect to the Judgment of others. . . .
>
>   In these Sentiments, Sir, I agree to this Constitution, with all its Faults, if they are such; because I think a General Government necessary for us. . . . I doubt too whether any other Convention we can obtain, may be able to make a better Constitution. . . . It therefore astonishes me, Sir, to find this System approaching so near to Perfection as it does; and I think it will astonish our Enemies, who are waiting with Confidence to hear that our Councils are Confounded, like those of the

Builders of Babel, and that our States are on the Point of Separation, only to meet, hereafter, for the Purpose of cutting one another's throats. Thus I consent, Sir, to this Constitution because I expect no better, and I am not sure that it is not the best.[46]

Over two centuries later, we can safely say that the Constitution has stood the test of time and fulfilled Franklin's fondest hopes. Almost inevitably, a mystic haze has formed around the document over the years, and words like *miracle* are used to describe its creation. No one present in Philadelphia at the time would have understood such a reverential gloss on the Constitution. Much later, several delegates recalled that "the hand of Providence" was at work. But Hamilton, Madison, and Washington all left town thinking they had failed to transform a confederation into a full-blooded nation.

Franklin's eloquent elegy served to remind them that perfection was never in the cards, that they had, in fact, designed the framework for a government that assumed human imperfection, which turned out to be an elemental insight denied his French friends. Within that realistic context, they had done their best. The fact that they had been unable to resolve the question of federal versus state sovereignty, or even to face the moral implications of the slavery question, did not mean that they had failed but rather that, in the current political context, those issues were irresolvable. The Constitution had created a framework in which the argument could continue. For the present, that was the most that history allowed, even more than Franklin, with all his seasoned wisdom, had allowed himself to expect.

Chapter 6

THE GREAT DEBATE

When the transient circumstances and fugitive performances which attend this crisis shall have disappeared, that work [the Federalist Papers] will merit the notice of Posterity, [because it] identified the principles underlying our noble experiment in permanent and classical form.

George Washington to Alexander Hamilton
AUGUST 28, 1788

p until the fall of 1787, the transition from a confederation of sovereign states to a nation-size republic had been instigated and managed by a quartet of prominent figures—Hamilton, Jay, Madison, and Washington. During the summer of that year, the list of leaders expanded, broadly speaking, to include all thirty-nine delegates who signed the Constitution. There were also several delegates who played a significant role in influencing the eventual shape of the final document, chiefly George Mason and Edmund Randolph, who harbored reservations that prevented them from signing, but the other key signers who most influenced the outcome were Gouverneur Morris and James Wilson, who might be regarded as significant supporting actors in the national story. Until September 1787, however, control over the debate about the future identity of the constellation of states called the United States had rested with a political elite, however broadly or narrowly defined, that had forced a conversation about the meaning of the American Revolution that otherwise would not have happened.

Starting in the fall of 1787 and continuing until the summer of 1788, this ongoing story entered a new chapter. Madison himself subsequently declared that it was the most important chapter of all:

> Whatever veneration might be entertained for the body of men who formed our constitution, the sense of that body could never be regarded as an oracular guide in . . . expanding the constitution. As the instrument came from them, it was nothing more than the draught of a plan, nothing but a dead

letter until life and validity were breathed into it, by the voice of the people, speaking through the several state conventions. If we were to look therefore, for the meaning of the instrument, we must look for it not in the general conventions, which proposed, but in the state conventions.[1]

In an elemental sense, Madison was surely right. For while the vast majority of American political leaders harbored a profound skepticism about the virtues of unbridled democracy, they all recognized that any credible American republic must be based on a popular foundation. There were seminal moments, then, when prominent leaders needed to step aside and let "the people" decide. (Awkward aside: Madison was on the record as not believing that such a thing as "the people" existed.) And this was one such moment, when ordinary citizens assumed control of the debate, selecting delegates to state ratifying conventions for what would be a national referendum on the proposed Constitution.[2]

Such a vibrantly democratic moment had happened once before, in the summer of 1776. In response to a resolution of the Continental Congress requesting each colony to revise its colonial charter into a state constitution, the colonial legislatures had forwarded the request to all the counties within their jurisdictions. This became a de facto referendum on independence throughout all the towns, villages, and hamlets up and down the Atlantic coast. In a sense, this was the first and most palpably popular declaration of independence, for the referendum produced a landslide verdict for secession from the British Empire.[3]

The political context in the fall of 1787 required a second democratic moment, when the core issue at stake was presented to the full citizenry for their approval or rejection. In 1776 the issue had been independence. In 1787–88 it was nationhood. And partly because the process was drawn out for eight months, and partly because the American electorate was more divided on nationhood than it was on independence, the arguments that ensued in the ratifying conventions and in town meetings and family parlors from Maine to Georgia were spirited, indeed ferocious affairs. Without much doubt, one can sensibly say that this was the greatest political debate in American history, because nothing less than a viable American nation-state was at issue.[4]

And because the vast majority of the American populace had been wholly oblivious to the secret conversations occurring in Philadelphia during the summer of 1787, the publication of the Constitution was a dramatic and traumatic event for which they were unprepared. They now needed to be folded into a conversation from which they had previously been excluded. Who knew that a few men would propose not a mere revision, but a complete overhaul of the current political arrangement under the Articles?

It needs to be noticed, though, in this democratic chapter that the range of options was severely circumscribed, just as it had been in 1776. Then the up-or-down issue was the Declaration of Independence. Now it was the recently drafted Constitution. It is quite likely that a majority of the American citizenry would have preferred a revision of the Articles, but that option was not available. The choice was between sticking with the Articles in their current moribund condition or going with the Constitution in its present form. It was, in effect, a take-it-or-leave-it decision.

And so while the democratic phase of the story was impressively open-ended and wide-ranging, the parameters of the possible had already been established by those favored few in Philadelphia, and before them by an even smaller cohort of nationalists who had worked behind the scenes to make the Constitutional Convention happen. The inevitable cacophony of that democratic process had to fit itself into one of two preordained categories: confederation or nation. "The people," to be sure, must have their say, but their vote must be either aye or nay.

The diverse histories of the ratifying conventions had one thing in common: namely, an effort by opponents of ratification to create a middle course that defied that up-or-down option. That strategy first became clear in late October, when the Virginia legislature was drafting its charge to the state convention. Patrick Henry, who was expected to lead the opposition, argued that the delegates be urged "to adopt—reject—or amend the proposed Constitution." A spirited debate then followed in which advocates of the Constitution successfully insisted on removal of the word *amend*. Although there were obviously huge political issues at stake in the ratification debates, tactical issues in the contested states determined the outcome, and the chief tactical goal of the nationalists was the refusal to permit critics of the Constitution to make ratification conditional upon amendments. As long as it remained a clear choice between the Articles and the Constitution, the nationalists enjoyed a distinct advantage.[5]

Three additional advantages also came their way, even before the ratification debates began. The Confederation Congress forwarded the Constitution to the state governments as requested and, after some confusion, did so unanimously. Many observers misinterpreted the unanimity of the vote as an endorsement of the Constitution itself rather than of the ratification process. "The appearance of unanimity will have its effects," Washington commented to Madison, knowing that the true intentions of the Confederation Congress were being misconstrued: "Not every one has opportunities to peep behind the curtain, and as the multitude often judge by externals, the appearance of unanimity in that body, on this occasion, will be of great importance."[6]

Second, ratification became much more likely when the Confederation Congress silently accepted Article VII of the Constitution, which declared that the new government would go into effect after nine states had ratified. Technically, this was an illegal provision, since the procedural rules under the Articles required a unanimous vote for any amendments. The delegates in Philadelphia, many of them veteran observers of the gridlock in the Confederation Congress, most especially Rhode Island's recalcitrance on the impost, realized a unanimous requirement for ratification would have been politically suicidal, since Rhode Island had already declared its intention to boycott the ratification process, just as it had boycotted the convention. They simply decided on their own that nine states constituted a sufficient consensus, probably drawing on the provision in the Articles requiring nine votes for all major legislation.[7]

There was a hidden as well as an obvious advantage to the nine-vote requirement, and Madison, ever the political operative, was the first to recognize it. "It is generally believed that nine States at least will embrace the plan," he predicted, "consequently that the tardy remainder must be reduced to the dilemma of either shifting for themselves or coming in without any credit for it." The chronological sequence of the state ratifying conventions only enhanced this momentum factor. Virginia and New York, two of the largest states where opposition was most formidable, came late in the schedule, so that political pressure to ratify would build in the spring and early summer of 1788 to recognize that opposition was a lost cause. Madison believed that political arguments would become irrelevant once nine states had ratified.[8]

Finally, before the debates began, the advocates for ratification won the rhetorical battle by claiming the title *Federalists*, which left their opponents with the limp label *Antifederalists*. This nomenclature was both inaccurate and grossly unfair to the "Antis." Both sides were really federalists, the difference being how they wished to apportion authority between the federal government and the states. (A more accurate set of labels would have been *nationalists* versus *confederationists*.) In the predebate skirmishes, then, the maneuvering for both votes and vocabulary went to the pro-Constitution side. It also helped that only twelve of the ninety American newspapers and magazines gave equivalent space to the opponents of ratification. The press was decidedly pronationalist.[9]

From the beginning, then, the "Antis" were placed on the political defensive. As Madison kept mentioning, their cause was further burdened by the fact that they did not agree on what they wanted in lieu of the Constitution. Was it more modest reform of the Articles, amendments to the proposed Constitution, or a second Constitutional Convention that would take into account their grievances? They agreed on what they were against, but not on what they were for. In that sense, the term *Antis* was accurate.

On the other hand, the opponents of ratification enjoyed one enormous ideological advantage: namely, that the government proposed in the Constitution defied the principles of the American Revolution as understood in 1776. Given the size and scale of a nation-size American republic, the very definition of representation would have to change. How, for example, could a representative in the House really know the needs and interests of his thirty thousand constituents? How could Virginians agree to be taxed because voters in New England decided to do so? At a time when distance made a huge difference, how could a faraway federal government possibly fathom the thoughts and feelings of farmers on the frontier?

The proposed Constitution, therefore, required a fundamental political and psychological shift in the meaning of the American Revolution. With one crucial exception, all the arguments that American colonists had made against Parliament and the king in 1776 applied equally to the government created in the Constitution in 1787. The obvious difference was that the colonists had not been represented in Parliament, whereas they were represented in the House and the Senate under the Constitution. But were they? It came back to how you defined representation. Given the local orientation of the vast majority of Americans, the Constitution was proposing the creation of a strange new world that defied their limited horizons.

The enemies of ratification, then, were speaking for the original impulse of the American Revolution. By all rights, to the extent that the ratification process accurately reflected the will of the American citizenry, the opponents should have enjoyed a clear political advantage. But they did not, because the framework for the debate had been controlled by a small group of nationalists, who were over-represented in most of the state ratifying conventions. As a result, on the eve of the ratification debates, the momentum belonged to the nationalists.[10]

⟨⟨⟨∘⟩⟩⟩

Despite the political and tactical advantages they enjoyed, none of the chief instigators of the political process that produced the Constitution was fully satisfied with the result. Washington, like Madison, preferred a clearer delineation of federal over state sovereignty, but after witnessing the debates in Philadelphia, he realized that compromise on that crucial question was unavoidable. "I am fully persuaded it is the best that can be obtained at the present moment," he explained to Benjamin Harrison, "under such diversity of ideas as prevail."[11]

His posture of studied indifference was just that, a posture. (Conspicuous aloofness came so naturally to Washington that it is often difficult to know when he was acting and when he was just being himself.) Throughout the fall of 1787 he was clearly acting, since his private correspondence is dominated by letters to and from Hamilton, Madison, Knox, and Lafayette on the prospects of ratification, most especially in the key states of Virginia and New York, where the opposition was likely to include some powerful figures. He and Madison shared their disappointment in the defection of George Mason to the other side, which Madison found bizarre and Washington found unforgivable. Mason had been a close neighbor and long-standing friend, but all communication now ceased between Mount Vernon and Gunston Hall. Washington had purchased an English translation of *Don Quixote* before leaving Philadelphia, an odd choice for a man indisposed to tilt at windmills; it was more appropriate for Mason, who was now making himself the Don Quixote of the ratification process.[12]

Washington was outraged when his remarks on the Constitution—namely, that he was "fully persuaded that it is the best that can be obtained at this time, and that it or disunion is before us"—were leaked to the press by Charles Carter, a correspondent he customarily consulted on agricultural matters. He chastised Carter for the indiscretion, claiming that he had played his last public role at the Constitutional Convention and now wished to return to his Cincinnatus mode. While utterly sincere, he was obviously not a disinterested spectator, since nothing less than the meaning of his revolutionary legacy was at stake.[13]

Hamilton, so unlike Washington in his preference for conspicuous engagement, had already gone on the offensive in New York. On the last day of the Constitutional Convention he had made a plea for a unanimous vote from his fellow delegates. "No man's ideas were more remote from the plan than his were known to be," Madison recorded in his notes, "but [Hamilton asked] is it possible to deliberate between anarchy and Convulsion on the one side, and the change of good to be expected on the other?" Hamilton realized that his preference for a more energetic and fully empowered federal government, with unlimited terms for the president and senators, was beyond the pale of political possibility. But even though he had once been the most outspoken critic of the lingering ambiguities about federal versus state sovereignty enshrined in the Constitution, he now pivoted in the face of political reality to make himself their most ardent defender.[14]

In a series of essays in *The New York Daily Advertiser*, he focused his fire on George Clinton, the most powerful politician in New York, whose network of political operatives upstate gave him nearly complete control of delegate selection to the ratifying convention. In a series of blistering polemics, Hamilton accused Clinton of preferring the preservation of his own power base in New York to the larger interests of American nationhood. "Such conduct in a man high in office," he accused, "argues greater attachment to his *own power* than to the *public good.*" Clinton's desire to maintain his own political bailiwick led him, wrote Hamilton, to the preposterous conclusion that "the current confederation is equal to the purpose of the union." It was clear to Hamilton that New York's size and commercial advantage should make it a major player in the newly configured American republic. But Clinton and his minions were committed to a more provincial agenda, rooted in their own local and state-based interests. The future beckoned, Hamilton lamented, but Clinton insisted upon living in the past.[15]

Hamilton loved a fight, but even he was surprised at the ad homi-nem character of the response from Clinton's devoted disciples. A pair of newspaper articles with the byline "Inspector" portrayed Hamil-ton as "Tom Shit," a bastard of mixed racial origins, and referred to Washington as his "immaculate daddy," both total fabrications that haunted Hamilton's reputation for the rest of his life and beyond. Critics also accused him of being an arrogant blowhard whose reputa-tion depended entirely on his association with Washington, who had eventually recognized that he was a pompous charlatan and removed him as aide-de-camp. This was a willful distortion—Washington's trust in Hamilton was nearly bottomless, and he had released him from his duties as aide at Hamilton's request, in order to assume a combat command at Yorktown. "They say that I palmed myself upon you and you dismissed me from your family," Hamilton wrote some-what plaintively to Washington. "This I confess hurt my feelings, and if it obtains credit, will require a contradiction."

Washington responded immediately with a letter that Hamilton quickly shared with the New York press: "I do therefore, explicitly declare that both charges are entirely unfounded." This should have sufficed to squash the blatant innuendo against Hamilton, but most newspaper editors in the state, who were in Clinton's pocket, refused to publish it. New York was clearly going to be a nasty political arena during the ratification debates, in which the power of the Clinton political machine made it the most challenging opponent to ratification, a place where argument was irrelevant because Clinton's supporters enjoyed more than a two-to-one majority and therefore felt no need to listen or compromise.[16]

Nothing in Hamilton's life had prepared him to accept defeat, so he remained convinced that New York would be dragged, kicking and screaming, into the new national order once nine states ratified. He summarized his thoughts in a diary-like essay entitled "Conjectures About the New Constitution." Ratification was likely, he surmised, since the alternatives were civil war or dissolution into several regional confederacies. Hamilton's thought process was inherently and instinctively futuristic, meaning that it depended on realistic calculations about where history was headed and then aligned itself with those prevailing currents. In this case, it meant that ratification was a foregone conclusion, as was Washington's election as the first president. After that, the picture blurred, but Hamilton speculated that the large states would be broken up, and all the states reduced to merely administrative agencies without any political power. If that did not occur, there would probably be a civil war based on sectional differences over slavery. His political instincts were characteristically bold and prescient.[17]

Because his selection as a delegate had been blocked by the Clinton partisans, Jay had not experienced the nerve-racking intensity of the debates in Philadelphia, so he reviewed the results of the convention from his perch in New York, where his major task was to provide a single voice for foreign policy amid a hapless Confederation Congress that was essentially living in limbo while it waited to learn whether it had been declared defunct. A letter to John Adams conveyed Jay's almost mystical conviction that the outcome of the looming debate was foreordained, much like the war for independence, and once you knew that, you could afford to be patient about the bumps in the road to the ultimate destination and be graceful in your attitude toward the beleaguered and misguided opposition.

> The public mind is much occupied by the Plan of federal Govt. recommended by the late Convention. . . . The majority seems at present to be in its Favor. For my part I think it much better than the one we have, and therefore that we will be Gainers in the Exchange, especially as there is Reason to hope that experience and the good Sense of the People will correct what may prove to be inexpedient in it. A compact like this, which is the result of accommodation and compromise, cannot be supposed to be perfectly consonant to the wishes of any of the Parties.[18]

Like Hamilton, Madison, and Washington, Jay preferred a stronger statement of federal sovereignty, but that had proved politically impossible. So be it. Unlike Madison, who loved to linger in the details, Jay tended to focus on the broad outlines of the outcome, which moved the United States from a powerless confederation of sovereign states to a more coherent and energetic federal government whose range of power would be determined in the future. Accusations by the opposition about the tyrannical tendencies of a consolidated national government could best be handled pragmatically, on a case-by-case basis, where they were likely to be exposed as paranoid delusions.

Jay knew that he was likely to be elected as a delegate to the New York ratifying convention, and in the end he received more votes than any other nominee. Not a man to harbor illusions, he also realized from the start that, because of Clinton's dominant role in New York politics, the nationalists were likely to be outgunned and outvoted in the New York convention. But he had a panoramic perspective on the ratification process. "I am inclined to think that the

Constitution will be adopted in this State," he wrote Washington, "especially if our eastern Neighbours should generally come into the Measure." In other words, ratification in New York would depend on what happened elsewhere, creating irresistible pressure to join the union once nine states ratified. His mind began with the assumption that ratification was inevitable, then plotted the only course for it to happen in New York. Events proved him right on both counts, and no one was prepared to be more gracious in victory than Jay.[19]

Unlike Jay, who had been watching from afar, Madison had spent the entire summer deeply engaged in the endless debates in Philadelphia, and he returned to his seat in the Confederation Congress both exhausted and deeply disappointed. Unlike Hamilton, who immediately shifted gears despite his personal reservations and moved into advocacy mode, Madison was temporarily paralyzed, blaming himself for the failure of the Constitution to resolve forever the sovereignty question. The opportunity to create a fully empowered national government, he wrote in code to Jefferson, had come and gone.[20]

Jefferson was somewhat mystified by Madison's message, in part because, even more than Jay, he enjoyed the luxury of distance from the debates in Philadelphia, and in part because he did not share Madison's robust national agenda. He confided to Madison that a federal veto of state laws struck him as unnecessarily excessive, "like mending a small hole by covering the whole garment." Jefferson always made it a practice to listen to the political advice of his younger protégé, so it is an intriguing but unanswerable question what side he would have taken if present in Philadelphia. His deepest convictions clearly lay on the confederation side of the political equation. Madison was Jefferson's most trusted political disciple, but for the moment they were not properly aligned.[21]

As he struggled to recover his political balance, Madison wrote to William Short, Jefferson's secretary in Paris, to ask what the European savants thought of the new Constitution:

I shall learn with much solicitude the comments of the philosophical statesmen of Europe on this new fabric of American
policy. Unless however their future criticisms should evince
a more thorough knowledge of our situation than many of
their past, my curiosity will not be rewarded with much
instruction.[22]

Madison knew full well that most European observers—with a
few French exceptions—expected and wanted the American experiment with a large-scale republic to fail. And again for the moment,
he was worried that their hopes would be fulfilled because of his own
failure to win the big battles in Philadelphia. He was living alone in
bachelor quarters in New York City, waiting for the Confederation
Congress, which was barely on life support, to gather a quorum. He
was in a funk.

What pulled him out of his sour mood was news from the field
that the "Great Debate" had begun in the newspapers, and the states
were beginning to select delegates for their conventions. "The newspapers in the middle & Northern States begin to teem with controversial publications," Madison reported to Edmund Randolph,
adding that the major criticism seemed to be that the Constitution
lacked a bill of rights. (One could invent many elaborate reasons
for the absence of a bill of rights, and Madison proceeded to do
just that, but the real reason was that the delegates in Philadelphia
were thoroughly exhausted after a summer of intense debates, and by
September they wanted to go home.) Madison entered his lawyer-
like mode again, just as he had before the Constitutional Convention, preparing rebuttals of the arguments beginning to emerge from
the opposition. His very real reservations about that document now
needed to be suppressed and concealed, lest they contaminate his
case and endanger the verdict.[23]

In the end, Madison believed that the verdict would be decided not by arguments but by the makeup of the state ratifying conventions, where the vast majority of delegates would vote their interests, which could not be changed by the eloquence of one side or the other. So he put on his other hat as backroom politician and began to assemble a state-by-state assessment of the likely voting blocs. Again, this was the kind of nitty-gritty politics that a Virginia statesman was supposed to regard as an affront to his dignity, but Madison found it invigorating.[24]

"The presumptive evidence is pretty strong with regard to New England," he concluded, meaning he predicted a sweep of all the states with the exception of Rhode Island, "whose folly and fraud have not yet finished their career." Reports from Pennsylvania suggested that it was not going to be a runaway victory, as he initially expected, but a clear victory nonetheless. New Jersey and Delaware could be safely counted in the win column, as could Maryland, unless Virginia faltered, which might then bring both Maryland and North Carolina in its train. Virginia looked likely to Madison but still problematic because of the opposition of Henry, Mason, and perhaps Randolph. New York would be very difficult because of Clinton's control of the upstate counties. Given the obvious political significance of Virginia and New York, the strategy should be to achieve the nine-state goal before their conventions met and thereby present their delegates with a fait accompli.[25]

All in all, Madison calculated that "the present appearance is in favor of the new Constitution." The momentum of the ratification process worked to the advantage of the "Pros" and the disadvantage of the "Antis," because pressure would build as each early state ratified, and quite fortuitously, the most questionable states would come at the end of the ratification sequence. Also, the supporters of ratification were united, "while the adversaries differ as much in their opposition as they do from the thing itself."[26]

At the same time that he was counting delegates in his obsessive Madisonian mode, his thought process, or perhaps his way of thinking about the ratification process, was beginning to change as he read the newspaper essays and editorials from multiple states. It gradually dawned on him that if he had gotten what he wanted at the Philadelphia convention, the prospects for ratification of the Constitution would have been remote in the extreme. In a long and quite extraordinary letter to Jefferson, the fullest and clearest exposition of what the Constitutional Convention had achieved that Madison ever wrote, he described the hybrid creature that the Constitution had created as part confederation and part nation. The delegates had, willy-nilly, managed "to draw a line of demarcation which would give to the General Government every power requisite for general purposes, and leave to the states every power which might be most beneficial to them."[27]

Left unsaid was that no one knew where that line existed, or what "general purposes" meant. Although it would take Madison several months to develop the full implications of this evolving idea, its outlines were already clear in the letter to Jefferson in late October 1787. The key insight might be called the beauty of ambiguity. Madison had misguidedly, he now realized, pushed for an unambiguous resolution of the sovereignty question during the convention. Now it was becoming clear to him that the great achievement of the convention, and of the Constitution as well, was to embrace the inconvenient truth that there was no consensus on the sovereignty question, either in the convention or in the country itself. So what they had created, albeit out of necessity rather then choice, was a political framework that deliberately blurred the sovereignty question.

Most historians and constitutional scholars over the last fifty years have agreed that Madison's preconvention preparations constituted an impressively creative moment that effectively set the agenda for the debate in Philadelphia that summer. Few have recognized that Madison's postconvention thinking constituted a second creative moment of equivalent or greater historical significance. For it produced a political perspective that had short-term consequences for the all-important ratification process and long-term consequences for how the Constitution should be comprehended as the defining document of the new, and eventually not so new, American republic.

In the short run, it meant that the advocates of ratification were defending the blueprint not for a new, wholly consolidated national government but rather for a halfway house that was partially federal and partially confederal. The multiple compromises reached in the Constitutional Convention over where to locate sovereignty accurately reflected the deep divisions in the American populace at large. There was a strong consensus that the state-based system under the Articles had proven ineffectual, but an equally strong apprehension about the political danger posed by any national government that rode roughshod over local, state, and regional interests, which were the familiar spaces where the vast majority of American lived out their lives. As Madison now realized, the Constitution created a federal structure that moved the American republic toward nationhood while retaining an abiding place for local and state allegiances. In that sense, it was a second American Revolution that took the form of an American Evolution, which allowed the citizenry to adapt gradually to its national implications.

In the long run—and this was probably Madison's most creative insight—the multiple ambiguities embedded in the Constitution made it an inherently "living" document. For it was designed not to offer clear answers to the sovereignty question (or, for that matter, to the scope of executive or judicial authority) but instead to provide a political arena in which arguments about those contested issues could continue in a deliberative fashion. The Constitution was intended less to resolve arguments than to make argument itself the solution. For judicial devotees of "originalism" or "original intent," this should be a disarming insight, since it made the Constitution the foundation for an ever-shifting political dialogue that, like history itself, was an argument without end. Madison's "original intention" was to make all "original intentions" infinitely negotiable in the future.[28]

The following chart provides a succinct summary, in chronological order, of the ratification process in all thirteen states:

STATE	DATE	YAY / NAY
Delaware	December 7, 1787	30–0
Pennsylvania	December 12, 1787	46–23
New Jersey	December 18, 1787	38–0
Georgia	December 31, 1787	26–0
Connecticut	January 8, 1788	128–40
Massachusetts	February 6, 1788	187–168 (with amendments)
Maryland	April 26, 1788	63–11
South Carolina	May 26, 1788	149–73
New Hampshire	June 21, 1788	57–47 (with amendments)
Virginia	June 29, 1788	89–79 (with amendments)
New York	July 26, 1788	30–27 (with amendments)
North Carolina	November 21, 1789	194–77 (with amendments)
Rhode Island	May 29, 1790	34–32 (with amendments)

At first glance, this list suggests that ratification of the Constitution enjoyed widespread popular support. Participation was broad-gauged, involving 1,646 delegates from all the states. In the end, not a single state refused to ratify, and majorities in seven states were overwhelming. In that sense, the Great Debate produced a resounding vote for American nationhood that approximated the resounding vote for American independence in the summer of 1776.

A closer look, however, tends to undermine such a comfortable conclusion. The vote in three of the largest states—Massachusetts, Virginia, and New York—was extremely close. A clear majority actually opposed ratification in New York, North Carolina, and Rhode Island, which grudgingly came along late in the game, after the nine-vote quota had been reached. The insistence on amendments in six of the states reflected a deep dissatisfaction with the all-or-nothing terms of the debate. The major achievement of the pro-ratification side was to insist that all amendments were only recommendations, that ratification could not be made contingent on their adoption. (Holding that line was Madison's all-consuming political goal throughout the ratification process.) A near majority in Massachusetts and Virginia, and a large majority in New York, North Carolina, and Rhode Island, preferred their amendments to be conditional, with ratification occurring only after a second convention took them into account.

To say, then, that ratification represented a clear statement about the will of the American people in 1787–88 would be grossly misleading. What ratification really represented was the triumph of superior organization, more talented leadership, and a political process that had been designed from the start to define the options narrowly (i.e., up or down), and the successful outcome broadly (i.e., nine states). And despite their built-in advantages, it was still a close call. A shift of six votes in Virginia would have probably produced a shock wave that left four states—Virginia, New York, North Carolina, and Rhode Island—out of the union. And even though nine states had ratified, so that the Constitution was legally adopted, it is difficult to imagine an American nation surviving in such a geographically splintered condition.

The chart also obscures the fact that the ratification debate in each state was driven by local and state-based concerns rather than by the larger question of confederation or nation. It seems almost sacrilegious to think it, much more to say it, but in the Great Debate overarching political principles became a minor theme in large part because the vast majority of delegates did not know how to think nationally, since nothing in their experience had prepared them to do so. In that sense, they were more representative of the American populace than their predecessors in Philadelphia. The net result was a twelve-ring circus—Rhode Island remaining an outlier—in which each state convention became a separate arena filled with performers playing to local constituencies.

In Massachusetts, for example, the outcome was much closer than Madison or Washington had predicted, partly because some delegates from the Maine district believed that ratification would endanger their looming bid for statehood, partly because farmers from the western towns and counties, some of them former Shaysites, preferred the vastly inflated state currency to pay off their debts and instinctively opposed any political initiative coming from Boston. The narrow margin of victory was rendered possible when John Hancock proposed a procedure that was subsequently copied by five other states: namely, the delegates would vote on ratification, then vote on recommended amendments to the Constitution. This allowed delegates with doubts to endorse ratification while still expressing their state-based reservations. In the end, six states submitted 124 proposed amendments, most of which were intended to impose restrictions on federal authority.[29]

While all states were different, among the big states New York was the most different of all. Governor George Clinton, the most popular politician in the state, was an adamant opponent of ratification, with patronage powers in the upstate counties that ensured an overwhelming majority in the convention. New York's economy was flourishing, in part because of a state tariff on imports that it did not wish to share, in part because of its policy of foreclosing on loyalist estates in violation of the Treaty of Paris. Ratification, therefore, would have undermined Clinton's power base and restricted New York's two major streams of revenue. Though both Jay and Hamilton were poised to deliver their eloquence to the New York ratification convention, Clinton's followers were impervious to argument.

Again, the most salient point to notice is that the debate over American nationhood in the ratifying conventions was driven by state and local concerns that were maddeningly diverse, thoroughly provincial, and utterly oblivious to the larger issues at stake. (Virginia, as we shall see, was somewhat of an exception.) Only one modern historian, Pauline Maier, has been willing and able to master the twelve separate stories in their excruciating detail. But the fact that there are twelve distinct stories is, in truth, the most revealing story of all, for it exposes the elemental fact that the vast majority of Americans were not yet capable of a national conversation as a coherent collective. Local and state borders were as far as they could see and, for the opponents of ratification, as far as any meaningful version of representative government should reach.[30]

The same men who had instigated the calling of the Constitutional Convention, recruited Washington to the task, and imposed the national agenda in Philadelphia now took the lead in attempting to orchestrate the ratification process. Between November 1787 and March 1788, Hamilton (51), Madison (29), and Jay (5), wrote eighty-five essays under the common pseudonym Publius entitled the Federalist Papers. It was a project conceived by Hamilton, who recruited Jay and Madison to the task. Over the ensuing centuries the Federalist Papers have assumed the stature of an iconic text, the classic expression of the great deliberation about the viability of a nation-size republican government.

In several senses, this reputation is both unwarranted and misleading. The Federalist Papers were, in fact, perhaps the supreme example of improvisational journalism, composed against tight deadlines without much time for deliberation at all. Madison later claimed that he was making changes as the printer set the type. And Hamilton, whose phenomenal output in such a brief time almost defies credibility, began the series writing on scrap paper atop a wooden box while traveling on a sloop between New York City and Albany.[31]

Even our modern inclination to see the Federalist Papers as the seminal statement of "the original intentions" of the framers is historically incorrect, since Publius represented only one side of the ratification debate—the winning side, to be sure, but a wholly partisan perspective. Finally, the Federalist Papers were aimed not at posterity but at a limited audience of the moment. As Madison later explained, Publius was intended "to promote the ratification of the new Constitution by the State of N. York, where it was powerfully opposed, and where success was deemed of critical importance." Scholarly studies of its distribution beyond New York suggest a very limited influence. It is highly likely the Federalist Papers have exercised a larger effect on our later perceptions of the debate over ratification than they did over the debate itself.[32]

All that said, the Federalist Papers remain an American masterpiece—mostly Hamilton's masterpiece—the classical statement for the viability of a nation-size republic. Washington was remarkably prescient on this score. When Hamilton presented him with a two-volume edition in August 1788, Washington offered the following opinion:

I have read every performance which has been printed on one side and the other on the question lately agitated and regarded the Production of your Triumvirate as best by far. . . . When the transient circumstances and fugitive performances which attend this crisis shall have disappeared, that work will merit the notice of Posterity, [because it] identified the principles underlying our noble experiment in permanent and classical form.[33]

Posterity has tended to confirm Washington's prediction, though it required more than a century for it to come true. In the twentieth century Madison's Federalist 10 became the most analyzed political essay in American history, so convincing in its argument for the viability of a large-scale republic that one is left to wonder why Montesquieu's argument on the other side was ever taken seriously. Or consider these words from Federalist 51, also an obligatory entry in any modern textbook on the origins of American government:

> But what is government itself but the greatest of all reflections on human nature? If men were angels, no government would be necessary. If angels were to govern men, neither external nor internal controls would be necessary. In framing a government which is to be administered by men over men, the greatest difficulty lies in this: You must first enable the government to control the governed; and in the next place oblige it to control itself. A dependence on the people is no doubt the primary control on government, but experience has taught mankind the necessity of auxiliary precautions.[34]

Parsing those last two words, "auxiliary precautions," might require a semester-long course in American political science. Madison was rather elliptically attempting to distinguish between a democracy and a republic, suggesting that the structure of the government proposed in the Constitution was designed to sift popular opinion through multiple layers of deliberation in order to distill the long-term interest of the American republic.

While how we read Publius today is not irrelevant, for historical purposes it is more relevant to recognize, as Washington suggested, that it was a distinctive voice in the ratification debates. No coordinated effort appeared on the other side. There was no such thing as the Antifederalist Papers. Even more relevant and revealing, almost all opponents of ratification wrote from a state-based perspective, and the vast majority of delegates in the ratifying conventions, including those who voted for ratification, did so for state-based reasons. Only Publius spoke from a national perspective.

One partial exception to the rule on the "Anti" side was Centinel, an otherwise obscure Philadelphia writer named Samuel Bryan. Centinel attacked a core assumption of Publius's, made most forcefully by Hamilton in Federalist 1, that the current government was about to dissolve into a series of regional confederacies: "This hobgoblin appears to have sprung from the deranged brain of Publius, a New York writer who, mistaking sound for argument, has with Herculean labour accumulated myriads of unmeaning sentences and mechanically endeavored to enforce conviction by a torrent of misplaced words. . . . The writer has devoted much time in combating chimeras of his own creation."[35]

Even Centinel, however, delivered his criticism from a Pennsylvania perspective. As far as he could tell, most of the citizens of his state were perfectly content with the current arrangement under the Articles. This did not meet the crux of Hamilton's argument about the growing national debt and the currently moribund condition of the Confederation Congress, because Centinel was essentially arguing that most Pennsylvanians did not care about such things. By insisting that the central issue required a national vision that transcended state and local mentalities, Publius was assuming that the Constitutional Convention had created a new political context within which local and state opinions needed to be subordinated. The new Constitution, then, was like a new ship of state prepared to carry most Americans to a more expansive definition of their identity, whether they wanted to go there or not.

By April 1788 it had become abundantly clear that Virginia would be the decisive state. Apart from its own importance and its keen sense of self-importance, the verdict in Virginia now loomed much larger because the early momentum for ratification had stalled when two states, New Hampshire and North Carolina, decided to postpone their conventions, and Maryland threatened to join them in order to await Virginia's decision. There was an interactive dimension to the ratification process. If Virginia did not ratify, the political momentum would shift dramatically against ratification.

Although Washington had taken a vow of abstinence after the Constitutional Convention—he would play no active role in the debates—he broke that vow, probably under prodding from Madison, by writing to friends in Maryland, urging a vote rather than a postponement. "An adjournment of your convention . . . will be tantamount to the rejection of the Constitution," he warned, because it would strengthen the opposition in Virginia, which was already perilously close to a majority. Any request of this sort from Washington was equivalent to a command, and Maryland voted for ratification (63–11) within the week. That meant that the political pressure would build in Virginia to become the ninth state and put ratification over the top. The problem was that the political elite in Virginia was evenly divided, and while both sides felt a keen obligation to lead, they wanted to lead in opposite directions.[36]

Madison went into his nose-counting mode soon after the delegates were elected to the Virginia convention, scheduled for Richmond in mid-June. After an initial burst of enthusiasm, during which he apprised both Jefferson and Washington that the "Pros" enjoyed a comfortable majority, he gradually became more circumspect. The northern part of the state was firmly "Pro," but the Tidewater counties, where the planter class was heavily in debt to British creditors whom they preferred to finesse, were firmly "Anti," with the delegates from the western counties and the Kentucky district holding the balance of power. It was going to be extremely close. Madison immediately began firing off letters to friends in Kentucky, arguing that their concerns about navigation rights on the Mississippi would be best served by joining the union.[37]

Another, less local way of looking at Virginia's voting patterns came from John Marshall, a devoted protégé of Washington's, a Revolutionary War hero, and a future chief justice of the Supreme Court. Marshall believed that a sizable majority of Virginians opposed ratification, "but they have chosen their most trusted local leaders as delegates, who by a small margin support it." In his judgment the will of the majority would defer to the more informed and trusted men in the Old Dominion. It was still a predemocratic world where that kind of elite analysis required no apology.[38]

The wild card that confounded any prediction of the outcome in Virginia was Patrick Henry, who was simultaneously the most popular politician in the state and the most famous orator of the age. Henry had boycotted the convention in Philadelphia, as Madison quite caustically put it to Washington, "in order to leave his conduct unfettered on another theatre, where the results of the [Virginia] Convention will receive its destiny from his omnipotence."[39]

Madison had been on the receiving end of Henry's eloquence on several occasions, so he knew what he was up against. Henry on his feet was a force of nature, part actor on the stage, part preacher in the pulpit. He could go on for hours at a time, without notes, often wandering off point, but always casting a spell. If argument was going to make a difference in the Virginia convention, and it was, Henry gave the "Antis" an advantage.

There was also bad blood between Henry and the Jefferson-Madison tandem. It dated from 1781, when Henry had led the effort to impeach Jefferson as governor for his somewhat hasty and headlong retreat from office to avoid capture by the invading British army. Henry had also used his political patronage to block Jefferson's resolution for religious freedom, which Madison was defending in the Virginia legislature. As Jefferson put it to Madison, there seemed no way to deal with Henry "except to ardently pray for his imminent death."[40]

The Virginia convention was destined to become one of the most significant and consequential debates in American history. The Virginia press, sensing the historical implications, had hired stenographers to record the words of all speakers, making it the most fully preserved of all the ratifying conventions. The two sides appeared evenly divided, especially when Edmund Randolph, the sitting governor, came over to the "Pro" side, while George Mason, one of the most respected constitutional thinkers in the state, had become a conspicuous spokesman and strategist for the "Antis."

Everyone realized, though, that the two titans in the Richmond debates were going to be Henry and Madison. To describe Madison as a "titan" seems incongruous, since he was a diminutive physical presence and on his feet was barely audible, speaking like a stilted professor who kept referring to notes stuffed in his hat, the oratorical opposite of the unscripted, free-floating Henry.

Appearances, however, were deceptive. Madison was accustomed to being the most fully prepared speaker in the room, the kind of frustrating opponent who somehow seemed to understand the implications of your argument better than you did. Unlike Henry, he had been present to hear all the debates in Philadelphia, and he possessed the fullest set of notes on those debates. Then the act of drafting twenty-nine essays as Publius had given his thoughts a final gloss. It was, in fact, an equal contest between a great orator and a great thinker. As Marshall so nicely put it, "Mr. Henry had without doubt the greatest power to persuade, [but] Mr. Madison had the greatest power to convince."[41]

———— ⚬⚬⚬ ————

Thanks largely to Henry's bravura performance, plus his instinctive desire to attack the central assumptions of Publius, the debate in the

Virginia convention achieved a singular status: it subordinated the local concerns of most delegates to the periphery and focused on the larger national issues at stake. Ironically, scholars have questioned the influence of Publius beyond New York. In Virginia, Publius was front and center but primarily as a target for all that the "Antis" opposed.

In his maiden speech on June 5, Henry fired a full salvo at the core premises of Publius. First, Henry claimed that the Constitutional Convention had itself been an unconstitutional gathering, because the delegates had exceeded their instructions by replacing the Articles rather than amending them. On this issue, he clearly had the historical facts on his side.[42]

Next, Henry questioned the alarmist presumption that America was on the verge of anarchy, with the Articles about to expire and dissolution into several regional confederacies the likely outcome. As far as Henry could tell, most Virginians were getting on with their lives with conspicuous serenity. The Confederation Congress was never supposed to function as a government, Henry observed, but as a clearinghouse for the political agenda of the states, and it had performed that limited mission quite well: "It carried us through a long and dangerous war. It rendered us victorious in that bloody conflict with a powerful nation. It had secured us a territory greater than any European monarchy possesses. And shall a government that strong and rigorous be accused of imbecility for want of energy?"[43]

This was revisionist history in a Virginia-writ-large vision of America, and Madison was quick to pounce on it as the kind of incredulous remarks made by someone who'd been living on another planet. Had Henry not noticed that, throughout the war, the states—Virginia included—had failed to meet their quota of money and men? Voluntary state requisitions had become a joke, producing a national debt approaching $70 million with no way to pay it, making American credit worthless among European bankers. All the European governments regarded the very term *United States* as a laughable irony, since each state made its own foreign policy.[44]

Madison then unfurled his familiar argument against the systemic weakness of the German, Swiss, and Dutch confederacies: "Does not the history of these confederacies coincide with the lessons drawn from our own experience?" He went on to answer his own rhetorical question: "A Government that relies on thirteen independent sovereignties for the means of its existence is a solecism in theory, and a mere nullity in practice."[45]

These were not arguments familiar to Henry, nor arguments often heard within the precincts of Virginia, which were the only precincts Henry cared about. He was an ardent confederationist who presumed that Virginia would remain the dominant nation-state and that both his own political power base and, as he saw it, the majority of Virginians had more to lose than gain by joining a larger union. In a very real sense, Henry and Madison were talking past each other, for they harbored fundamentally different views of America's future. The great virtue of the Henry-Madison debate was to make that fundamental difference abundantly clear.

Henry did not believe that there was such a thing as "the American people," only Virginians, Pennsylvanians, New Englanders, or South Carolinians. And on this score he was, once again, historically correct. He spoke eloquently and passionately for the hallowed conviction that the American Revolution committed the United States to a version of republican government that was proximate and personal. And any larger union of states that made representation distant and impersonal defied the political experience of most Virginians and the core principles of '76. Again, the facts were on his side.

In retrospect, we can see clearly that Henry spoke for the past and Madison spoke for the future. But Henry deserves full attention for making the case for what we might call the first American Revolution with such clarity. "Have they said, 'we the states' . . . this would be a confederation. . . . The question turns, Sir, on that poor little thing, the expression 'We, the people,' instead of the States of America." Henry was right. That was the core issue.

In an extremely revealing aside, Henry posed the following question: "Suppose every delegate from Virginia in the new government opposed a law levying a tax, but it passes. So you are taxed not by your own consent, but by the people who have no connection with you." In Henry's political universe, non-Virginians were not fellow citizens but foreigners, whose interests were not aligned with the values of the Old Dominion. Any wholly national government that attempted to unite the states created a domestic version of Parliament, which was precisely the kind of arbitrary and unrepresentative government that Americans had spent so much blood and treasure to escape.[46]

The watchword of Henry's critique of the Constitution was *consolidation*, a term loaded with ideological and quasi-paranoid implications. It conjured up the image of a political monster devouring the liberties of the citizenry, an inherently tyrannical behemoth with an avaricious appetite that, once in place, could not be controlled or stopped. (Modern-day Tea Partiers share this political legacy, with its deep roots in the hostility to any robust expression of government power at the federal level.) "You make the citizens of this country to become the subjects of one consolidated empire in America," Henry warned. "When I come to examine those features sir, they appear to me horribly frightful. Among other deformities it has an awful squinting; it squints towards monarchy."[47]

In several senses, then, Henry had history on his side in this critique of the Constitution. But there was one elemental difference between the political context in 1776 and that in 1787–88. The American colonists had not been represented in Parliament. Their definition of what constituted representation would have to change, to be sure, but the delegates gathered in Philadelphia did not regard themselves as repudiating so much as expanding the meaning of the

American Revolution. And Henry had the misfortune to draw as an opponent the one man in America most articulate in making that argument.

In some better world, Madison would have attacked the central premise of Henry's argument that there was, as yet, no such thing as "We the people of the United States." He would have said, "I have seen the future and it works"—in effect, we are a single people who only need time within a common government to discover our collective interest. (This, by the way, was Washington's opinion.) But Madison was less a political visionary than a practical politician who needed to win the votes in Richmond and put Virginia over the top. For that reason, he chose to attack the flanks of Henry's argument. Henry had argued that the Constitution created a consolidated federal government that rode roughshod over the power of states. Madison argued that Henry did not know what he was talking about, that the political architecture created in Philadelphia mandated shared sovereignty between the federal government and the states.

"It is, in a manner unprecedented," Madison observed. "It stands by itself. In some respects it is a government of a federal nature; in others it is of a consolidated nature," meaning that the Constitution granted enumerated powers to the national government, but left all else to the province of the states. The phrase "We the people" did not refer to "the people composing one great body—but the people composing thirteen separate sovereignties." The Senate represented the states, and its members would be elected by the state legislatures. The states appointed the electors who chose the president. All constitutional amendments required ratification by a supermajority of the states. This was an enormous concession on Madison's part, on the one hand a recognition that Henry was right in saying that no national ethos currently existed but, on the other hand, a deft deferral of the ultimate verdict to the future by describing the Constitution as a framework within which some version of state and national sovereignty would continue to coexist.[48]

All the arguments that Madison made in Richmond on behalf of shared sovereignty represented a repudiation of the arguments he had made in Philadelphia in favor of a clear statement of sovereignty at the federal level. But the political circumstances had changed, and Madison, ever the political animal, had changed with them. If he had to abandon some of his fondest convictions to win ratification in Virginia, he was fully prepared to do so.

Once the boogeyman of "consolidation" had been defanged, Henry realized his only hope was to load up Virginia's ratification with so many amendments that a second convention would need to be called, which then, he hoped, would end up revising the Articles rather than replacing them. But erosion of support in the western counties and Kentucky meant that he did not have the votes.

While delivering his final speech on June 29, proposing forty new amendments to the Constitution, Henry was interrupted by a violent thunderstorm, suggesting that even the gods favored ratification. The final vote was close but decisive (89–79). A caucus of the defeated "Antis" voted to mount a challenge to the verdict, holding out hope for a second convention. But Henry refused to lend his support to what he realized was a lost cause. He had done his best, he said, they had all done their best, and though they surely had represented Virginia's political interest, they had lost. And so for now "they had better go home." For better and for worse, the Constitution was destined to become the law of the land.[49]

Given the size and commercial significance of New York, it seems both awkward and irreverent to notice that the decision in Virginia made New York a mere epilogue in the ratification story, but it was. Actually, New Hampshire had acted with unexpected vigor to ratify as the ninth state, making Virginia the tenth. Ratification was now assured, altering the political chemistry and leaving New York with a rather somber choice. It could join Rhode Island as a renegade state and attempt to go it alone, a posture that was simultaneously honorable and suicidal, or it could, albeit reluctantly, join the union.[50]

Before the verdict in Virginia was clear, both Jay and Hamilton, though vastly outnumbered, had done their best to make the case for ratification. Jay had written an essay, widely circulated in the New York press, that actually outdid Publius in making the most comprehensive argument for what was at stake, in language that was, even more than that of Publius, simultaneously accessible and lyrical. It was a new revolutionary moment, as Jay saw it, and Americans needed to come together in 1788 as they had in 1776. The downside was that, if they failed to do so, the outcome would be just as catastrophic as defeat would have been in the war against Great Britain. Jay also won adherents even among his opponents on the floor at Poughkeepsie with a diplomatic demeanor that made him impossible to hate. ("Please, sir, explain your position to me again, since I do so much wish to understand it.")[51]

As might be expected, Hamilton was brilliant in a more aggressive mode, impervious to the political odds against which he was arguing; as Jefferson later said, he was "a host unto himself." But Hamilton's greatest contribution, at least in practical terms, was to establish a series of riders between Richmond and Poughkeepsie to apprise New York of the verdict in Virginia. Given the numbers in the New York convention, there was no way that Jay and Hamilton could win the debate. Their primary political task was to delay the vote in New York until the Virginia vote had created a fait accompli. They were successful in this task, and New York voted for ratification by the narrowest of margins (30–27), in truth against its will.

Reading Jay's correspondence during the New York debates again calls attention to his almost preternatural confidence that, against all odds, victory was never in doubt. He apparently believed what he had written to the New York citizenry, that providential forces were at work in the ratification process just as they had been in the war for independence. And given the extraordinarily fortuitous way that history happened in New York, it is difficult to dismiss Jay's incomparable serenity as anything less than some secular version of divine inspiration.[52]

If the verdict in New York turned out to be a political epilogue in the ratification story, the incredulity of the Clintonites at losing a battle in which they possessed a clear majority created an epilogue to the epilogue. New York's endorsement of ratification included a series of recommended amendments to the Constitution, and a statement that ratification had occurred "in full confidence that the necessary amendments would be adopted." Madison immediately rejected New York's terms, arguing that they constituted "conditional ratification, that it does not make N. York a member of the New Union, and consequently she should not be received on that plan." Madison's point was that states could make recommended amendments, but they could not make ratification conditional upon acceptance of those amendments. New York was attempting to conflate recommendations with conditions. Madison wrote Hamilton, urging him to apprise all the New York delegates that the Constitution must be adopted "in toto, and for ever . . . and any condition whatsoever must visciate the ratification."[53]

New York's somewhat mischievous intentions were fully exposed in a circular letter sent by Governor Clinton to all the states, arguing that there needed to be a second convention if the multiple amendments recommended by six of the states were not acted on promptly by the newly elected government. There was also a veiled threat that New York intended to secede from the union if its recommended amendments were ignored. Ever the aggressor, Hamilton then proceeded to issue his own not-so-veiled threat that if New York seceded from the union, the New York City region would secede from New York.[54]

Both Washington and Madison regarded New York's circular letter as a last-ditch attempt to subvert ratification of the Constitution. Washington thought the letter would have "an insidious tendency . . . to serve as a standard to which the disaffected might resort." As he put it to Madison, "to be shipwrecked in sight of the Port would be the severest of all aggravations." Madison concurred, describing New York's circular letter as an "act of desperation with a most pestilent tendency."[55]

Somewhat strangely, Jay endorsed the circular letter and even had a major hand in its drafting. He had made a career out of being his own man, and in this instance, much as in his handling of the Mississippi Question, he concluded that a temporary concession would do no harm, especially if you knew that your cause would triumph in the end. "I think we should not have much danger to apprehend of it," he apprised Washington, "especially if the new Government should in the mean Time recommend itself to the People by the wisdom of its Proceedings, which I flatter myself will be the Case."[56]

Jay apparently believed that New York was engaging in a political tantrum, an exercise in bravado in response to the unacceptable fact of its political irrelevance in the ratification process. Since they had provided no deadline for acceptance of their amendments, Jay observed, the Clintonites were clearly bluffing. Best to humor them, harmlessly endorse their sense of significance, then fold them into the union with their honor intact.

Although Madison, who for good reasons regarded himself as the chief conductor of the ratification symphony, spent most of August and September 1788 worrying that New York's desperate gambit might transform the music of ratification into a cacophony, events proved Jay's judgment correct. New York had no desire to become a larger version of Rhode Island.

———— ∞ ————

Once ratification was assured, Washington tried to explain how a political movement for a national government, which only two years earlier had appeared hopeless, had somehow managed to overcome the odds and triumph. "A multiplicity of circumstances . . . appear to have cooperated in bringing about the happy resolution," he observed, citing Shays' Rebellion as a near calamity that prompted the calling of the Constitutional Convention, "which then ushered us to permanent national felicity." In the same ironic vein, he thought that the very hopelessness of the task, and the strength of the opposition, "had called forth abilities which would otherwise not perhaps been exerted that have thrown new lights on the science of Government [i.e., the Federalist Papers], that have given the rights of man a full and fair discussion."[57]

Washington had developed a flair for providential interpretations during the war, when he had firsthand experience with the way American independence, what he called "The Cause," had experienced multiple moments when everything was at stake, and providence—the fates, pure luck, whatever one wished to call it— had come to the rescue just when all seemed lost. He was now bringing that same providential perspective to the ratification of the Constitution. In both instances, as he saw it, America seemed to be destiny's child.

A more secular and less spiritual interpretation would emphasize the role of what historians, somewhat awkwardly, call human agency. In Washington's version of how history happened, the gods were always in control. And perhaps they were. But on this earth, rather than in the heavens, four men made history happen in a series of political decisions and actions that, in terms of their consequences, have no equal in American history. And they were not quite through.

Chapter 7

FINAL PIECES

You will permit me to say that it is indispensible you should lend yourself to its [the government's] first operation. It is of little use to have introduced a system if the weightiest influence is not given to its firm establishment, in the outset.

Alexander Hamilton to George Washington
AUGUST 13, 1788

amilton took the lead during the final phase of the story, which was all about ensuring that the new federal government was administered by men of talent who were committed to making the experiment with a large-scale republican government work. Down in Virginia, Patrick Henry was already moving to avenge his defeat in Richmond by pressuring the legislature to select for the Senate men who had opposed ratification, thereby blocking Madison's election, though he could not prevent Madison's election to the House. Up in New York, George Clinton was pursuing the same strategy, designed to make the New York delegation a Trojan horse within the new federal fortress, all the while pressing for a second convention as described in his "circulatory letter," which was obviously a recipe for reversing the verdict recently reached in the ratification process.[1]

Hamilton again focused most of his fire on New York, launching a campaign to oppose Clinton's candidates for the Senate and the Electoral College. He also published fourteen essays in the *Daily Advertiser* under the pseudonym "H.R.," attacking Clinton's character, his obstructionist political motives, and his corrupt system of patronage. Beyond much doubt, Hamilton was the most skilled political polemicist in America, and he brought the same incredible energy he had displayed as Publius to the task at hand. The Constitution, he believed, was only words on parchment, outlining the framework for a new kind of American republic. Unless those words and framework were implemented by representatives devoted to its success, not men seeking to sabotage its very survival, all the work of the past two years would be for naught.[2]

There was one person who was utterly indispensable, the only man in America capable of transcending the local, state, and regional divisions, the "singular figure" whom every American could agree embodied the American Revolution in all its multiple manifestations. Like everyone else, Hamilton assumed that George Washington would become the first president of the United States, and a number of delegates to the Constitutional Convention and state ratifying conventions had voted to endorse the Constitution primarily on the presumption that Washington would head the new federal government.

There was, however, one man in America who did not share that presumption, and it happened to be Washington himself. Ever since the spring of 1788, when the prospects for ratification began to look likely, Washington had seen fit to apprise all who inquired that he was permanently embedded beneath his vines and fig tree at Mount Vernon and had no desire or intention to budge. "I am so wedded to a state of retirement," he explained, "and find the occupations of a rural life so congenial with my feelings, that to be drawn into public life at this advanced age would be a sacrifice that could afford no compensation."[3]

Eloquent testimonials in the Ciceronian style to the bucolic pleasures of retirement were a familiar refrain within the planter class of Virginia. But Washington was not just posing within that rhetorical tradition. "As the great searcher of human hearts is my witness," he insisted, "I have no wish which aspires beyond the humble and happy lot of living and dying a private citizen on my own farm."[4]

It fell to Hamilton to apprise his old commander that, whether he knew it or not, he really had no choice:

I take it for granted, Sir, you have concluded to comply with what will no doubt be the general call of your country in relation to the new government. You will permit me to say that it is indispensible you should lend yourself to its first operation. It is of little use to have introduced a system if the weightiest influence is not given to its firm establishment, in the outset.[5]

In effect, once he stepped back onto the public stage in Philadelphia, he had committed himself to the success of the nation-size republican experiment, and there was now no way he could avoid leading the launch.

Washington thanked his old aide-de-camp for this "manly advice" but confessed that it left him feeling deeply depressed, overwhelmed by "a kind of gloom," and he wanted Hamilton to know that acceptance of the presidency "would be attended with more diffidence and reluctance than ever I experienced before in my life."[6]

Hamilton knew Washington well enough to realize that he was not being coy. So he made another kind of argument designed to appeal to his historical aspirations. If the new federal government should fail, he observed, "the framers of it will have to encounter the disrepute of having brought about a revolution in government . . . that was not worth the effort. They pulled down one Utopia, it will be said, to build another." If that should happen, Hamilton warned, Washington's place in history would be compromised, an outcome that "will suggest to your mind greater hazard to that fame which must be and ought to be dear to you." But in the end, Hamilton concluded, all of Washington's anguish was irrelevant, because "the crisis which brought you again into public view has left you no alternative but to comply."[7]

No president in American history wanted to be president less than Washington. And yet, as Hamilton made clear to him, no man in America was so essential to enhance the prospects for success of the emerging nation. As Henry Lee, Washington's old cavalry commander, put it, "It is a sacrifice on your part, unjustifiable from any personal point of view. But on the other hand, no alternative seems to be presented."[8]

Washington attempted to find an escape route by declaring that any announcement of his candidacy would be regarded as a conspicuous expression of his ambition, which in his political universe was dishonorable behavior that essentially disqualified him from office. He liked to refer to the fable about the fox "who inveighed against the sourness of grapes, because he could not reach them."[9]

This was a desperate gambit on his part, an effort to dodge the inevitable, but also utterly irrelevant because there was no need for him to stand for office or declare his candidacy. There were, as yet, no political primaries or nominating conventions. The electors in each state were free to select anyone they wished. The winner became the president, and the runner-up became the vice president. The only way that Washington could have avoided election was by refusing to serve if chosen. And Hamilton had already told him why he could not do that. Washington did confide to Knox that "my movement to the Chair of Government will be accompanied by feelings not unlike those of a culprit who is going to the place of his execution." But it was a virtual certainty that he would be elected in a landslide.[10]

Virtual certainty, however, was not enough for Hamilton. From Hamilton's perspective, Washington's election was utterly essential if the American experiment was to succeed. He began to conjure up a nightmare scenario in which, as he put it, "the defect in the Constitution which renders it possible that the man intended for Vice President may in fact turn up President." This was an extremely far-fetched fear, and events eventually proved it utterly illusory. But it was a measure of Hamilton's obsession with ensuring Washington's election that he decided to take no chances. So he moved behind the scenes to rig the election.[11]

Political polls, of course, did not exist, but there was an informed consensus that John Adams was likely to finish second and become vice president, probably with unanimous support in New England

and most of the northern states. Hamilton lobbied friends in Delaware, New Jersey, and Pennsylvania to throw away their electoral votes for Adams in favor of lesser candidates, in order to prevent an accidental Adams presidency. Hamilton claimed that he had nothing against Adams, indeed would welcome him as the first vice president. But Adams was not Washington—no one was—and even the slightest risk that Adams might sneak in ahead of Washington was a risk not worth running.

In the end, it made no difference. When the electoral votes were counted, all sixty-nine electors voted for Washington, making him the unanimous choice. Adams finished second with thirty-four electoral votes, probably five or ten votes less than he would have received without Hamilton's machinations.

Hamilton had unnecessarily given credence to the view that the transition from confederation to nation was an inherently corrupt conspiracy. Neither Washington, nor Madison, nor Jay would have countenanced what he did. Indeed, Washington would have been outraged that Hamilton had placed a dishonorable stain on his presidency. But at the time Hamilton cared not a whit about such hostile accusations. The only relevant fact was that Washington would be at the helm of the American ship of state when she sailed.

There was one final ingredient that needed to be added to the institutional equation in order to ensure the prospects for success. Over the course of the ratification debate, it had become abundantly clear that the biggest mistake made by the delegates at the Constitutional Convention had been to omit a bill of rights from the final draft of the document. As mentioned earlier, the underlying reasons for this failure were more prosaic than profound: basically, the delegates were exhausted after a summer of intense work and wanted to go home.

During the ratification debates, both Madison and James Wilson developed elaborate political arguments to justify the absence of a bill of rights, essentially insisting that there was no need for such a thing because the Constitution gave only enumerated powers to the new federal government, making explicit guarantees of personal rights (i.e., the right to a jury trial, freedom of the press, freedom of speech) unnecessary since they were already embedded in the state constitutions. Madison added the somewhat strained argument that assembling such a list of rights was actually dangerous, because one could never know if the list would be sufficiently comprehensive and complete.

But as the debates in the state ratifying conventions demonstrated, many reluctant delegates did not buy that argument, and the major reason given by those opposing ratification was the absence of a bill of rights that would provide a clear zone of immunity from federal intrusion into their private lives and into the more proximate authority of their local and state governments. Of the 124 different amendments proposed by six states, the vast majority focused on fears of federal power, which a bill of rights would have considerably mollified.[12]

If Hamilton took the lead in ensuring that Washington would be the first president, Madison took the lead in correcting the mistake that he and the other delegates in Philadelphia had made by failing to provide a bill of rights. His motives were almost entirely political. While we tend to regard (and capitalize) the Bill of Rights as a secular version of the Ten Commandments handed down by God to Moses, Madison saw it as a weapon to be wielded against opponents of the Constitution, like Henry and Clinton, who were pushing the second convention proposal, which Madison regarded as a thinly veiled attempt to undo all that he and his fellow collaborators had accomplished.[13]

There would be no need for a second convention if the first Congress passed a bill of rights that addressed the legitimate concerns of those who had opposed ratification. He announced a shift in his position in January 1789. "Whatever opinion may be entertained at this point," he wrote, "it is evident that the change of situation produced by the establishment of the Constitution, leaves me in common with the other friends of the Constitution, free, and consistent in espousing such a revisal of it, as will either make it better in itself, or without making it worse, will make it appear better to those who now dislike it." The first Congress, not a second convention, was the proper place to amend the Constitution, and he vowed to lead that effort: "It is, accordingly, my sincere opinion, and wish, that in order to effect these purposes, the Congress, which is to meet in March, should undertake the salutary work." By having the revisions to the Constitution occur in the first Congress, the authority of the new federal government would actually be enhanced, whereas the unspoken agenda of second convention advocates was to undermine that authority. Madison's chief goal was to disarm the outright opponents of the Constitution and to demonstrate his good faith with those reluctant ratifiers who had recommended all those amendments, thereby drawing them into the fold just as Jay had envisioned.[14]

While Madison's motives for switching his position were thoroughly political, his thinking about the role of a bill of rights in the Constitution was intellectually complicated. His experience with the state governments under the Articles led him to the conclusion that the major threat to individual liberty and the rights of minorities came from below rather than above—that is, from popular majorities rather than from government. And he did not think that a bill of rights could do much to prevent those abuses. This put him at odds with his avowed mentor in Paris, whose experience in France had led him to the opposite conclusion. The Jefferson-Madison correspondence in late 1788 and early 1789 provides a convenient window through which to view two dramatically different ways of thinking about what became the Bill of Rights.[15]

Madison had spent the last two years thoroughly immersed in the political campaign to draft the Constitution and oversee its ratification. Jefferson, on the other hand, was an ocean away in Paris, and although Madison had kept him informed of the state-by-state developments in the ratification process, Jefferson was blissfully oblivious to the supercharged political atmosphere that Madison was trying to manage.

This helps to explain the rather strange proposal that Jefferson made in February 1788, when ratification remained problematic: "I sincerely wish that the first nine conventions, may receive [the Constitution], and the last four reject it. The former will secure it finally, while the latter will oblige them to offer a declaration of rights in order to complete the union. We shall thus have all its good, without its principal defect."[16]

One can only imagine the sense of horror that seized Madison when he read these words, for they came perilously close to the second convention option that he regarded as the political equivalent of a poison pill designed to kill the Constitution under the pretext of amending it. Jefferson obviously thought that the absence of a bill of rights was a fatal flaw in the document and, though he probably did not realize it, was willing to put ratification at risk in order to include what he called a "declaration of rights."

There are two discernible reasons for Jefferson's obsession with a bill of rights, one quite specific, the other more general and revelatory of how his mind worked. On the specific side, he was currently engaged in conversations with Lafayette and other French reformers who were attempting to draft a declaration of rights for a new French constitution. All of them regarded such a declaration as an utterly essential statement of the principles on which the French Revolution should proceed. Jefferson was especially invested in this project, since, at least as he saw it, the goal was to bring the values of the Declaration of Independence, his very words, to the revolution in France. Finding the language to define basic human rights, then, was very much on Jefferson's mind.

More generally, Jefferson did not think about constitutions, or even government itself, in the same way as Madison or, for that matter, any other prominent American statesman of his time. As for constitutions, he regarded them as temporary political frameworks, merely transitory arrangements that should be revised or replaced every twenty years to reflect the interests and values of a new generation. As for government, he wanted it small, weak, and as close to invisible as possible. The trouble with most Europeans, he observed, was that they were bred to prefer "a government [they] can feel." His mind and heart longed for a world in which government would not be felt, indeed one in which it almost disappeared.[17]

In effect, Madison and his fellow nationalists had been working to create a constitution that was most admirable for the energetic qualities that Jefferson despised and denounced. A bill of rights was so important to Jefferson because its essential function was to define what government could *not* do, creating a political zone where individual rights were free to roam beyond the surveillance and restrictions of kings, courts, legislatures, and judges. This was Jefferson's ideal, in truth his utopian vision, and it was as far removed from Madison's interest-driven political universe as night from day.[18]

Madison confessed that he and his mentor seemed to be on different pages: "I have never thought the omission [of a bill of rights] a material defect, nor for any other reason than it is anxiously desired by others. . . . I have not viewed it in an important light." Moreover, Madison went on to describe all bills of rights as "parchment barriers," easily ignored and violated "by overbearing majorities in every state." In Virginia, for example, Madison claimed that the Declaration of Rights "has been violated in every instance where it has been opposed to a popular current."

Jefferson's problem, as Madison saw it, was that he believed that the primary threat to personal rights came from government. That might be true in Europe, "but in our Governments the real power lies in the majority of the community." So the real threat came "from acts in which the Government is the mere instrument of the major number of the constituents." As a result, Madison concluded that a bill of rights, "however strongly marked on paper, will never be regarded when opposed to the decided sense of the public." He did not foresee the active role of the Supreme Court as the ultimate arbiter of either the Constitution or the Bill of Rights.[19]

It is unlikely that Jefferson understood what Madison was saying, since the idea that the greatest threat to the rights of the people could be popular opinion was impossible to imagine from a Jeffersonian perspective. At any rate, Jefferson never addressed Madison's argument and simply held firm to his core conviction: "As to the bill of rights, however, I still think it should be added." In response to Madison's claim that no bill of rights could possibly cover all the possible abuses, Jefferson countered that "half a loaf is better than no bread."[20]

As we have seen, Madison had reached the same conclusion by January 1789, though not for the reasons Jefferson had offered. He apparently made up his mind to lead the movement for a bill of rights during his campaign for a seat in the House. It was a difficult campaign because Henry had persuaded James Monroe, another Jefferson protégé and sometime friend of Madison, to run against him, and redefine the borders of Madison's district—what would later be called "gerrymandering"—to tilt the playing field.

It didn't work—Madison won handily, 1,308 to 972—but in the course of the campaign he came under relentless pressure from his erstwhile constituents to support the recommended amendments of the Virginia convention. That pushed him over the line. He let it be known that if elected, he would take up the cause of amendments. "It is my sincere desire," he now vowed, "that the Constitution ought to be revised, and that the first Congress meeting under it ought to

prepare and recommend to the States for ratification, the most satisfactory provisions for all essential rights, particularly the rights of
conscience in the fullest latitude, the freedom of the press, trials by
jury, security against general warrants, etc."[21]

In truth, he still did not share Jefferson's faith in the efficacy of
written lists of rights, and he believed that the greatest protection of
individual rights was already embedded in the political framework
created by the Constitution. But the political reasons for going forward were now clearer than ever: his Virginia constituents wanted
amendments; a bill of rights would undermine the subversive second convention movement; and reluctant ratifiers in six states would
learn that he was listening. As he put it to Jefferson, such an act of
conciliation would "extinguish opposition to the system, or at least
break the force of it by detaching the deluded opponents from their
designing leaders." In short, he viewed the movement for a bill of
rights not as an opportunity to glimpse the abiding truths, but as the
final step in the ratification process.[22]

Madison was in an excellent position to act on his promise. He
was generally recognized as the "first man" in the House. His central
role at the Constitutional Convention, his contribution to the Federalist Papers, and then his prominence at the Virginia convention
had made him, for the first time, a conspicuous national figure. Soon
after his inauguration, Washington had asked him to draft a letter to
the members of Congress, expressing his desire to work closely with
them. The members of Congress, not knowing of Madison's involve-
ment, asked him to draft their reply to Washington. It was Madison
writing to Madison. He had become the second most prominent
figure in the new government.[23]

In early March 1789, just five days after Washington had taken the
oath of office, Madison announced his intention to propose amend-

ments to the Constitution later in the month. He then entered into one of those intense periods of Madisonian preparation, taking the Virginia Declaration of Rights and all of the amendments recommended by the states into his study for deliberation. To call Madison the "Father of the Constitution" is quite plausible, but it is also arguable, given the significant roles played by others in Philadelphia, chiefly Gouverneur Morris. But there is no question that Madison was the "Father of the Bill of Rights." He wrote the first draft single-handedly, ushered it through the House, and negotiated with leaders in the Senate as they reduced the seventeen amendments proposed by the House to twelve.[24]

Several congressmen commented on Madison's nearly obsessive dedication to the passage of a bill of rights, blaming his compulsion on a misguided fear that the threat of a second convention loomed if he failed to act promptly. Theodore Sedgwick, a representative from western Massachusetts, believed that Madison was "constantly haunted by the ghost of Patrick Henry." And Robert Morris, now a senator from Pennsylvania, thought that Madison "got so cursedly frightened in Virginia that he dreamed of amendments ever since." They had a point. The movement for a second convention was already beginning to fade, as Jay had predicted it would. But just as Hamilton had chosen to take no risk in ensuring Washington's election, Madison felt an urgent need to pass a bill of rights before the disciples of Henry and Clinton could mobilize their forces. He was almost surely exaggerating the threat, but given the arduous trail he had traveled to reach a political version of the promised land, he was in no mood to take any chances.[25]

Madison spent several weeks in the late spring of 1789 working on the amendments and trying to decide where they should be inserted into the text of the Constitution. Apparently he harbored the conviction that including them within the document rather than adding them at the end would enhance the body of the text instead of just tacking them on as a tail. "There is a neatness and propriety in incorporating the amendments to the Constitution itself," he explained, "so that the amendments are interwoven into those parts in which they naturally belong."[26]

During the debate in the House, Roger Sherman of Connecticut called attention to the problem with this approach: namely, it revised the document that the framers in Philadelphia had signed without their authorization or knowledge. In effect, it created the illusion that the amendments had been drafted at the Constitutional Convention. (By now, Madison surely wished that they had.) The more appropriate way to proceed, Sherman argued, was to regard the amendments as a separate codicil to the original text of the Constitution, which was, in fact, what they were.[27]

Madison immediately recognized this as an unanswerable argument and conceded the point, which also relieved him of the daunting task of deciding how to corkscrew a series of civil rights and restrictions on federal power into the original text of the Constitution. The result was to give the Bill of Rights a separate status as an epilogue that accurately reflected the concerns of so many delegates at the ratifying conventions. Over time this separate placement allowed the Bill of Rights to assume an iconic status of its own, as the legal version of the liberal values first articulated in the Declaration of Independence, and as the classic statement of rights beyond the reach of government, the American version of the Magna Carta. Small wonder, then, that Jefferson regarded it as more important than the Constitution itself.[28]

If we wish to recover Madison's mentality during the congressional debates over what became the Bill of Rights—what we might call Madison's "original intentions"—the best place to look is the opening speech he delivered on June 8 to the House, in which he presented the fruits of his quite massive editorial labors during the spring months. Several representatives objected to considering a revision of the Constitution at this time. As James Jackson of Georgia put it, the Constitution was like "a ship that has never yet put to sea. . . . Upon experiment she may prove faultless, or her defects might be very obvious." It was too early to start tampering with the text.[29]

What's more, Congress had more pressing issues to resolve. It needed to set up a federal revenue system, translate the vagaries in the Constitution into a workable federal judiciary, create executive departments and define their authority—in short, get the government up and going. Madison's proposal that the House put itself into a committee-of-the-whole format to debate his draft of a bill of rights would mean that it could not focus on all those other important duties.

Madison eventually relented on the tactical questions by abandoning his committee-of-the-whole proposal and allowing his suggested amendments to be sent to a special committee, which would permit the House to proceed with its other business. But he insisted on the principle that a bill of rights must be an immediate priority. And he was explicit about his reasons for doing so:

> It cannot be a secret to the gentlemen of this house, that, notwithstanding the ratification of this system of government by eleven of the thirteen United States, yet there is a great number of our constituents who are dissatisfied with it; among whom are many respectable for their talents, their patriotism, and respectable for the jealousy they have for their liberty. . . . There is a great body of the people falling under this description. . . . We ought not to disregard their inclination, conform to their wishes, and expressly declare the great rights of mankind secured under this constitution.[30]

He also noted that there were still two states, North Carolina and Rhode Island, that had failed to ratify, and it behooved the newly created federal government to persuade them, as he put it, "to throw themselves into the bosom of the new confederacy." In short, while the new government surely needed to be up and going, it was imperative to perform this one piece of unfinished business that, in effect, would complete the ratification process.[31]

Madison's predominantly political motives in the summer of 1789 have, for understandable reasons, faded into oblivion over the ensuing years, so that what we remember are the amendments enshrined in the current Bill of Rights (see Appendix C). Madison's original list of amendments contained the standard set of rights we have come to expect, most of which were already recognized in many of the state constitutions. The major ones included the right of free speech, a free press, freedom of religion, freedom from unwarranted searches and seizures, the right to a jury trial within a reasonable period of time, and the explicit presumption that powers not delegated to the federal government were reserved for the states. Madison bundled several of these rights together in what became nine draft amendments. The House unbundled several of his composite paragraphs to produce seventeen amendments, subsequently reduced to twelve by the Senate, and then to ten in the state ratification process.[32]

But if we are truly to grasp Madison's original intentions in the crucible of this creative moment, there are four features of his first draft that are worthy of attention. Perhaps the initial item to notice is the absence of a certain amendment that had been proposed by all the states that had made recommendations.

Six states had urged a return to the arrangement under the Articles whereby federal tax requests would be regarded as voluntary rather than mandatory by the states. Each state had proposed a different scheme whereby the states and the federal government could negotiate their differences, but the core idea was to move at least halfway back to state sovereignty on the essential question of taxation. Since the failure to fund the federal budget and debt was a central reason for the fiscal chaos under the Articles, Madison believed that this recommended amendment struck at the heart of the union. His way of handling the problem was simply to ignore it. Though it had been a unanimous recommendation from six states, it disappeared in Madison's editing process.

Second, moving in exactly the opposite direction, Madison proposed an amendment of his own that no state had recommended: "No state shall violate the equal rights of conscience, or the freedom of the press, or the trial by jury in criminal cases." At the Constitutional Convention he had tried and failed to enact a provision allowing for a federal veto of state laws. Now he was trying to smuggle that same principle into his bill of rights under the guise of ensuring federal standards for agreed-upon human rights at the state level. It would take the Supreme Court over a century to recognize federal jurisdiction in the Madisonian manner. And history proved Madison right when, as he had predicted to Jefferson, more abuses of individual rights would occur at the state than at the federal level.[33]

But the Senate deleted this proposed amendment for the same reason that the delegates in Philadelphia had rejected its earlier version. They were not ready for such a conspicuous projection of federal power over the state governments. Madison deeply regretted this rejection, saying that he regarded it to be "the most valuable amendment on the whole list." Nevertheless, a clear majority in both branches of Congress believed it went too far.[34]

Third, and not wholly unrelated, Madison criticized the part of the Constitution that declared that "the number of representatives shall not exceed the proportion of one for every thirty thousand persons. . . . It is the sense of the people of America that the number of representatives should be increased." Here he referred to recommended amendments from several states on this score, all of which were rooted in the conviction that the new version of representation as defined in the Constitution lacked the personal familiarity they had experienced at the state level under the Articles.[35]

Madison was attempting to convey the honest concerns of delegates in several state ratifying conventions that the geographic size of congressional districts needed to be reduced and the number of representatives increased in order to sustain a meaningful sense of representative government as they understood it. But as Madison surely realized, the problem was inherently unsolvable, because any federal legislature that contained as many representatives as these critics wanted would be an impossibly unwieldy body that would only become more so as the population increased. What had to change was not the ratio of representatives to constituents but the way those constituents thought about representation. It was a problem of scale. Once you moved from a local and state to a national orientation, basic attitudes toward government itself needed to change. Nothing came of this proposal because, in truth, nothing could, but the issue exposed the most palpable and practical way the transition from confederation to nation required a radical change in thinking about how the political architecture of an American republic should be configured.

Finally, under the rubric of his fourth proposed amendment, Madison wrote the following words: "The right of the people to keep and bear arms shall not be infringed; a well armed, and well regulated militia being the best security of a free country; but no person religiously scrupulous of bearing arms, shall be compelled to render military service in person." This eventually, after some editing in the Senate, became the Second Amendment in the Bill of Rights, and its meaning has provoked more controversy in our own time than it did in 1789.[36]

Madison was responding to recommended amendments from five states, calling for the prohibition of a permanent standing army on the grounds that it had historically proven to be an enduring threat to republican values. It is clear that Madison's intention in drafting his proposed amendment was to assure those skeptical souls that the defense of the United States would depend on state militias rather than a professional, federal army. In Madison's formulation, the right to bear arms was not inherent but derivative, depending on service in the militia. The recent Supreme Court decision (*Heller v. District of Columbia,* 2008) that found the right to bear arms an inherent and nearly unlimited right is clearly at odds with Madison's original intentions.[37]

During the debates in the House, several delegates, mostly from southern states, accused Madison of cherry-picking from the recommended amendments of the state ratifying conventions so as to minimize rather than maximize the restraints on federal power. Aedanus Burke of South Carolina described Madison's proposed amendments as "whip-syllabub," a popular dessert of the day that was "frothy and full of wind, formed only to please the palate." Burke, who was apparently enjoying a metaphoric epiphany, also characterized the proposed amendments as "a tub thrown out to the whale," a tactic used by sailors trying to divert a whale from attacking their ship.[38]

Thomas Tudor Tucker, also of South Carolina, wanted to know why Madison had failed to include the amendment, proposed by all the states that had recommended amendments, to regard all federal taxes as voluntary requirements in the initial solicitation. Most critics seemed to be saying that Madison's proposed amendments did not accurately reflect the deepest concerns of their constituents about the enhanced powers of the federal government but instead were gestures of appeasement toward what were, in fact, the diminished powers of the states. And, in truth, that was precisely what Madison intended: namely, to make the fewest concessions possible to the opposition in order to ensure the greatest level of support for the new government.[39]

The most basic of Madison's intentions in drafting and defending the Bill of Rights, then, were neither constitutional nor philosophical, but political. He had no sense that he was writing what has now become enshrined as the semi-sacred creedal statement of America's core political values. As he explained to Jefferson on several occasions, he really did not think the Constitution needed a bill of rights.

What he called "the nauseus business of amendments" was primarily intended to win over those disaffected and reluctant Americans by identifying in specific ways the constitutional constraints on federal power. He was always very clear about that: "It is to be wished that the discontented part of our fellow Citizens could be reconciled to the Government they have opposed, and by means as little unacceptable to those who approve the Constitution in its present form. The amendments proposed in the H. of Rep. had this two-fold object in view."[40]

He did not regard himself as a political philosopher but rather as a political strategist attempting to secure the success of a quite daring project that he, Hamilton, Jay, and Washington had launched against great odds three years earlier. Over the ensuing decades and centuries, to be sure, the Bill of Rights has ascended to an elevated region in the American imagination. But in its own time, and in Madison's mind, it was only an essential epilogue that concluded a brilliant campaign to adjust the meaning of the American Revolution to a national scale.

—————

It makes sense to end the story in the summer of 1789. By then the Constitution had been ratified, Washington was ensconced as the first president, the Bill of Rights was on the way to ratification, and the framework for a truly national government was in place. Only a few years earlier, no one could have predicted this outcome or the chain of events that led to it. But there it was. The American Revolution now meant not just independence but nationhood. And though a majority of the American populace was either opposed or indifferent to this remarkable transition, the institutions necessary to make it happen were now established, and the American citizenry were beginning to grow into the nation-size house constructed for them. It would take at least a full generation before they felt comfortable living there and had arranged the political furniture to their satisfaction.[41]

All the men who had led the movement toward nationhood, with one major exception, were centrally involved in the effort to implement and institutionalize that vision in the following decade. Washington's role was paramount, for he made the American presidency a powerful office that combined the symbolic authority of an elected monarch with the substantive role of prime minister responsible for overseeing domestic and foreign policy. No one other than Washington could have done this so seamlessly and successfully, although he would spend both presidential terms wishing he was back at Mount Vernon.

Hamilton became the first secretary of the treasury. Washington had initially offered the job to Robert Morris, who declined in order to serve in the Senate. Hamilton proceeded to implement a comprehensive financial plan closely modeled on what Morris had attempted as the superintendent of finance: namely, a national bank, federal assumption of all state debts, and a long-range plan to retire the national debt and restore American credit internationally. In part because he came at the start, he is generally regarded as the greatest secretary of the treasury in American history. By the time he came under the fatal gaze of Aaron Burr on the plains of Weehawken in 1804, however, his commanding presence within the Federalist Party was in decline, as was the party itself.

Washington so respected Jay that he offered him any post he wished in the new government. Jay turned down the opportunity to become the first secretary of state—Jefferson then got that job—in favor of an appointment as the first chief justice of the Supreme Court. But his major contribution was in foreign policy, where he negotiated an agreement that avoided war with Great Britain in a landmark treaty that bore his name. He later went on to serve as governor of New York, where his foremost achievement was a law putting slavery on the road to extinction in what had begun to call itself the Empire State.

Madison was the exception. In the early months of Washington's presidency, Madison continued to serve as his closest confidant and liaison in Congress. But for reasons that have baffled historians ever since, by 1791 Madison had switched sides and joined with Jefferson to lead the opposition against Hamilton's financial plan as well as the entire domestic and foreign policy agenda of the Federalist Party. The former champion of an ultranationalist vision now embraced a Virginia-writ-large conception of the union. This conversion process culminated in Madison's *Virginia Resolutions* (1798), where he articulated a states-rights interpretation of the Constitution, essentially making the same arguments that Patrick Henry had made and Madison had opposed at the Virginia convention, and that later became the position of the Confederacy in 1861.

It was one of the most breathtaking turnarounds in American political history, and the easiest way to explain it is to observe that, upon Jefferson's return from France, Madison chose to harness all his formidable powers of argument to the political agenda of his mentor and hero. That is surely part of the explanation but hardly the whole. One would need to explore Madison's sudden realization that Hamilton's financial plan favored the commercial North over the agrarian South and his sense of loyalty to his constituents in Virginia. But that is another Madison and, as they say, another story.[42]

Looking back at this story with all the advantages of hindsight, certain features that were invisible or blurry at the start become clearer for all to see at the end.[43]

First, while Washington was an invaluable trophy without whom the Constitutional Convention never could have succeeded, he was also more than that. His assessment of America's prospects in his Circular Letter of 1783 was the clearest argument for a national government as the essential prerequisite for harnessing America's nearly infinite potential. Both Jay and Hamilton had glimpsed the outlines of the same vision somewhat earlier, but Washington's substantive and not just symbolic role in making the case for a federal government capable of securing the energies released by the American Revolution was crucial, in part because his vision turned out to be right, in part because no one could deliver the message with greater credibility. He was the Foundingest Father of them all because of his central role in winning both independence and American nationhood.

Second, the brand of leadership exhibited by the four most committed nationalists came to them naturally, because it represented a repetition of the roles they had all played just a few years earlier in winning American independence. In both instances they were prepared to make an all-or-nothing wager on behalf of a cause that appeared highly problematic at the time. In 1776 they were risking their lives. In 1787 they were risking their reputations and their place in American history. They were accustomed to winning such wagers, and in both instances their confidence was buoyed by the belief that they knew where history was headed. Indeed, they all regarded nationhood as the second chapter in the same larger story about American destiny in a script that had been written by what both Washington and Jay called providence. Although hagiographic depictions of the founders as quasi-divine creatures with supernatural powers of mind and heart are no longer credible, the quartet of unbridled nationalists central to this story all believed that, while they themselves were not gods, the gods were on their side.

Third, the success that these mere men enjoyed in imposing their more expansive definition of the American Revolution was the beneficiary of history in another, more time-bound sense of that term. While modern-day critics of the founders and the constitutional settlement they brokered often deliver their critical judgments from our present perspective, and the politically correct posture it permits, the more historically correct conclusion is to begin with the recognition that the founders inhabited a premodern world that cannot be understood, much less judged, in modern terms.

More specifically, the founders occupied a transitional moment in the history of Western civilization that was postaristocratic and predemocratic. On the one hand, this meant that politics in America was open to a whole class of talented men—women were still unimaginable as public figures—who would have languished in obscurity throughout Europe because they lacked the proper bloodlines and inherited wealth. Hamilton is the best example of this egalitarian ethos, and even Washington would never have risen beyond the rank of major in the British army. The presentistic tendency to contrast egalitarian assumptions at that time and now, and then to find the founding generation hopelessly elitist, is deeply flawed historically. Measured against the political and social standards of their own time, the founding generation was the beneficiary of an American society that offered greater access to latent talent than any other society in the world.

On the other hand, on the predemocratic side of the historical equation, political leadership in this premodern world remained blissfully oblivious to democratic mythology about the uncommon wisdom of the common man or the superior virtue of that mysterious congregation called "the people." Hamilton and Madison were the most outspoken critics of any democratic perspective that assumed that the majority of the American citizenry could be expected to behave virtuously or to subordinate their own personal agendas to some larger definition of the public interest. These were not merely theoretical conclusions but hard-earned lessons learned by Hamilton while serving in the Continental Army and by Madison while serving in the Confederation Congress. Both believed that any government based on unadulterated democratic assumptions would be founded on a seductive illusion that had been exposed as such during the war and then in the state governments under the Articles.

Perhaps the best way to describe their achievement, then, is to argue that they maximized the historical possibilities of their transitory moment. They were comfortable and unembarrassed in their role as a political elite, in part because their leadership role depended on their revolutionary credentials, which they had earned, not on bloodlines that they had inherited. They were unapologetic in their skepticism about unfettered democracy, because that skepticism was rooted in their recent experiences as soldiers and statesmen, and no democratic mythology had yet emerged to place them on the defensive.

They straddled an aristocratic world that was dying and a democratic world that was just emerging, theoretically an awkward posture that they managed to make into a graceful synthesis they called a republic. The Constitution they created and bequeathed to us was necessarily a product of that bimodal moment and mentality, and most of the men featured in this story would be astonished to learn that it abides, with amendments, over two centuries later. It has endured not because it embodies timeless truths that the founders fathomed as tongues of fire danced over their heads, but because it manages to combine the two time-bound truths of its own time: namely, that any legitimate government must rest on a popular foundation, and that popular majorities cannot be trusted to act responsibly, a paradox that has aged remarkably well.

Not their hubris but their humility has made the lasting difference. They knew they did not have all the answers, and any political elite that thought it did was surely destined to find itself languishing on the trash heap of history, as the French philosophes and then the Marxist ideologues eventually discovered. Their genius was to answer the political challenges of their own moment decisively, meaning that the confederation must be replaced by the nation, but also to provide a political platform wide enough to allow for considerable latitude within which future generations could make their own decisions. Like wise parents, they allowed their children, which is to say us, to maximize our own moments for ourselves within the capacious republican framework they designed. Which was precisely what Lincoln did in 1863 at Gettysburg, acting in their name.

The last word must belong to Jefferson, even though he had the good fortune to be safely ensconced in Paris during the summer of 1787, had no role in making the Constitution happen, and went to his maker believing that federal authority over domestic policy was a betrayal of the American Revolution rather than a rescue. Jefferson also had the good fortune to live into the third decade of the nineteenth century and therefore to be asked countless times what he thought his remarkable generation had wrought. And because he also happened to be the most lyrical prose stylist of the era, his eulogy needs to be noticed:

> Some men look at constitutions with sanctimonious reverence, and deem them like the ark of the covenant, too sacred to be touched. They ascribe to the preceding age a wisdom more than human, and suppose what they did to be beyond amendment. I knew that age well; I belonged to it and labored with it. It deserved well of its country. . . . But I know also, that laws and institutions must go hand in hand with the progress of the human mind. As that becomes more developed, more enlightened, as new discoveries are made, new truths discovered . . . institutions must advance also, and keep pace with the times. We might as well require a man to wear still the coat which fitted him as a boy as civilized society to remain ever under the regime of their barbarous ancestors.[44]

Jefferson spoke for all the most prominent members of the revolutionary generation in urging posterity not to regard their political prescriptions as sacred script. It is richly ironic that one of the few original intentions they all shared was opposition to any judicial doctrine of "original intent." To be sure, they all wished to be remembered, but they did not want to be embalmed.

APPENDIX A: THE ARTICLES OF CONFEDERATION AND PERPETUAL UNION

★ ~ *1777* ~ ★

To all to whom these Presents shall come, we the undersigned Delegates of the States affixed to our Names send greeting.

Whereas the Delegates of the United States of America, in Congress assembled, did, on the 15th day of November, in the Year of Our Lord One thousand Seven Hundred and Seventy seven, and in the Second Year of the Independence of America, agree to certain articles of Confederation and perpetual Union between the States of New-hampshire, Massachusetts-bay, Rhodeisland and Providence Plantations, Connecticut, New York, New Jersey, Pennsylvania, Delaware, Maryland, Virginia, North-Carolina, South-Carolina, and Georgia in the words following, viz. "Articles of Confederation and perpetual Union between the states of New-hampshire, Massachusetts-bay, Rhode island and Providence Plantations, Connecticut, New-York, New-Jersey, Pennsylvania, Delaware, Maryland, Virginia, North-Carolina, South-Carolina and Georgia".

Article I.

The Stile of this Confederacy shall be "The United States of America."

Article II.

Each state retains its sovereignty, freedom, and independence, and every power, jurisdiction, and right, which is not by this Confederation expressly delegated to the United States, in Congress assembled.

Article III.

The said States hereby severally enter into a firm league of friendship with each other, for their common defence, the security of their liberties, and their mutual and general welfare, binding themselves to assist each other, against all force offered to, or attacks made upon them, or any of them, on account of religion, sovereignty, trade, or any other pretence whatever.

Article IV.

The better to secure and perpetuate mutual friendship and intercourse among the people of the different States in this Union, the free inhabitants of each of these States, paupers, vagabonds, and fugitives from justice excepted, shall be entitled to all privileges and immunities of free citizens in the several States; and the people of each State shall free ingress and regress to and from any other State, and shall enjoy therein all the privileges of trade and commerce, subject to the same duties, impositions, and restrictions as the inhabitants thereof respectively, provided that such restrictions shall not extend so far as to prevent the removal of property imported into any State, to any other State, of which the owner is an inhabitant; provided also that no imposition, duties or restriction shall be laid by any State, on the property of the United States, or either of them.

If any person guilty of, or charged with treason, felony, or other high misdemeanor in any State, shall flee from justice, and be found in any of the United States, he shall, upon demand of the Governor or executive power of the State from which he fled, be delivered up and removed to the State having jurisdiction of his offence.

Full faith and credit shall be given in each of these States to the records, acts and judicial proceedings of the courts and magistrates of every other State.

Article V.

For the more convenient management of the general interests of the United States, delegates shall be annually appointed in such manner as the legislature of each State shall direct, to meet in Congress on the first Monday in November, in every year, with a power reserved to each State, to recall its delegates, or any of them, at any time within the year, and to send others in their stead for the remainder of the year.

No State shall be represented in Congress by less than two, nor more than seven members; and no person shall be capable of being a delegate for more than three years in any term of six years; nor shall any person, being a delegate, be capable of holding any office under the United States, for which he, or another for his benefit, receives any salary, fees or emolument of any kind.

Each State shall maintain its own delegates in a meeting of the States, and while they act as members of the committee of the States.

In determining questions in the United States in Congress assembled, each State shall have one vote.

Freedom of speech and debate in Congress shall not be impeached or questioned in any court, or place out of Congress, and the members of Congress shall be protected in their persons from arrests and imprisonments, during the time of their going to and from, and attendence on Congress, except for treason, felony, or breach of the peace.

Article VI.

No State, without the consent of the United States in Congress assembled, shall send any embassy to, or receive any embassy from, or enter into any conference, agreement, alliance or treaty with any King, Prince or State; nor shall any person holding any office of profit or trust under the United States, or any of them, accept of any present, emolument, office or title of any kind whatever from any King, Prince or foreign State; nor shall the United States in Congress assembled, or any of them, grant any title of nobility.

No two or more States shall enter into any treaty, confederation or alliance whatever between them, without the consent of the United States in Congress assembled, specifying accurately the purposes for which the same is to be entered into, and how long it shall continue.

No State shall lay any imposts or duties, which may interfere with any stipulations in treaties, entered into by the United States in Congress assembled, with any King, Prince or State, in pursuance of any treaties already proposed by Congress, to the courts of France and Spain.

No vessel of war shall be kept up in time of peace by any State, except such number only, as shall be deemed necessary by the United States in Congress assembled, for the defence of such State, or its trade; nor shall any body of forces be kept up by any State, in time of peace, except such number only, as in the judgement of the United States in Congress assembled, shall be deemed requisite to garrison the forts necessary for the defence of such State; but every State shall always keep up a well-regulated and disciplined militia, sufficiently armed and accoutered, and shall provide and constantly have ready for use, in public stores, a due number of filed pieces and tents, and a proper quantity of arms, ammunition and camp equipage.

No State shall engage in any war without the consent of the United States in Congress assembled, unless such State be actually invaded by enemies, or shall have received certain advice of a resolution being formed by some nation of Indians to invade such State, and the danger is so imminent as not to admit of a delay till the United States in Congress assembled can be consulted: nor shall any State grant commissions to any ships or vessels of war, nor letters of marque or reprisal, except it be after a declaration of war by the United States in Congress assembled, and then only against the Kingdom or State and the subjects thereof, against which war has been so declared, and under such regulations as shall be established by the United States in Congress assembled, unless such State be infested by pirates, in which case vessels of war may be fitted out for that occasion, and kept so long as the danger shall continue, or until the United States in Congress assembled, shall determine otherwise.

Article VII.

When land-forces are raised by any State for the common defence, all officers of or under the rank of colonel, shall be appointed by the legislature of each State respectively, by whom such forces shall be raised, or in such manner as such State shall direct, and all vacancies shall be filled up by the State which first made the appointment.

Article VIII.

All charges of war, and all other expences that shall be incurred for the common defence or general welfare, and allowed by the United States in Congress assembled, shall be defrayed out of a common treasury, which shall be supplied by the several States in proportion to the value of all land within each State, granted to or surveyed for any person, as such land and the buildings and improvements thereon shall be estimated according to such mode as the United States in Congress assembled, shall from time to time direct and appoint.

The taxes for paying that proportion shall be laid and levied by the authority and direction of the legislatures of the several States within the time agreed upon by the United States in Congress assembled.

Article IX.

The United States in Congress assembled, shall have the sole and exclusive right and power of determining on peace and war, except in the cases mentioned in the sixth article—of sending and receiving ambassadors— entering into treaties and alliances, provided that no treaty of commerce shall be made whereby the legislative power of the respective States shall be restrained from imposing such imposts and duties on foreigners, as their own people are subjected to, or from prohibiting the exportation or importation of any species of goods or commodities, whatsoever—of establishing rules for deciding in all cases, what captures on land or water shall be legal, and in what manner prizes taken by land or naval forces in the service of the United States shall be divided or appropriated—of granting letters of marque and reprisal in times of peace—appointing courts for the trial of piracies and felonies committed on the high seas and establishing courts for receiving and determining finally appeals in all cases of captures, provided that no member of Congress shall be appointed a judge of any of the said courts.

The United States in Congress assembled shall also be the last resort on appeal in all disputes and differences now subsisting or that hereafter may arise between two or more States concerning boundary, jurisdiction or any other cause whatever; which authority shall always be exercised in the manner following. Whenever the legislative or executive authority or lawful agent of any State in controversy with another shall present a petition to Congress stating the matter in question and praying for a hearing, notice thereof shall be given by order of Congress to the legislative or executive authority of the other State in controversy, and a day assigned for the appearance of the parties by their lawful agents, who shall then be directed to appoint by joint consent, commissioners or judges to constitute a court for hearing and determining the matter in question: but if they cannot agree, Congress shall name three persons out of each of the United States, and from the list of such persons each party shall alternately strike out one, the petitioners beginning, until the number shall be reduced to thirteen; and from that number not less than seven, nor more than nine names as

Congress shall direct, shall in the presence of Congress be drawn out by lot, and the persons whose names shall be so drawn or any five of them, shall be commissioners or judges, to hear and finally determine the controversy, so always as a major part of the judges who shall hear the cause shall agree in the determination: and if either party shall neglect to attend at the day appointed, without showing reasons, which Congress shall judge sufficient, or being present shall refuse to strike, the Congress shall proceed to nominate three persons out of each State, and the secretary of Congress shall strike in behalf of such party absent or refusing; and the judgement and sentence of the court to be appointed, in the manner before prescribed, shall be final and conclusive; and if any of the parties shall refuse to submit to the authority of such court, or to appear or defend their claim or cause, the court shall nevertheless proceed to pronounce sentence, or judgement, which shall in like manner be final and decisive, the judgement or sentence and other proceedings being in either case transmitted to Congress, and lodged among the acts of Congress for the security of the parties concerned: provided that every commissioner, before he sits in judgement, shall take an oath to be administered by one of the judges of the supreme or superior court of the State, where the cause shall be tried, 'well and truly to hear and determine the matter in question, according to the best of his judgement, without favour, affection or hope of reward': provided also, that no State shall be deprived of territory for the benefit of the United States.

All controversies concerning the private right of soil claimed under different grants of two or more States, whose jurisdictions as they may respect such lands, and the States which passed such grants are adjusted, the said grants or either of them being at the same time claimed to have originated antecedent to such settlement of jurisdiction, shall on the petition of either party to the Congress of the United States, be finally determined as near as may be in the same manner as is before prescribed for deciding disputes respecting territorial jurisdiction between different States.

The United States in Congress assembled shall also have the sole and exclusive right and power of regulating the alloy and value of coin struck by their own authority, or by that of the respective States—fixing the standard of weights and measures throughout the United States—regulating the trade and managing all affairs with the Indians, not members of any of the States, provided that the legislative right of any State within its own limits be not infringed or violated—establishing or regulating post offices from one State to another, throughout all the United States, and exacting such postage on the papers passing thro' the same as may be requisite to defray the expences of the said office—appointing all officers of the land forces, in the service of the United States, excepting regimental officers—appointing all the officers of the naval forces, and commissioning all officers whatever in the service of the United States—making rules for the government and regulation of the said land and naval forces, and directing their operations.

The United States in Congress assembled shall have authority to appoint a committee, to sit in the recess of Congress, to be denominated 'A Committee of the States', and to consist of one delegate from each State; and to appoint such other committees and civil officers as may be necessary for managing the general affairs of the United States under their direction—to appoint one of their number to preside, provided that no person be allowed to serve in the office of president more than one year in any term of three years; to ascertain the necessary sums of money to be raised for the service of the United States, and to appropriate and apply the same for defraying the public expences—to borrow money, or emit bills on the credit of the United States, transmitting every half-year to the respective States an account of the sums of money so borrowed or emitted—to build and equip a navy—to agree upon the number of land forces, and to make requisitions from each State for its quota, in proportion to the number of white inhabitants in such State; which requisition shall be binding, and thereupon the legislature of each State shall appoint the regimental officers, raise the men and cloath, arm and equip them in a soldier like manner, at the expence of the United States; and the officers and men so cloathed, armed and equipped shall march to the place appointed, and within the time agreed on by the United States in Congress assembled. But if the United States in Congress assembled shall, on consideration of circumstances judge proper that any State should not raise men, or should raise a smaller number than its quota, and that any other State should raise a greater number of men than the quota thereof, such extra number shall be raised, officered, cloathed, armed and equipped in the same manner as the quota of such State, unless the legislature of such State shall judge that such extra number cannot be safely spared out in the same, in which case they shall raise, officer, cloath, arm and equip as many of such extra number as they judge can be safely spared. And the officers and men so cloathed, armed and equipped, shall march to the place appointed, and within the time agreed on by the United States in Congress assembled.

The United States in Congress assembled shall never engage in a war, nor grant letters of marque and reprisal in time of peace, nor enter into any treaties or alliances, nor coin money, nor regulate the value thereof, nor ascertain the sums and expences necessary for the defence and welfare of the United States, or any of them, nor emit bills, nor borrow money on the credit of the United States, nor appropriate money, nor agree upon the number of vessels of war, to be built or purchased, or the number of land or sea forces to be raised, nor appoint a commander in chief of the army or navy, unless nine States assent to the same: nor shall a question on any other point, except for adjourning from day to day be determined, unless by the votes of a majority of the United States in Congress assembled.

The Congress of the United States shall have power to adjourn to any time within the year, and to any place within the United States, so that no period of adjournment be for a longer duration than the space of six months, and shall publish the journal of their proceedings monthly, except such parts thereof relating to treaties, alliances or military operations, as in their judgement require secrecy; and the yeas and nays of the delegates of each State on any question shall be entered on the journal, when it is desired by any delegate; and the delegates of a State, or any of them, at his or their request shall be furnished with a transcript of the said journal, except such parts as are above excepted, to lay before the legislatures of the several States.

Article X.

The Committee of the States, or any nine of them, shall be authorized to execute, in the recess of Congress, such of the powers of Congress as the United States in Congress assembled, by the consent of nine States, shall from time to time think expedient to vest them with; provided that no power be delegated to the said Committee, for the exercise of which, by the Articles of Confederation, the voice of nine States in the Congress of the United States assembled is requisite.

Article XI.

Canada acceding to this confederation, and joining in the measures of the United States, shall be admitted into, and entitled to all the advantages of this Union: but no other colony shall be admitted into the same, unless such admission be agreed to by nine States.

Article XII.

All bills of credit emitted, monies borrowed, and debts contracted by, or under the authority of Congress, before the assembling of the United States, in pursuance of the present confederation, shall be deemed and considered as a charge against the United States, for payment and satisfaction whereof the said United States, and the public faith are hereby solemnly pledged.

Article XIII.

Every State shall abide by the determinations of the United States in Congress assembled, on all questions which by this confederation are submitted to them. And the Articles of this Confederation shall be inviolably observed by every State, and the Union shall be perpetual; nor shall any alteration at any time hereafter be made in any of them; unless such alteration be agreed to in a Congress of the United States, and be afterwards confirmed by the legislatures of every State.

And Whereas it hath pleased the Great Governor of the World to incline the hearts of the legislatures we respectively represent in Congress, to approve of, and to authorize us to ratify the said Articles of Confederation and perpetual Union, Know Ye that we the undersigned delegates, by virtue of the power and authority to us given for that purpose, do by these presents, in the name and in behalf of our respective constituents, fully and entirely ratify and confirm each and every of the said Articles of Confederation and perpetual Union, and all and singular the matters and things therein contained: And we do further solemnly plight and engage the faith of our respective constituents, that they shall abide by the determinations of the United States in Congress assembled, on all questions, which by the said Confederation are submitted to them. And that the Articles thereof shall be inviolably observed by the States we respectively represent, and that the Union shall be perpetual.

In Witness whereof we have hereunto set our hands in Congress. Done at Philadelphia in the State of Pennsylvania the ninth day of July in the Year of our Lord One Thousand Seven Hundred and Seventy-eight, and in the Third Year of the independence of America.

On the part of & behalf of the State of New Hampshire:
> Josiah Bartlett
> John Wentworth. Junr; August 8th, 1778

On the part and behalf of the State of Rhode-Island and Providence Plantations:
> William Ellery
> Henry Marchant
> John Collins

On the part and behalf of the State of New York:
> Jas Duane
> Fra: Lewis
> Wm Duer
> Gouvr Morris

On the part and behalf of the State of Pennsylvania:
> Robert Morris
> Daniel Roberdeau
> Jon. Bayard Smith
> William Clingar
> Joseph Reed; 22d July, 1778

On the part and behalf of the State of Maryland:
> John Hanson; March 1, 1781
> Daniel Carroll, do.

On the part and behalf of the State of North Carolina:
> John Penn; July 21st, 1778
> Corns Harnett
> Jno Williams

On the part and behalf of the State of Georgia:
> Jno Walton; 24th July, 1778
> Edwd Telfair
> Edwd Langworthy

On the part of & behalf of the State of Massachusetts Bay:

John Hancock
Samuel Adams
Elbridge Gerry
Francis Dana
James Lovell
Samuel Holten

On the part and behalf of the State of Connecticut:

Roger Sherman
Samuel Huntington
Oliver Wolcott
Titus Hosmer
Andrew Adams

On the Part and in Behalf of the State of New Jersey, November 26th, 1778:

Jno Witherspoon
Nathl Scudder

On the part and behalf of the State of Delaware:

Thos McKean; Febr 22d, 1779
John Dickinson; May 5th, 1779
Nicholas Van Dyke

On the part and behalf of the State of Virginia:

Richard Henry Lee
John Banister
Thomas Adams
Jno Harvie
Francis Lightfoot Lee

On the part and behalf of the State of South Carolina:

Henry Laurens
William Henry Drayton
Jno Mathews
Richd Hutson
Thos Heyward, junr.

APPENDIX B: CONSTITUTION
OF THE UNITED STATES

★ ~ *1787* ~ ★

We the People of the United States, in Order to form a more perfect Union, establish Justice, insure domestic Tranquility, provide for the common defence, promote the general Welfare, and secure the Blessings of Liberty to ourselves and our Posterity, do ordain and establish this Constitution for the United States of America.

Article. I.

Section. 1. All legislative Powers herein granted shall be vested in a Congress of the United States, which shall consist of a Senate and House of Representatives.

Section. 2. The House of Representatives shall be composed of Members chosen every second Year by the People of the several States, and the Electors in each State shall have the Qualifications requisite for Electors of the most numerous Branch of the State Legislature.

No Person shall be a Representative who shall not have attained to the Age of twenty five Years, and been seven Years a Citizen of the United States, and who shall not, when elected, be an Inhabitant of that State in which he shall be chosen.

[Representatives and direct Taxes shall be apportioned among the several States which may be included within this Union, according to their respective Numbers, which shall be determined by adding to the whole Number of free Persons, including those bound to Service for a Term of Years, and excluding Indians not taxed, three fifths of all other Persons.]* The actual Enumeration shall be made within three Years after the first Meeting of the Congress of the United States, and within every subsequent Term of ten Years, in such Manner as they shall by Law direct. The Number of Representatives shall not exceed one for every thirty Thousand, but each State

---

* Brackets indicate language later modified by amendment.

shall have at Least one Representative; and until such enumeration shall be made, the State of New Hampshire shall be entitled to chuse three, Massachusetts eight, Rhode-Island and Providence Plantations one, Connecticut five, New-York six, New Jersey four, Pennsylvania eight, Delaware one, Maryland six, Virginia ten, North Carolina five, South Carolina five, and Georgia three.

When vacancies happen in the Representation from any State, the Executive Authority thereof shall issue Writs of Election to fill such Vacancies.

The House of Representatives shall chuse their Speaker and other Officers; and shall have the sole Power of Impeachment.

Section. 3. The Senate of the United States shall be composed of two Senators from each State, [chosen by the Legislature thereof,] for six Years; and each Senator shall have one Vote.

Immediately after they shall be assembled in Consequence of the first Election, they shall be divided as equally as may be into three Classes. The Seats of the Senators of the first Class shall be vacated at the Expiration of the second Year, of the second Class at the Expiration of the fourth Year, and of the third Class at the Expiration of the sixth Year, so that one third may be chosen every second Year; [and if Vacancies happen by Resignation, or otherwise, during the Recess of the Legislature of any State, the Executive thereof may make temporary Appointments until the next Meeting of the Legislature, which shall then fill such Vacancies.]

No Person shall be a Senator who shall not have attained to the Age of thirty Years, and been nine Years a Citizen of the United States, and who shall not, when elected, be an Inhabitant of that State for which he shall be chosen.

The Vice President of the United States shall be President of the Senate, but shall have no Vote, unless they be equally divided.

The Senate shall chuse their other Officers, and also a President pro tempore, in the Absence of the Vice President, or when he shall exercise the Office of President of the United States.

The Senate shall have the sole Power to try all Impeachments. When sitting for that Purpose, they shall be on Oath or Affirmation. When the President of the United States is tried, the Chief Justice shall preside: And no Person shall be convicted without the Concurrence of two thirds of the Members present.

Judgment in Cases of Impeachment shall not extend further than to removal from Office, and disqualification to hold and enjoy any Office of honor, Trust or Profit under the United States: but the Party convicted shall nevertheless be liable and subject to Indictment, Trial, Judgment and Punishment, according to Law.

Section. 4. The Times, Places and Manner of holding Elections for Senators and Representatives, shall be prescribed in each State by the Legislature thereof; but the Congress may at any time by Law make or alter such Regulations, except as to the Places of chusing Senators.

The Congress shall assemble at least once in every Year, and such Meeting shall be [on the first Monday in December,] unless they shall by Law appoint a different Day.

Section. 5. Each House shall be the Judge of the Elections, Returns and Qualifications of its own Members, and a Majority of each shall constitute a Quorum to do Business, but a smaller Number may adjourn from day to day, and may be authorized to compel the Attendance of absent Members, in such Manner, and under such Penalties as each House may provide.

Each House may determine the Rules of its Proceedings, punish its Members for disorderly Behaviour, and, with the Concurrence of two thirds, expel a Member.

Each House shall keep a Journal of its Proceedings, and from time to time publish the same, excepting such Parts as may in their Judgment require Secrecy; and the Yeas and Nays of the Members of either House on any question shall, at the Desire of one fifth of those Present, be entered on the Journal.

Neither House, during the Session of Congress, shall, without the Consent of the other, adjourn for more than three days, nor to any other Place than that in which the two Houses shall be sitting.

Section. 6. The Senators and Representatives shall receive a Compensation for their Services, to be ascertained by Law, and paid out of the Treasury of the United States. They shall in all Cases, except Treason, Felony and Breach of the Peace, be privileged from Arrest during their Attendance at the Session of their respective Houses, and in going to and returning from the same; and for any Speech or Debate in either House, they shall not be questioned in any other Place.

No Senator or Representative shall, during the Time for which he was elected, be appointed to any civil Office under the Authority of the United States, which shall have been created, or the Emoluments whereof shall have been encreased during such time; and no Person holding any Office under the United States, shall be a Member of either House during his Continuance in Office.

Section. 7. All Bills for raising Revenue shall originate in the House of Representatives; but the Senate may propose or concur with Amendments as on other Bills.

Every Bill which shall have passed the House of Representatives and the Senate, shall, before it become a Law, be presented to the President of the United States; If he approve he shall sign it, but if not he shall return it, with his Objections to that House in which it shall have originated, who shall enter the Objections at large on their Journal, and proceed to reconsider it. If after such Reconsideration two thirds of that House shall agree to pass the Bill, it shall be sent, together with the Objections, to the other House, by which it shall likewise be reconsidered, and if approved by two thirds of that House, it shall become a Law. But in all such Cases the Votes of both Houses shall be determined by Yeas and Nays, and the Names of the Persons voting for and against the Bill shall be entered on the Journal of each House respectively. If any Bill shall not be returned by the President within ten Days (Sundays excepted) after it shall have been presented to him, the Same shall be a Law, in like Manner as if he had signed it, unless the Congress by their Adjournment prevent its Return, in which Case it shall not be a Law.

Every Order, Resolution, or Vote to which the Concurrence of the Senate and House of Representatives may be necessary (except on a question of Adjournment) shall be presented to the President of the United States; and before the Same shall take Effect, shall be approved by him, or being disapproved by him, shall be repassed by two thirds of the Senate and House of Representatives, according to the Rules and Limitations prescribed in the Case of a Bill.

Section. 8. The Congress shall have Power To lay and collect Taxes, Duties, Imposts and Excises, to pay the Debts and provide for the common Defence and general Welfare of the United States; but all Duties, Imposts and Excises shall be uniform throughout the United States;

To borrow Money on the credit of the United States;

To regulate Commerce with foreign Nations, and among the several States, and with the Indian Tribes;

To establish an uniform Rule of Naturalization, and uniform Laws on the subject of Bankruptcies throughout the United States;

To coin Money, regulate the Value thereof, and of foreign Coin, and fix the Standard of Weights and Measures;

To provide for the Punishment of counterfeiting the Securities and current Coin of the United States;

To establish Post Offices and post Roads;

To promote the Progress of Science and useful Arts, by securing for limited Times to Authors and Inventors the exclusive Right to their respective Writings and Discoveries;

To constitute Tribunals inferior to the supreme Court;

To define and punish Piracies and Felonies committed on the high Seas, and Offences against the Law of Nations;

To declare War, grant Letters of Marque and Reprisal, and make Rules concerning Captures on land and Water;

To raise and support Armies, but no Appropriation of Money to that Use shall be for a longer Term than two Years;

To provide and maintain a Navy;

To make Rules for the Government and Regulation of the land and naval Forces;

To provide for calling forth the Militia to execute the Laws of the Union, suppress Insurrections and repel Invasions;

To provide for organizing, arming, and disciplining, the Militia, and for governing such Part of them as may be employed in the Service of the United States, reserving to the States respectively, the Appointment of the Officers, and the Authority of training the Militia according to the discipline prescribed by Congress;

To exercise exclusive Legislation in all Cases whatsoever, over such District (not exceeding ten Miles square) as may, by Cession of particular States, and the Acceptance of Congress, become the Seat of the Government of the United States, and to exercise like Authority over all Places purchased by the Consent of the Legislature of the State in which the Same shall be, for the Erection of Forts, Magazines, Arsenals, dock-Yards and other needful Buildings;—And

To make all Laws which shall be necessary and proper for carrying into Execution the foregoing Powers, and all other Powers vested by this Constitution in the Government of the United States, or in any Department or Officer thereof.

Section. 9. The Migration or Importation of such Persons as any of the States now existing shall think proper to admit, shall not be prohibited by the Congress prior to the Year one thousand eight hundred and eight, but a Tax or duty may be imposed on such Importation, not exceeding ten dollars for each Person.

The Privilege of the Writ of Habeas Corpus shall not be suspended, unless when in Cases of Rebellion or Invasion the public Safety may require it.

No Bill of Attainder or ex post facto Law shall be passed.

[No Capitation, or other direct, Tax shall be laid, unless in Proportion to the Census or enumeration herein before directed to be taken.]

No Tax or Duty shall be laid on Articles exported from any State.

No Preference shall be given by any Regulation of Commerce or Revenue to the Ports of one State over those of another: nor shall Vessels bound to, or from, one State, be obliged to enter, clear, or pay Duties in another.

No Money shall be drawn from the Treasury, but in Consequence of Appropriations made by Law; and a regular Statement and Account of the Receipts and Expenditures of all public Money shall be published from time to time.

No Title of Nobility shall be granted by the United States: And no Person holding any Office of Profit or Trust under them, shall, without the Consent of the Congress, accept of any present, Emolument, Office, or Title, of any kind whatever, from any King, Prince, or foreign State.

Section. 10. No State shall enter into any Treaty, Alliance, or Confederation; grant Letters of Marque and Reprisal; coin Money; emit Bills of Credit; make any Thing but gold and silver Coin a Tender in Payment of Debts; pass any Bill of Attainder, ex post facto Law, or Law impairing the Obligation of Contracts, or grant any Title of Nobility.

No State shall, without the Consent of the Congress, lay any Imposts or Duties on Imports or Exports, except what may be absolutely necessary for executing it's inspection Laws: and the net Produce of all Duties and Imposts, laid by any State on Imports or Exports, shall be for the Use of the Treasury of the United States; and all such Laws shall be subject to the Revision and Controul of the Congress.

No State shall, without the Consent of Congress, lay any Duty of Tonnage, keep Troops, or Ships of War in time of Peace, enter into any Agreement or Compact with another State, or with a foreign Power, or engage in War, unless actually invaded, or in such imminent Danger as will not admit of delay.

Article. II.

Section. 1. The executive Power shall be vested in a President of the United States of America. He shall hold his Office during the Term of four Years, and, together with the Vice President, chosen for the same Term, be elected, as follows

Each State shall appoint, in such Manner as the Legislature thereof may direct, a Number of Electors, equal to the whole Number of Senators and Representatives to which the State may be entitled in the Congress: but no Senator or Representative, or Person holding an Office of Trust or Profit under the United States, shall be appointed an Elector.

[The Electors shall meet in their respective States, and vote by Ballot for two Persons, of whom one at least shall not be an Inhabitant of the same State with themselves. And they shall make a List of all the Persons voted for, and of the Number of Votes for each; which List they shall sign and certify, and transmit sealed to the Seat of the Government of the United States, directed to the President of the Senate. The President of the Senate shall, in the Presence of the Senate and House of Representatives, open all the Certificates, and the Votes shall then be counted. The Person having the greatest Number of Votes shall be the President, if such Number be a Majority of the whole Number of Electors appointed; and if there be more than one who have such Majority, and have an equal Number of Votes, then the House of Representatives shall immediately chuse by Ballot one of them for President; and if no Person have a Majority, then from the five highest on the List the said House shall in like Manner chuse the President. But in chusing the President, the Votes shall be taken by States, the Representation from each State having one Vote; A quorum for this Purpose shall consist of a Member or Members from two thirds of the

States, and a Majority of all the States shall be necessary to a Choice. In every Case, after the Choice of the President, the Person having the greatest Number of Votes of the Electors shall be the Vice President. But if there should remain two or more who have equal Votes, the Senate shall chuse from them by Ballot the Vice President.]

The Congress may determine the Time of chusing the Electors, and the Day on which they shall give their Votes; which Day shall be the same throughout the United States.

No Person except a natural born Citizen, or a Citizen of the United States, at the time of the Adoption of this Constitution, shall be eligible to the Office of President; neither shall any person be eligible to that Office who shall not have attained to the Age of thirty five Years, and been fourteen Years a Resident within the United States.

[In Case of the Removal of the President from Office, or of his Death, Resignation, or Inability to discharge the Powers and Duties of the said Office, the Same shall devolve on the Vice President, and the Congress may by Law provide for the Case of Removal, Death, Resignation or Inability, both of the President and Vice President, declaring what Officer shall then act as President, and such Officer shall act accordingly, until the Disability be removed, or a President shall be elected.]

The President shall, at stated Times, receive for his Services, a Compensation, which shall neither be increased nor diminished during the Period for which he shall have been elected, and he shall not receive within that Period any other Emolument from the United States, or any of them.

Before he enter on the Execution of his Office, he shall take the following Oath or Affirmation:—"I do solemnly swear (or affirm) that I will faithfully execute the Office of President of the United States, and will to the best of my Ability, preserve, protect and defend the Constitution of the United States."

Section. 2. The President shall be Commander in Chief of the Army and Navy of the United States, and of the Militia of the several States, when called into the actual Service of the United States; he may require the Opinion, in writing, of the principal Officer in each of the executive Departments, upon any Subject relating to the Duties of their respective Offices, and he shall have Power to grant Reprieves and Pardons for Offenses against the United States, except in Cases of Impeachment.

He shall have Power, by and with the Advice and Consent of the Senate, to make Treaties, provided two thirds of the Senators present concur; and he shall nominate, and by and with the Advice and Consent of the Senate, shall appoint Ambassadors, other public Ministers and Consuls, Judges of the supreme Court, and all other Officers of the United States, whose Appointments are not herein otherwise provided for, and which shall be established by Law: but the Congress may by law vest the Appointment of such inferior Officers, as they think proper, in the President alone, in the Courts of Law, or in the Heads of Departments.

The President shall have Power to fill up all Vacancies that may happen during the Recess of the Senate, by granting Commissions which shall expire at the End of their next Session.

Section. 3. He shall from time to time give to the Congress Information of the State of the Union, and recommend to their Consideration such Measures as he shall judge necessary and expedient; he may, on extraordinary Occasions, convene both Houses, or either of them and in Case of Disagreement between them with Respect to the Time of Adjournment, he may adjourn them to such Time as he shall think proper; he shall receive Ambassadors and other public Ministers; he shall take Care that the Laws be faithfully executed, and shall Commission all the Officers of the United States.

Section. 4. The President, Vice President and all civil Officers of the United States, shall be removed from Office on Impeachment for, and Conviction of, Treason, Bribery, or other high Crimes and Misdemeanors.

Article. III.

Section. 1. The judicial Power of the United States, shall be vested in one supreme Court, and in such inferior Courts as the Congress may from time to time ordain and establish. The Judges, both of the supreme and inferior Courts, shall hold their Offices during good Behaviour, and shall, at stated Times, receive for their Services, a Compensation, which shall not be diminished during their Continuance in Office.

Section. 2. The judicial Power shall extend to all Cases, in Law and Equity, arising under this Constitution, the Laws of the United States, and Treaties made, or which shall be made, under their Authority;—to all Cases affecting Ambassadors, other public Ministers and Consuls;—to all Cases of admiralty and maritime Jurisdiction;—to Controversies to which the United States shall be a Party;—to Controversies between two or more States;—[between a State and Citizens of another State;]—between Citizens of different States,—between Citizens of the same State claiming Lands under Grants of different States, [and between a State or the Citizens thereof, and foreign States, Citizens or Subjects.]

In all Cases affecting Ambassadors, other public Ministers and Consuls, and those in which a State shall be Party, the supreme Court shall have original Jurisdiction. In all the other Cases before mentioned, the supreme Court shall have appellate Jurisdiction, both as to Law and Fact, with such Exceptions, and under such Regulations as the Congress shall make.

The Trial of all Crimes, except in Cases of Impeachment; shall be by Jury, and such Trial shall be held in the State where the said Crimes shall have been committed; but when not committed within any State, the Trial shall be at such Place or Places as the Congress may by Law have directed.

Section. 3. Treason against the United States, shall consist only in levying War against them, or in adhering to their Enemies, giving them Aid and Comfort. No Person shall be convicted of Treason unless on the Testimony of two Witnesses to the same overt Act, or on Confession in open Court.

The Congress shall have Power to declare the Punishment of Treason, but no Attainder of Treason shall work Corruption of Blood, or Forfeiture except during the Life of the Person attainted.

Article. IV.

Section. 1. Full Faith and Credit shall be given in each State to the public Acts, Records, and judicial Proceedings of every other State. And the

Congress may by general Laws prescribe the Manner in which such Acts, Records and Proceedings shall be proved, and the Effect thereof.

Section. 2. The Citizens of each State shall be entitled to all Privileges and Immunities of Citizens in the several States.

A Person charged in any State with Treason, Felony, or other Crime, who shall flee from Justice, and be found in another State, shall on Demand of the executive Authority of the State from which he fled, be delivered up, to be removed to the State having Jurisdiction of the Crime.

[No Person held to Service or Labour in one State, under the Laws thereof, escaping into another, shall, in Consequence of any Law or Regulation therein, be discharged from such Service or Labour, but shall be delivered up on Claim of the party to whom such Service or Labour may be due.]

Section. 3. New States may be admitted by the Congress into this Union; but no new State shall be formed or erected within the Jurisdiction of any other State; nor any State be formed by the Junction of two or more States, or Parts of States, without the Consent of the Legislatures of the States concerned as well as of the Congress.

The Congress shall have power to dispose of and make all needful Rules and Regulations respecting the Territory or other Property belonging to the United States; and nothing in this Constitution shall be so construed as to Prejudice any Claims of the United States, or of any particular State.

Section. 4. The United States shall guarantee to every State in this Union a Republican Form of Government, and shall protect each of them against Invasion; and on Application of the Legislature, or of the Executive (when the Legislature cannot be convened), against domestic Violence.

Article. V.

The Congress, whenever two thirds of both houses shall deem it necessary, shall propose Amendments to this Constitution, or, on the Application of the Legislatures of two thirds of the several States, shall call a Convention for proposing Amendments, which, in either Case, shall be valid to all Intents and Purposes, as Part of this Constitution, when ratified by the

Legislatures of three fourths of the several States, or by Conventions in three fourths thereof, as the one or the other Mode of Ratification may be proposed by the Congress; Provided that no Amendment which may be made prior to the Year One thousand eight hundred and eight shall in any Manner affect the first and fourth Clauses in the Ninth Section of the first Article; and that no State, without its Consent, shall be deprived of its equal Suffrage in the Senate.

Article. VI.

All Debts contracted and Engagements entered into, before the Adoption of this Constitution, shall be as valid against the United States under this Constitution, as under the Confederation.

This Constitution, and the Laws of the United States which shall be made in Pursuance thereof; and all Treaties made, or which shall be made, under the Authority of the United States, shall be the supreme Law of the Land; and the Judges in every State shall be bound thereby, any Thing in the Constitution or Laws of any State to the Contrary notwithstanding.

The Senators and Representatives before mentioned, and the Members of the several State Legislatures, and all executive and judicial Officers, both of the United States and of the several States, shall be bound by Oath or Affirmation, to support this Constitution; but no religious Test shall ever be required as a Qualification to any Office or public Trust under the United States.

Article. VII.

The Ratification of the Conventions of nine States, shall be sufficient for the Establishment of this Constitution between the States so ratifying the Same.

Done in Convention by the Unanimous Consent of the States present the Seventeenth Day of September in the Year of our Lord one thousand seven hundred and Eighty seven and of the Independance of the United States of America the Twelfth In Witness whereof We have hereunto subscribed our Names,

G°.Washington — Presd.t and deputy from Virginia

New Hampshire	John Langdon
	Nicholas Gilman
Massachusetts	Nathaniel Gorham
	Rufus King
Connecticut	Wm. Saml. Johnson
	Roger Sherman
New York	Alexander Hamilton
New Jersey	Wil: Livingston
	David Brearley
	Wm. Paterson
	Jona: Dayton
Pennsylvania	B Franklin
	Thomas Mifflin
	Robt. Morris
	Geo. Clymer
	Thos. FitzSimons
	Jared Ingersoll
	James Wilson
	Gouv Morris
Delaware	Geo: Read
	Gunning Bedford jun
	John Dickinson
	Richard Bassett
	Jaco: Broom
Maryland	James McHenry
	Dan of St Thos. Jenifer
	Danl. Carroll
Virginia	John Blair
	James Madison Jr.
North Carolina	Wm. Blount
	Richd. Dobbs Spaight
	Hu Williamson
South Carolina	J. Rutledge
	Charles Cotesworth Pinckney
	Charles Pinckney
	Pierce Butler
Georgia	William Few
	Abr Baldwin

Attest William Jackson Secretary

APPENDIX C: THE BILL OF RIGHTS

—⟨∞⟩—

The Bill of Rights: Amendments I–X
Passed by Congress September 25, 1789
Ratified December 15, 1791

Amendment I - Congress shall make no law respecting an establishment of religion, or prohibiting the free exercise thereof; or abridging the freedom of speech, or of the press; or the right of the people peaceably to assemble, and to petition the Government for a redress of grievances.

Amendment II - A well regulated Militia, being necessary to the security of a free State, the right of the people to keep and bear Arms, shall not be infringed.

Amendment III - No Soldier shall, in time of peace be quartered in any house, without the consent of the Owner, nor in time of war, but in a manner to be prescribed by law.

Amendment IV - The right of the people to be secure in their persons, houses, papers, and effects, against unreasonable searches and seizures, shall not be violated, and no Warrants shall issue, but upon probable cause, supported by Oath or affirmation, and particularly describing the place to be searched, and the persons or things to be seized.

Amendment V - No person shall be held to answer for a capital, or otherwise infamous crime, unless on a presentment or indictment of a Grand Jury, except in cases arising in the land or naval forces, or in the Militia, when in actual service in time of War or public danger; nor shall any person be subject for the same offence to be twice put in jeopardy of life or limb; nor shall be compelled in any criminal case to be a witness against himself, nor be deprived of life, liberty, or property, without due process of law; nor shall private property be taken for public use, without just compensation.

Amendment VI - In all criminal prosecutions, the accused shall enjoy the right to a speedy and public trial, by an impartial jury of the State and district wherein the crime shall have been committed, which district shall have been previously ascertained by law, and to be informed of the nature and cause of the accusation; to be confronted with the witnesses against him; to have compulsory process for obtaining witnesses in his favor, and to have the Assistance of Counsel for his defence.

Amendment VII - In Suits at common law, where the value in controversy shall exceed twenty dollars, the right of trial by jury shall be preserved, and no fact tried by a jury shall be otherwise re-examined in any Court of the United States, than according to the rules of the common law.

Amendment VIII - Excessive bail shall not be required, nor excessive fines imposed, nor cruel and unusual punishments inflicted.

Amendment IX - The enumeration in the Constitution, of certain rights, shall not be construed to deny or disparage others retained by the people.

Amendment X - The powers not delegated to the United States by the Constitution, nor prohibited by it to the States, are reserved to the States respectively, or to the people.

ACKNOWLEDGMENTS

At a certain age one looks back to the beginning and realizes that a few teachers put you on the path you have traveled. In my case, four historians were my mentors: Edmund Morgan, C. Vann Woodward, Elting Morison, and William McFeely.

More to the matter at hand, six colleagues read the entire manuscript and made critical suggestions that I could not afford to ignore, even though on occasion I resisted their advice: Robert Dalzell, just retired from Williams College, whose narrative instincts were always impeccable; Susan Dunn, also of Williams, whose cheers in the margins were accompanied by deft criticisms offered with uncommon grace; David Hendrickson of Colorado College, who shared his unsurpassed knowledge of the secondary literature; Michael Neff, a former student and recent graduate of Harvard Law School, who has an eagle eye for generalizations that need to be qualified; another former student, Chelsea Michta, now reading history at Cambridge University, who helped me with the appendices and with the various dictionary definitions of *coup;* and Stephen Smith, former editor of the *Washington Examiner,* whose verbal agility in that problematic place where substance meets style is almost magical.

I have been the beneficiary of the massive documentary projects long in process to publish the papers of the most prominent American founders. This book could not have been written without the labor-intensive work done by editors of the George Washington, James Madison, Thomas Jefferson, Robert Morris, and John Jay papers. A special thanks to Jennifer Steinshorne at the Jay Papers for digital access to materials not yet published.

My editor at Knopf, Dan Frank, proved an able successor to the late, great Ash Green. Dan pushed me hard with probing questions at the start, then ushered the manuscript through the corridors of power with guile and gusto.

Ike Williams, my literary agent, grasped the core argument of the book before I did, always took my calls, and from his listening post in Boston kept me abreast of all trade rumors involving the Red Sox, Patriots, and Celtics.

My longtime assistant, Linda Chesky Fernandes, continued to conceal my technological incompetence and began each day asking "What do you need?" I always answered "Nothing but unconditional love."

That came naturally from my wife, Ellen Wilkins Ellis, offered in her Mississippi accent, often with a steel magnolia edge, suggesting that it was time to come back from the eighteenth century.

Most of the book was written in my study at Amherst in longhand, though not with a quill pen. My only research assistants were two devoted Labradoodles, an aging but still feisty Jack Russell, and a bothersome cat who kept walking across the piles of papers on my desk.

There are professional and personal reasons for the dedication to Pauline Maier, who passed away while I was writing the final draft. On the former score, Pauline's last book has established itself as the authoritative account of the ratification process of 1787–88, which helped to guide me through the otherwise bewildering state-by-state debates over the Constitution. On the latter score, Pauline was a spirited, intellectually passionate friend and colleague for thirty years, who was never afraid to tell me what she thought. She preached that history was an argument without end, and she practiced what she preached. I can hear her now, shouting from above, "Joe, are you sure about the title?"

Joseph J. Ellis
Amherst, Massachusetts
MAY 12, 2015

NOTES

The following endnotes represent my attempt to cite the primary and secondary sources that most influenced my interpretation of the founding era. Several generations of American historians have moseyed on down this trail before me, leaving a legacy of scholarship that merits at least a nod of recognition. Here are some seminal studies that somehow never made it into the endnotes:

Akkil Reed Amar, *America's Constitution: A Biography* (New York, 2005); Herman Belz et al., eds., *To Form a More Perfect Union: The Critical Ideas of the Constitution* (Charlottesville, Va., 1992); Robert Dahl, *How Democratic Is the American Constitution?* (New Haven, Conn., 2003); Jackson Turner Main, *The Antifederalists: Critics of the Constitution* (Chapel Hill, N.C., 1961); Forrest McDonald, *We the People: The Economic Origins of the Constitution* (Chicago, 1958), and *E Pluribus Unum: The Formation of the American Republic, 1776–1790* (Boston, 1965); Clinton Rossiter, *1787: The Grand Convention* (New York, 1966); David Stewart, *The Summer of 1787* (New York, 2007); Carl Van Doren, *The Great Rehearsal* (New York, 1948); Gordon Wood, *The Creation of the American Republic* (Chapel Hill, N.C., 1969), and *Revolutionary Characters: What Made the Founders Different* (New York, 2006). For whatever reasons, I have not quoted from these texts, but there is no question that my thinking over the years has been influenced by them.

ABBREVIATIONS

Titles

AP Robert J. Taylor et al., eds., *The Papers of John Adams*, 12 vols. to date (Cambridge, Mass., 1983–)

DA Lyman H. Butterfield et al., eds., *The Diary and Autobiography of John Adams* (Cambridge, Mass., 1966)

DHRC Merrill Jensen, John P. Kaminski, and Gaspar J. Saladino, eds., *Documentary History of the Ratification of the Constitution*, 26 vols. to date (Madison, Wis., 1976–)

FP Barbara Oberg et al., eds., *The Papers of Benjamin Franklin*, 27 vols. to date (New Haven, Conn., 1959–)

GP Richard K. Showman, ed., *The Papers of General Nathaniel Greene*, 7 vols. to date (Chapel Hill, N.C., 1976–)

HP Harold C. Syrett and Jacob E. Cooke, eds., *The Papers of Alexander Hamilton*, 26 vols. (New York, 1961–79)

JCC W. C. Ford et al., eds., *Journals of the Continental Congress*, 24 vols. (Washington, D.C., 1904–37)

JER *Journal of the Early Republic*

JP Elizabeth M. Nuxoll et al., eds. *The Selected Papers of John Jay*, 3 vols. to date (Charlottesville, Va., 2010–)

LDC Paul H. Smith et al., eds., *Letters of Delegates to Congress, 1774–1789*, 29 vols. (Washington, D.C., 1976–2000)

MP William T. Hutchinson et al., eds., *The Papers of James Madison*, 20 vols. to date (Chicago and Charlottesville, Va., 1962–)

PMHB *The Pennsylvania Magazine of History and Biography*

PRM E. James Ferguson et al., eds., *The Papers of Robert Morris*, 9 vols. (Pittsburgh, 1973–99)

PWCS W. W. Abbott and Dorothy Twohig, eds., *The Papers of George Washington: Confederation Series* (Charlottesville, Va., 1992–97)

PWR W. W. Abbott, Dorothy Twohig, and Philander D. Chase, eds., *The Papers of George Washington: Revolutionary War Series*, 20 vols. to date (Charlottesville, Va., 1985–)

RL James Morton Smith, ed., *The Republic of Letters: The Correspondence Between Thomas Jefferson and James Madison, 1776–1826*, 3 vols. (New York, 1995)

TJP Julian Boyd et al., eds., *The Papers of Thomas Jefferson*, 30 vols. to date (Princeton, N.J., 1950–)

VMHB   *Virginia Magazine of History and Biography*

WMQ   *William and Mary Quarterly,* 3rd series

Works   Charles Francis Adams, ed., *The Works of John Adams,* 10 vols. (Boston, 1950–60)

WW   James C. Fitzpatrick, ed., *Writings of George Washington,* 39 vols. (Washington, D.C., 1931–39)

Persons

AA	Abigail Adams
AH	Alexander Hamilton
GW	George Washington
JA	John Adams
JJ	John Jay
JM	James Madison
RM	Robert Morris
TJ	Thomas Jefferson

PREFACE: *PLURIBUS* TO *UNUM*

1. David C. Hendrickson, *Peace Pact: The Lost World of the American Founding* (Lawrence, Kan., 2003).

2. Edmund S. Morgan, *The Birth of the Republic, 1763–89* (Chicago, 1956), is the seminal statement of the constitutional issues at stake in the 1760s. Pauline Maier, *American Scripture: Making the Declaration of Independence* (New York, 1997), is the standard work on the subject.

3. James D. Drake, *The Nation's Nature: How Continental Assumptions Gave Rise to the United States of America* (Charlottesville, Va., 2011), is a splendid meditation on the role of space and distance in the founding era.

4. Bernard Bailyn, *Ideological Origins of the American Revolution* (Cambridge, Mass., 1967), is the seminal study of the conspiratorial and on occasion irrational mentality that shaped the American response to British policy during the decade before the outbreak of war in 1775.

5. The evidence for this argument is offered in some detail in Chapters 1–3 below. Not all historians agree. Richard Morris, *The Forging of the Union, 1781–1789* (New York, 1987), purports to detect an incipient national ethos in 1776 and beyond. Jack Rakove, *The Beginnings of National Politics: An Interpretive History of the Continental Congress*

(Baltimore, 1979), despite the title, makes a more careful case for the survival of a national mentality after the heady days of 1775–76. For the argument that the Constitution created a national framework for an American population that lacked a national identity, see John M. Murrin, "'A Roof Without Walls': The Dilemma of American National Identity," in Richard Beeman, Stephen Botein, and Edward C. Carter, eds., *Beyond Confederation: Origins of the Constitution and National Identity* (Chapel Hill, N.C., 1987), 333–48.

6. Merrill Jensen, *The Articles of Confederation: An Interpretation of the Social-Constitutional History of the American Revolution* (New York, 1940); Merrill Jensen, *The New Nation: The History of the United States During the Confederation* (New York, 1950). For a sophisticated analysis of the Progressive School, see Richard Hofstadter, *The Progressive Historians* (New York, 1968). The Progressive School still has dedicated disciples. See, for example, Woody Holton, *Unruly Americans and the Origins of the Constitution* (New York, 2007).

7. For an argument along somewhat the same lines, see Max M. Edling, *A Revolution in Favor of Government: The U.S. Constitution and the Making of the American State* (Oxford, 2003).

8. Full citations of the multivolume editions of the founders' papers are listed in the key to abbreviations beginning on page 251.

9. Gordon S. Wood, *The Radicalism of the American Revolution* (New York, 1992), makes the strongest case for the egalitarian impact of the revolution, which eroded the hierarchical assumptions prevalent in the colonial era and thereby created the democratic culture that Tocqueville described in the 1830s. My intention here is not to refute Wood's argument so much as amend it. The democratizing process that Wood describes had only begun its work in the 1780s, so the mentality of the most prominent founders was still embedded in a network of predemocratic assumptions that remained skeptical about the wisdom of the common man and the embrace of majority rule. The Constitution that they crafted, then, accurately reflects their desire to tap the energies of democracy while also controlling its inevitable excesses.

10. Two of the most recent studies of slavery and the Constitution offer good examples of both interpretive options. George William Van Cleve, *A Slaveholders' Union: Slavery, Politics and the Constitution in*

the Early Republic (Chicago, 2010), leans toward the inevitability of it all. David Waldstreicher, *Slavery's Constitution: From Revolution to Ratification* (New York, 2009), is a blistering indictment of the founders for failing to make the moral choice.

CHAPTER 1: THE ARTICLES AND THE VISION

1. Thomas Rodney, diary, 1 March 1781, *LDC* 17:3.

2. Josiah Tucker, *Cai Bono* (London, 1781), 11–12. See also David C. Hendrickson, *Peace Pact: The Lost World of the American Founding* (Lawrence, Kan., 2003), 11–12.

3. My interpretation here is much influenced by Hendrickson, *Peace Pact.* See Appendix A, p. 221.

4. Ibid. Two of the most important books on the government under the Articles of Confederation announce in their titles the exact opposite of what the Articles created. Jack Rakove, *The Beginnings of National Politics: An Interpretive History of the Continental Congress* (Baltimore, 1979), and Merrill Jensen, *The New Nation: The History of the United States During the Confederation* (New York, 1950), are both major works that contain invaluable information not to be found elsewhere. But both insist on the existence of a national ethos beyond the heady years of 1775–76—Jensen rather brazenly, Rakove more obliquely—that strikes me as misguided. State and local priorities were in the saddle by the fall of 1776, and they dictated the state-based structure of the Articles. Rakove seems to grasp this, despite his title. Jensen does not.

5. The Adams prescription for state governments is in *AP* 4:65–73. My earlier effort to explain the influence of *Thoughts on Government* is in *American Creation: Triumphs and Tragedies at the Founding of the Republic* (New York, 2007), 46–49. The point here is that there was a commonly accepted formula for a viable and balanced republican government in place that most of the states followed. The failure of the Articles to embody that formula suggested that they were never intended to function as a government because a truly national government remained unimaginable.

6. Appendix A, pp. 223–24.

7. Rakove, *Beginnings of National Politics,* 63–86, is at his best here, in the earliest stages of the war, when the revolutionary fires still burned brightly. For the Rush quotation, see *DA* 2:247.

8. *LDC* 4:233–50, for the Dickinson Draft. Merrill Jensen, *The Articles of Confederation: An Interpretation* (Madison, Wis., 1941), 126–39, tends to emphasize the nationalistic features of the document. Hendrickson, *Peace Pact*, 127–37, emphasizes the confederationist elements.

9. *DA* 2:245–46; *JP* 1:320–23.

10. *LDC* 4:338–39.

11. *JCC* 5:425–31, 546–56; *FP* 22:536–38, for the editorial note on Franklin's role in the debate.

12. *LDC* 4:242; *DA* 2:245; *FP* 22:538.

13. *DA* 2:249; *JP* 1:323–27.

14. *DA* 2:241–43, 249–50; *JP* 1:462–65.

15. JA to Hezekiah Niles, 13 February 1818, *Works* 10:283.

16. JA to Joseph Hawley, 25 August 1776, *LDC* 5:60–62.

17. Burke's "Remarks" are in *LDC* 3:419–21, 433–77. There is a spirited scholarly debate over the significance and influence of Burke's amendment; it is nicely synthesized in Hendrickson, *Peace Pact*, 343–44. Historians who detect a lurking nationalistic dimension in the Dickinson Draft regard Burke's role in demanding a clear statement of state sovereignty as crucial. But Hendrickson does not think the Dickinson Draft was that nationalistic to begin with and therefore sees Burke's amendment as a mere clarification of the broad consensus on the confederation model. I tend to agree with Hendrickson.

18. See the expressions of wartime urgency in *LDC* 7:251–58, 98, 254, 348.

19. On the essential but threatening role of the Continental Army, see Charles Royster, *A Revolutionary People at War: The Continental Army and the American Character* (Chapel Hill, N.C., 1979), and Robert K. Wright, *The Continental Army* (Washington, D.C., 1983).

20. Editorial Note, *GP* 1:307, for the recommendation of the committee to raise eighty-eight battalions; *JCC* 5:810–11, 842–44, for the congressional vote approving the recommendations; John Hancock to GW, 9 October 1776, *PWR* 6:515–16, for the manpower potential of the American population.

21. For a sample of Washington's steady stream of complaints about lack of support for the Continental Army, see the following: GW to Board of War, 11 November 1778, *WW* 13:244–46; GW to Benjamin Harrison, 18–30 December 1778, *WW* 13:463–68; GW to Committee of Conference, 13 January 1779, *WW* 14:3–12.

22. GW to Joseph Jones, 31 May 1780, *WW* 18:453; GW to Fielding

Lewis, 6 July 1780, *WW* 19:131. On the same theme see *WW* 17:425–28; 18:207–11; 21:213–16, 318–21.

23. Circular Letter to the States, 26 August 1779, *WW* 16:173–74, for the initial effort to appeal to state governments.

24. This character sketch is primarily based on the research done for my biography *His Excellency: George Washington* (New York, 2004). The scholarship on Washington defies any neat synthesis, but four books strike me as seminal: Ron Chernow, *Washington: A Life* (New York, 2010); Marcus Cunliffe, *George Washington: Man and Monument* (Boston, 1958); Peter Henriques, *Realistic Visionary: A Portrait of George Washington* (Charlottesville, Va., 2006); and Don Higgenbotham, ed., *George Washington Reconsidered* (Charlottesville, Va., 2001).

25. Ellis, *His Excellency,* 73–74, for the instructions to his manager at Mount Vernon.

26. GW to Burwell Bassett, 19 June 1775, *PWR* 1:19–20.

27. On the potency of Washington as a unifying symbol, see Barry Schwartz, *George Washington: The Making of a Symbol* (New York, 1987).

28. GW to John Armstrong, 10 January 1783, *WW* 26:26–27.

29. GW to Benjamin Harrison, 4 March 1783, *WW* 26:184–85.

30. Circular Letter to the States, 8 June 1783, *WW* 26:483–88.

31. *WW* 26:492–96.

32. Ellis, *His Excellency,* 151–57.

33. My thinking on this theme was first prompted by W. W. Abbot's essay, "George Washington, the West, and the Union," in Higgenbotham, *George Washington Reconsidered,* 198–211.

CHAPTER 2: THE FINANCIER AND THE PRODIGY

1. John Witherspoon to Richard Henry Lee, 19 May 1781, *LDC* 17:250, for the quorum problem. See also Roger Sherman to Jonathan Trumbull, Jr., 15 September 1781, *LDC* 18:48.

2. Charles Thomson's Notes of Delegates, 8 August 1782, *LDC* 19:41–42, for Lee's role as obstructionist. A nice character sketch of Lee is in Thomas Fleming, *The Perils of Peace: America's Struggle for Survival After Yorktown* (New York, 2007), 50–54.

3. Samuel Huntington to The States, 1 June 1781, *LDC* 17:283–85; see also *LDC* 17:319–21 and 18:72–79.

4. James Madison's Observations, 1 May 1782, *LDC* 18:481–82.

5. Charles Thomson's Notes of Debates, 27 August 1782, *LDC* 19:98.

6. JM to TJ, 15 November 1781, *LDC* 18:205–6. The land claims debate dominated the records of Congress. See *JCC* 19:99–100, 208–13, 253–64; 20:502, 526, 534; 21:781–84, 1032. See also *JCC* 21:124–25, for the claims of the Virginia delegation.

7. *LDC* 18:462–63, for the Butler quotation. See also *JCC* 22:191–94, for the Vermont debate.

8. E. James Ferguson, *The Power of the Purse: A History of American Public Finance* (Chapel Hill, N.C., 1961), 109–20, for the currency inflation. The Congress set the rate of dollars to specie at 40 to 1, but the rate kept escalating until it reached 500 to 1.

9. Charles Thomson to RM, 29 June 1781, *LDC* 17:362; Samuel Osgood to Samuel Holton, 14 May 1782, *LDC* 18:511–12.

10. *JCC* 19:311, 421–27.

11. Samuel Huntington to Certain States, 14 May 1781, *LDC* 17:235. The correspondence among delegates in the spring and summer of 1781 is littered with lamentations about the ballooning debt and depreciating currency.

12. Morris has waited too long for a modern biographer who can recover his stature in the 1780s. He has found him in Charles Rappleye, *Robert Morris: Financier of the American Revolution* (New York, 2010). In his introduction, Rappleye mentions my previous work on the founders, noting its failure to give Morris his due. While there are mitigating factors, I plead guilty. Clarence L. VerSteeg, *Robert Morris: Revolutionary Financier* (New York, 1972), is still useful.

13. Diary, 8 February 1781, *PRM* 1:8. See the early chapters of Rappleye, *Morris*, for the controversy over Morris's purported privateering.

14. Benjamin Franklin to RM, 26 July 1781, *PRM* 1:5.

15. RM to Philip Schuyler, 29 May 1781, *PRM* 1:92–93.

16. This character sketch is based on Rappleye, *Morris*, and my reading in *MP*.

17. On the concept of credit in a capitalistic economy, see James Grant, *Money of the Mind* (New York, 1992). See also Thomas K. McCraw, *The Founders and Finance: How Hamilton, Gallatin and Other Immigrants Forged a New Economy* (Cambridge, Mass., 2012), 56–73.

18. RM to Benjamin Harrison, 15 January 1782, *PRM* 4:32.

19. *JCC* 22:1186–87; *PRM* 1:83.

20. RM to Benjamin Franklin, 13 July 1781, *PRM* 1:283.

21. RM to Jonathan Trumbull, Jr., 31 July 1782, *PRM* 6:133; RM to Governors, 19 October 1781, *PRM* 3:83.

22. RM to Governors, 27 July 1781, *PRM* 1:396.

23. RM and Richard Peters to GW, 13 August 1781, *PRM* 2:50–55; Diary, 21 August 1781, *PRM* 2:73–81; GW to RM, 6 September 1781, *PRM* 2:205. On the fortuitous circumstances that made victory at Yorktown possible, see Richard M. Ketchum, *Victory at Yorktown: The Campaign That Won the Revolution* (New York, 2004), 1–28.

24. Report on the Public Credit, 29 July 1781, *PRM* 6:36–84; *JCC* 22:429–47; RM to Gouverneur Morris, 3 April 1782, *PRM* 4:510.

25. Arthur Lee to Samuel Adams, 6 August 1782, *LDC* 19:25–26.

26. Lee's essay, under the pseudonym Lucius, appeared in the *Freeman's Journal* in March 1783, available in *PRM* 7:502–6, 559, 595, 685–89.

27. Rappleye, *Morris,* 319–26; David Howell to William Greene, 30 July 1782, *LDC* 18:678–84; David Howell to RM, 31 July–2 August 1782, *LDC* 18:691–92.

28. RM to Daniel Jennifer, 11 June 1782, *PRM* 5:379; Rappleye, *Morris,* 300.

29. RM to Matthew Ridley, 9 September 1782, *PRM* 6:552.

30. JM to Edmund Pendleton, 7 February 1782, *LDC* 18:327.

31. This generalization is based on my reading of *MP* from August 1782 to March 1783, when he served as a Virginia delegate to the Confederation Congress. Much more will be forthcoming on Madison as his role in the story grows. The best brief character sketch of Madison is in Stanley Elkins and Eric McKitrick, *The Age of Federalism: The Early Republic, 1788–1800* (New York, 1993), 79–92.

32. AH to RM, 30 April 1781, *HP* 2:604–35.

33. RM to AH, 26 May 1781, *HP* 2:645–46; RM to AH, 28 August 1782, *HP* 3:152–56; RM to AH, *HP* 3:166.

34. The character sketch is based on the early chapters of Ron Chernow's magisterial *Alexander Hamilton* (New York, 2004) and the first three volumes of *HP*.

35. The quotation is from AH to Edward Stevens, 11 November 1769, *HP* 1:4.

36. *HP* 2:649–52.

37. *HP* 2:669–74.

38. *HP* 3:103.

39. Resolution Calling for a Convention of the States to Revise and

Amend the Articles of Confederation, 20 July 1782, *HP* 3:110–13. See *JCC* 23:476; 24:285; 25:523, for the fate of Hamilton's resolution.

40. GW to James McHenry, 12 September 1782, *WW* 25:151.

41. *HP* 3:243–45; *PRM* 7:248–50, for an editorial note on the meeting with McDougall; *JCC* 24:291–93.

42. The standard account is Richard H. Kohn, *Eagle and Sword: The Beginning of a Military Establishment in America* (New York, 1975), 17–39. See also the scholarly article by Kohn, "The Inside History of the Newburgh Conspiracy: America and the Coup d'État," *WMQ* 27 (1970): 187–220. Rappleye, *Morris*, 331–38, makes a persuasive case that Robert Morris was not the chief instigator, Gouverneur Morris was.

43. AH to GW, 13 February 1783, *HP* 3:254.

44. Remarks on the Revenue and the Situation of the Army, 20 February 1783, *HP* 3:264.

45. GW to AH, 11 March 1783, *HP* 3:286–87; GW to AH, 4 April 1783, *HP* 3:315–16.

46. GW to AH, 4 March 1783, *HP* 3:277–79.

47. To the Officers of the Army, 15 March 1783, *WW* 26:222–23.

48. Henry Knox to Gouverneur Morris, 21 February 1783, *PRM* 7:448; AH to GW, 17 March 1783, *HP* 3:292; AH to GW, 24 March 1783, *HP* 3:304–5.

49. GW to AH, 31 March 1783, *HP* 3:310.

50. Charles Royster, *A Revolutionary People at War: The Continental Army and the American Character* (Chapel Hill, N.C., 1979), 341–51, recovers this poignant moment, as does Fleming, *Perils of Peace*, 298–322. See GW to Theodore Bland, 4 April 1783, *WW* 26:285, for the quotation.

51. RM to AH et al., 14 April 1783, *HP* 3:323–24.

52. RM to President of Congress, 24 January 1783, *PRM* 7:368; RM to Horatio Gates, 28 January 1783, *PRM* 7:378.

53. Kenneth Bowling, "New Light on the Philadelphia Mutiny of 1783," *PMHB* 101 (1977): 419–35; see also Fleming, *Perils of Peace*, 290–91.

54. Report on Conference with the Supreme Council of Pennsylvania, 20 June 1783, *HP* 3:399–400; Resolutions on Measures to Be Taken in Consequence of the Pennsylvania Mutiny, *HP* 3:401–2.

55. AH to JM, 29 June 1783, *HP* 3:408–9.

56. AH to Nathanael Greene, 10 June 1783, *HP* 3:376.

57. AH to JJ, 25 July 1783, *HP* 3:416–17.

CHAPTER 3: THE DOMAIN

1. Samuel Flagg Bemis, *The Diplomacy of the American Revolution* (Bloomington, Ind., 1957), 212–13, claims that "the greatest victory in the annals of American diplomacy was won at the outset by Franklin, Jay and Adams."

2. See Walter Stahr, *John Jay* (New York, 2006), 171, for the exchange between the French and English negotiators. While Jay's contributions to the American founding have hardly gone unnoticed, my keen sense is that his significance has not been fully appreciated. The ongoing publication of his papers by the University of Virginia Press, just begun, will most likely move him to the first rank of founders. Stahr's solid biography is a first step in that direction.

3. Aranda Notes, *JP* 2:270–72. See also Richard Morris, *The Peacemakers: The Great Powers in the Search for American Independence* (New York, 1965), 309–10.

4. JJ to Robert Livingston, 17 November 1782, *LDC* 6:11–49.

5. *DA* 3:37–38, 81, 85; JA to James Lloyd, 6 February 1815, *Works* 10–115.

6. The sketch is based on my reading of *JP*, volumes 1–3; Stahr, *John Jay*, 1–212; and Richard Morris, *Seven Who Shaped Our Destiny: The Founding Fathers as Revolutionaries* (New York, 1973), 150–88.

7. JJ to Sarah Jay, 21 and 29 July 1776, *JP* 1:305–7. During the British occupation of New York, Jay organized a spy network to expose covert loyalists and intercept British intelligence, leading the CIA to name a conference room in his honor as "America's first counter-intelligence chief."

8. Willi Paul Adams, *The First State Constitution: Republican Ideology and the Making of the State Constitution in the Revolutionary Era* (Lantham, Md., 2001), 1–24.

9. JJ to Egbert Benson, 26 August 1782, *JP* 2:326.

10. JJ to Lafayette, 3 January 1779, *LDC* 11:409; JJ to AH, 28 September 1783, *HP* 3:459–60.

11. JJ to Samuel Huntington, 6 November 1780, *LDC* 4:133–39.

12. *JCC* 15:1052–53.

13. William Ellery to Francis Dana, 3 December 1783, *LDC* 21:177; David Howell to William Greene, 5 February 1784, *LDC* 21:341.

14. Deed of the Virginia Cession, 1 March 1784, *TJP* 6:578.

15. Plan for Government of the Western Territory, 3 February–23 April 1784, *TJP* 6:580–616; *JCC* 26:118–20, 246–47, 255–60, 274–79.

16. *TJP* 6:604. See also Dumas Malone, *Jefferson the Virginian* (Boston, 1948), 412–14, and, old but still valuable, Thomas Perkins Abernethy, *Western Lands and the American Revolution* (Charlottesville, Va., 1937), 274–310.

17. TJ to Thomas Hutchins, 24 January 1784, *LDC* 21:305–6.

18. GW to James Duane, 7 September 1783, *LDC* 21:101–4. For the Ordinance of 1784, see Merrill Jensen, *The New Nation: The History of the United States During the Confederation* (New York, 1950), 350–59, and Peter Onuf, *Statehood and Union: A History of the Northwest Ordinance* (Bloomington, Ind., 1992), 4–5. See also Virginia Delegates to Benjamin Harrison, 1 November 1783, *LDC* 21:128–29, for the chaotic consequences of unregulated migration.

19. Wilcomb Washburn, ed., *The American Indian and the United States: A Documentary History*, 4 vols. (New York, 1973), 4:2267–77, for the treaties. Reginald Horseman, *Expansion and American Indian Policy, 1783–1812* (East Lansing, Mich., 1967), is the standard work. Two books by David K. Richter recover the Native American perspective on American policy, *Facing East from Indian Country: A Native History of Early America* (Cambridge, Mass., 2001), and *Before the Revolution: America's Ancient Pasts* (Cambridge, Mass., 2011).

20. Philip Schuyler to President of Congress, 29 July 1781, *JCC* 13:601–7.

21. Elizabeth Fenn, *Pox Americana: The Great Smallpox Epidemic of 1775–82* (New York, 2001).

22. Quoted in editorial note, TJ to Francis Hopkinson, *LDC* 21:363.

23. The Jefferson quotation is in *LDC* 21:494; Benjamin Harrison to GW, 8 January 1784, *PWCS* 1:22–23; Jacob Read to GW, 13 August 1784, *LDC* 21:768.

24. Henry Knox to GW, 23 November 1784, *PWCS* 2:144.

25. GW to Benjamin Harrison, 10 October 1784, *PWCS* 2:92.

26. *American Museum* (February 1787), 1:160.

27. Ibid., 238.

28. David Howell to Jonathan Arnold, 21 February 1784, *LDC* 21:381.

29. For Washington's worries that Congress would mishandle westward expansion, see GW to Richard Henry Lee, 15 March 1785, *PWCS* 2:437–40.

30. Don Juan Miralles to José de Galvez, 28 December 1778, *LDC* 11:381–83, for Jay's unflattering opinion of Spanish power on the North American continent.

31. JJ to JA, 14 October 1785, *JP* 4. The editors of *Jay Papers* graciously gave me access to the unpublished correspondence being prepared for publication at the University of Virginia Press; therefore, citations lack pagination for the fourth volume.

32. JJ to John Lovell, 10 May 1785, *JP* 4.

33. Circular to the Governors or Presidents of the States, 29 January 1785, ibid.; JJ to Richard Henry Lee, 23 January 1785, *JP* 4.

34. Report to Congress, 13 September 1786, *JP* 4, for Jay's position on the debt and loyalist issues.

35. Report on State Laws, 13 October 1786, *JP* 4; JJ to JA, 1 May 1786, *JP* 4; JJ to GW, 27 June 1786, *PWCF* 4:130–32; Charles F. Hobson, "The Recovery of British Debts in the Federal Court of Virginia," *VMHB* 94 (1984): 176–79.

36. JJ to JA, 1 November 1786, *JP* 4.

37. Gardoqui: Notes of a Conference with John Jay, 4 February 1786, *JP* 4.

38. *JCC* 29:657–58, for the instructions to Jay; Report to Congress, 3 August 1786, *JP* 4.

39. JJ to Diego de Gardoqui, 4 October 1785, *JP* 4, for the diplomatic refusal to accept gifts for Sarah Jay; Report to Congress, 3 August 1786, *JP* 4; JJ to Richard Henry Lee, 15 August 1786, *JP* 4.

40. JJ to Diego de Gardoqui, 10 May 1786; Gardoqui to JJ, 25 May 1786, *JP* 4.

41. Charles Pinckney, Speech in Congress, 10 August 1786, *JP* 4. The French chargé d'affaires, Louis Guillama Otto, recorded the debate quite fully in Otto to Vergennes, 10 September 1786, *JP* 4.

42. JJ to John Hancock, 29 May 1786, *JP* 4, for Jay's insistence on complete secrecy during his negotiations with Gardoqui. James Monroe to Patrick Henry, 12 August 1786, *JP* 4, for Monroe's conspiratorial theory.

43. James Monroe to Benjamin Harrison, 26 March 1784, *LDC* 21:460–61, for Monroe's estimate of Virginia's debt.

44. Proceeding in Congress, 31 August 1786, *JP* 4; Charles Pinckney to JJ, 1–3 September 1786, *JP* 4.

45. GW to Henry Lee, Jr., 18 June 1786, *PWCS* 4:117–18.

46. JJ to GW, 27 June 1786, *JP* 4.

47. JJ to JA, 18 August 1786, *JP* 4.

48. JJ to GW, 16 March 1786, *JP* 4.

49. GW to JJ, 18 March 1786, *JP* 4.

CHAPTER 4: THE COURTING

1. GW to Lafayette, 10 May 1786, *PWCS* 4:42.
2. Unsubmitted Resolution Calling for a Convention, July 1783, *HP* 3:420–26.
3. John Francis Mercer to JM, 26 November 1784, *MP* 8:152–53; William Grayston to JM, 28 May 1786, *MP* 9:61–66.
4. JM to James Monroe, 19 March 1786, *MP* 8:505.
5. JM to TJ, 12 August 1786, *MP* 9:96; JM to TJ, 12 August 1786, *MP* 8:502–3. See also JM to James Monroe, 14 March 1786, *MP* 8:497–98.
6. Address at the Annapolis convention, 14 September 1786, *HP* 3:687.
7. Ibid., 689.
8. Leonard R. Richards, *Shays' Rebellion: The American Revolution's Final Battle* (Philadelphia, 2002).
9. JM to George Muter, 7 January 1787, *MP* 9:230–31.
10. GW to Henry Lee, 31 October 1786, *PWCS* 4:318. See also the multiple reports Washington received on Shays' Rebellion, all exaggerated, in *PWCS* 4:240–41, 281–82, 297, 300–1, 417–18, 460–62.
11. Samuel Higginson to Henry Knox, 12 November 1786, *LDC* 9:155.
12. JM to Edmund Randolph, 25 February 1787, *MP* 9:299; Notes on Debates, 21 February 1787, *LDC* 9:291–92; *Boston Independent Chronicle*, 15 February 1787.
13. JM to GW, 8 November 1786, *MP* 9:166–67.
14. GW to JJ, 15 August 1786, *PWCS* 4:213.
15. GW to Lafayette, 8 December 1784, *PWCS* 2:175–76.
16. The quotation is from GW to Francis Hopkinson, 16 May 1785, *PWCS* 2:561–62. For other remarks on the aging process, see *PWCS* 3:50; 4:39–40, 150.
17. GW to JM, 18 November 1786, *PWCS* 5:382–83.
18. JM to GW, 7 December 1786, 24 December 1786, *MP* 9:199–200, 224–25.
19. JJ to GW, 7 January 1787, *JP* 4.
20. Edmund Randolph to GW, 6 December 1786, *PWCS* 4:445; JM to Edmund Randolph, 15 April 1787, *MP* 9:378.
21. GW to Edmund Randolph, 9 April 1787, *PWCS* 5:135–36; GW to Henry Knox, 25 February 1787, *PWCS* 5:52–53.
22. GW to AH, 3 March 1783, *PWCS* 1:276–77; GW to James Warren, 7 October 1785, *PWCS* 3:299; GW to JM, 30 November 1785, *PWCS* 3:420.

23. GW to Henry Knox, 5 December 1784, 28 February 1785, *PWCS* 2:170–72, 400; Henry Knox to GW, 14 January 1787, *PWCS* 5:518–23; GW to Henry Knox, 8 March 1787, *PWCS* 6:74–75.

24. David Humphreys to GW, 20 January 1787, *PWCS* 4:526–30; David Humphreys to GW, 24 March 1787, *PWCS* 5:102–4.

25. GW to Henry Knox, 27 April 1787, *PWCS* 5:157–59.

26. Henry Knox to GW, 19 March 1787, *PWCS* 5:95–98.

27. JM to GW, 18 March 1787, and GW to JM, 28 March 1787, *PWCS* 5:94–95, 114–17.

28. JJ to GW, 7 January 1787, *PWCS* 4:502–4.

29. JM to GW, 16 April 1787, *PWCS* 5:144–50. See also Notes on the Sentiments of Government of John Jay, Henry Knox, and James Madison, April 1787, *PWCS* 5: 163–66.

30. This sketch is based on my reading of the first nine volumes of *MP*. Among the biographies, I found the following most helpful: Jack N. Rakove, *James Madison and the Creation of the American Republic* (Glenview, Ill., 1990), is the most succinct life story; Richard Brookhiser, *James Madison* (New York, 2011), is best on Madison as a career politician; Lance Banning, *The Sacred Fire of Liberty: James Madison and the Founding of the Federal Republic* (Ithaca, N.Y., 1995), sees him as a prominent political thinker; the introductory essay at the start of each section of correspondence in James Morton Smith, ed., *The Republic of Letters: The Correspondence Between James Madison and Thomas Jefferson, 1776–1826*, 3 vols. (New York, 1995), taken together, constitute a biography of considerable distinction; and finally, Drew R. McCoy's *The Last of the Fathers: James Madison and the Republican Legacy* (Cambridge, U.K., 1989) just might be the wisest book of all. The quotation is from McCoy, *Last of the Fathers*, xiii.

31. This paragraph is heavily indebted to my earlier sketch of Madison's character in *Founding Brothers: The Revolutionary Generation* (New York, 2000), 53–54.

32. JM to Edmund Randolph, 11 March 1783, *MP* 6:327.

33. JM to Richard Henry Lee, 25 December 1784, *MP* 8:201.

34. JM to James Monroe, 7 August 1785, *MP* 8:333–36.

35. JM to James Monroe, 9 April 1786, *MP* 9:25–26.

36. Notes on Debates, 19 February–26 April 1787, *MP* 1:275–76.

37. GW to TJ, 30 May 1787, *PWCS* 5:208.

CHAPTER 5: MADISON'S MOMENT

1. My interpretation of Madison's way of thinking has been most influenced by Marvin Meyers, ed., *The Mind of the Founder: The Political Thought of James Madison* (Hanover, N.H., and London, 1981); Richard Brookhiser, *James Madison* (New York, 2011); and Drew R. McCoy, *The Last of the Fathers: James Madison and the Republican Legacy* (Cambridge, U.K., 1989).

2. JM to GW, 16 April 1787, *MP* 9:383.

3. JM to Edmund Randolph, 8 April 1787, *MP* 9:368.

4. Ibid., 370. See also JM to TJ, 15 March 1787, *MP* 9:317–22.

5. JM to Edmund Randolph, *MP* 9:369, 371.

6. For Madison's surveys of the state delegations, see JM to Edmund Randolph, 11 March 1787, *MP* 9:307–8; JM to GW, 18 March 1787, *MP* 9:314–17. For the futile effort by Hamilton to enlarge the New York delegation, see "Remarks on a Motion that Five Delegates be Appointed to the Constitutional Convention," 16 April 1787, *HP* 4:148.

7. See, for example, Douglass Adair's critique of Beard in Trevor Colbourn, ed., *Fame and the Founding Fathers: Essays by Douglass Adair* (New York, 1974), 3–26.

8. "Notes on Ancient and Modern Confederacies," April–June, 1786, *MP* 9:3–24.

9. "Vices of the Political System of the United States," *MP* 9:345–58.

10. Ibid., 354–55. See also David C. Hendrickson, *Peace Pact: The Lost World of the American Founding* (Lawrence, Kan., 2003), 211–19.

11. On the question of what representation meant for the revolutionary generation, see two books by Edmund S. Morgan, *The Stamp Act Crisis* (Chapel Hill, N.C., 1953), and *Inventing the People: The Rise of Popular Sovereignty in England and America* (New York, 1988).

12. "Vices of the Political System of the United States," *MP* 9:357–58.

13. In his skeptical attitude toward unbridled democracy, Madison was a typical late-eighteenth-century thinker. It is possible to discover the roots of democracy in the revolutionary era, and Gordon Wood has done so with considerable sophistication in *The Radicalism of the American Revolution* (New York, 1992). But I would argue that the world of the founders remained decisively predemocratic, and that Madison's analysis of state governments in the 1780s was a clear expression of those predemocratic values.

14. *MP* 9:357–59.
15. The scholarly literature on this subject is substantial, best synthesized in Larry D. Kramer, "Madison's Audience," *Harvard Law Review* 112 (January 1999): 611–99. See also Douglass Adair's seminal essay "'That Politics May be Reduced to a Science': David Hume, James Madison, and the Tenth Federalist," in Colbourn, *Fame and the Founding Fathers*, 107–23.
16. The Progressive School of historians interpreted the adoption of the Constitution as an elitist betrayal of the democratic impulses inherent in the American Revolution. It seems abundantly clear that, in the months before the Constitutional Convention, Madison believed that he was trying to rescue the American Revolution, not so much from democracy as from a fatal aversion to government itself. His novel argument about large-scale republics was a centerpiece of that rescue operation because it claimed that geography and demography would obviate the need for coercive government.
17. One can see Madison groping toward this pluralistic view of American society as a swirling collection of interest groups and factions in "Vices," but his clearest and fullest expression of the idea came after the convention in a remarkable letter to Jefferson. See JM to TJ, 24 October 1787, *MP* 10:212–13.
18. David Hume, *Idea of a Perfect Commonwealth* (London, 1754), 7–20. For the Madison quotation and an excellent exegesis of the "filtration" argument, see F. H. Buckley, *The Once and Future King: The Rise of Crown Government in America* (New York, 2014), 18–20.
19. TJ to Edmund Pendleton, 26 August 1776, *JP* 1:506–7.
20. Editorial note on "James Madison at the Federal Convention," 27 May–17 September 1787, *MP* 10:3–10.
21. Madison's version of their preconvention conversations is summarized in JM to TJ, 6 June 1787, *MP* 10:29–30.
22. "Virginia Plan," 29 May 1787, *MP* 10:15–17.
23. Gaillard Hunt and James Brown Scott, eds., *The Debates in the General Convention . . . Reported by James Madison* (New York, 1920), 27–31. Hereafter cited as *Debates*.
24. My version of the debates in the convention draws upon Madison's notes in *Debates* and on five secondary accounts by distinguished historians: Max Farrand, *The Framing of the Constitution of the United States* (New Haven, Conn., 1913), which is old and venerable; Cath-

erine Drinker Bowen, *Miracle at Philadelphia* (Boston, 1966), which lacks notes but possesses the most narrative verve; Jack N. Rakove, *Original Meanings: Politics and Ideas in the Making of the Constitution* (New York, 1996), which is not so much a narrative as a first-rate, topically organized analysis; Carol Berkin, *A Brilliant Solution: Inventing the American Constitution* (New York, 2003), which is written with a nice edge and is the most succinct account; and finally Richard Beeman, *Plain, Honest Men: The Making of the American Constitution* (New York, 2009), which is a superb scholarly synthesis that also ranks up there with Bowen's *Miracle* for readability.

25. *Debates*, 18–21. Buckley, *Once and Future King*, 13–14, called my attention to the implications of the one-state-one-vote decision, though I make more of it than he does.

26. *Debates*, 21.

27. In the summer of 2013 I spent two days taking the tour of Independence Hall multiple times and talking with tourists about their impressions. Three common features dominated their responses: this was sacred space; it was much smaller than they had imagined; and it was unbearably hot.

28. Beeman, *Plain, Honest Men*, 56–58. See also Berkin, *Brilliant Solution*, 211–61, for brief sketches of all the delegates.

29. George Bancroft, *History of the Formation of the Constitution of the United States of America*, 2 vols. (New York, 1882), 2:284.

30. Richard Hofstadter, *The Progressive Historians* (New York, 1968), 15–20.

31. For the absolute dread of monarchy, see Hendrickson, *Peace Pact*, 40–47. Thomas Paine's *Common Sense* and Thomas Jefferson's *Declaration* defined the antimonarchical agenda for the revolutionary generation.

32. "Virginia Plan," 29 May 1787, *MP* 10:17; Buckley, *Once and Future King*, 8–9.

33. *HP* 4:181–95, for Hamilton's speech on June 18. For the frustrating and confusing debates about executive power in the convention, see Bowen, *Miracle at Philadelphia*, 40–54; Beeman, *Plain, Honest Men*, 107–22; Berkin, *Brilliant Solution*, 116–48; and Ron Chernow, *Alexander Hamilton* (New York, 2004), 231.

34. Lincoln made his remarks in the Cooper Union speech on February 27, 1860. Just as he had political reasons to detect an incipient

American nationalism in 1776, it was important for him to believe that the founders agreed with his view that slavery must and would end.

35. The Madison quotation is in Max Farrand, ed., *The Records of the Federal Convention of 1787*, 4 vols. (New Haven, Conn., 1937), 1:486–87. On the role of slavery in the convention, see Paul Finkelman, *Slavery and the Founders: Race and Liberty in the Age of Jefferson* (London, 1996), 1–30; and my effort in *Founding Brothers: The Revolutionary Generation* (New York, 2000), 81–119. For the current version of the neoabolitionist argument condemning the framers, see David Waldstreicher, *Slavery's Constitution: From Revolution to Ratification* (New York, 2009).

36. Beeman, *Plain, Honest Men*, 176–85, and Rakove, *Original Meanings*, 73–74, 92–93, are especially good on the three-fifths clause. It is important to recognize that it was intended not as a moral statement about the lesser human value of slaves but as a political compromise about how to count them as part persons, part property for the purpose of representation in the House and then in the Electoral College. The political advantage it gave the southern states in presidential elections is the main reason that Jefferson was referred to as "the Negro president" after his narrow victory in the election of 1800.

37. Farrand, *Records of the Federal Convention*, 1:605; 2:221–23, 364–66; Ellis, *Founding Brothers*, 91–93.

38. Dickinson's observation was made in notes he kept at the convention but never delivered. Quoted in James H. Hutson, *Supplement to Max Farrand's "The Records of the Federal Convention of 1787"* (New Haven, Conn., 1987), 158.

39. Beeman, *Plain, Honest Men*, 146–62, provides the best synthesis of this extended moment.

40. GW to AH, 10 July 1787, *PWCS* 5:257.

41. Beeman, *Plain, Honest Men*, 188–97.

42. JM to TJ, 6 September 1787, *MP* 10:163–66.

43. GW to Lafayette, 18 September 1787, *PWCS* 5:334; in a similar vein, GW to Henry Knox, 19 August 1787, *PWCS* 5:297.

44. Buckley, *Once and Future King*, 32–45, also makes a case for Morris, as does Richard Brookhiser in *Gentleman Revolutionary: Gouverneur Morris, the Rake Who Wrote the Constitution* (New York, 2003), 78–93.

45. JM to Jared Sparks, 8 April 1831, in Farrand, *Records of the Federal Con-*

vention, 3:499. For the fullest discussion of Morris's editorial changes, see Brookhiser, *Gentleman Revolutionary,* 90–93.

46. Franklin's speech is reproduced in Edmund S. Morgan, ed., *Not Your Usual Founding Father: Selected Readings from Benjamin Franklin* (New Haven, Conn., 2006), 286–87.

CHAPTER 6: THE GREAT DEBATE

1. JM in Congress, 6 April 1796, *MP* 16:295–96.
2. The authoritative scholarly study of the ratification process is Pauline Maier, *Ratification: The People Debate the Constitution, 1787–88* (New York, 2010). The documents for each state ratifying convention are published in *DHRC,* a massive editorial project nearing completion.
3. The fullest account of the referendum on independence in the spring and summer of 1776 is Pauline Maier, *American Scripture: Making the Declaration of Independence* (New York, 1997), 217–34. I offer a more succinct version of the story in *American Creation: Triumphs and Tragedies at the Founding of the Republic* (New York, 2007), 49–51.
4. This is a huge claim, I realize, but the only serious alternative is the Lincoln-Douglas debates in 1858, and they could never have happened if the debates over ratification had gone the other way.
5. The decision of the Virginia legislature is described in GW to JM, 5 November 1787, *MP* 10:242–43.
6. GW to JM, 10 October 1787, *MP* 10:189.
7. Maier, *Ratification,* 25–49.
8. JM to Edmund Pendleton, 28 October 1787, *MP* 10:223–24.
9. Maier, *Ratification,* 74–75; Jeffrey L. Pasley, *"The Tyranny of Printers": Newspaper Politics in the Early American Republic* (Charlottesville, Va., 2001), 33–43.
10. One delegate to the Pennsylvania convention, Robert Whitehill, claimed that only one in twenty residents in the western counties of the state had even read the Constitution. *DHRC* 2:65–72.
11. GW to Lafayette, 18 September 1787, and GW to Benjamin Harrison, 24 September 1787, *PWCS* 5:334, 339.
12. See the letters, *PWCS* 5:297, 365–66, 366–68, 368–69; 6:95–97; JM to GW, 18 October 1787, *MP* 10:196–97.
13. GW to Charles Carter, 7 December 1787, *PWCS* 5:492.
14. Remarks on Signing the Constitution, 17 September 1787, *HP* 4:253.
15. To the *Daily Advertiser,* 20 July 1787, *HP* 4:229–32.

16. AH to GW, 11–15 October 1787, and GW to AH, 18 October 1787, *HP* 4:280–81, 284–85; Ron Chernow, *Alexander Hamilton* (New York, 2004), 245.

17. "Conjectures About the New Constitution," 17–30 September 1787, *HP* 4:275–76.

18. JJ to JA, 16 October 1787, *JP* 3.

19. JJ to GW, 3 February 1787, *JP* 3.

20. JM to TJ, 6 September 1787, *MP* 10:163–64.

21. TJ to JM, 20 June 1878, *MP* 10:64.

22. JM to William Short, 24 October 1787, *MP* 10:220–22.

23. JM to Edmund Randolph, 21 October 1787, *MP* 10:199–200.

24. The fullest state-by-state assessment is in JM to Ambrose Madison, 8 November 1787, *MP* 10:243–44.

25. JM to Archibald Stuart, 30 October 1787, *MP* 10:232.

26. JM to Ambrose Madison, 30 September 1787, *MP* 10:179–80.

27. JM to TJ, 24 October 1787, *MP* 10:208.

28. Madison is a much-studied thinker, and for this moment in his career three books strike me as seminal: Marvin Meyers, *The Mind of the Founder: Sources of the Political Thought of James Madison* (Hanover, N.H., 1981); Lance Banning, *The Sacred Fire of Liberty: James Madison and the Founding Federal Republic* (Ithaca, N.Y., 1995); and Drew R. McCoy, *The Last of the Fathers: James Madison and the Republican Legacy* (Cambridge, U.K., 1989). My interpretation here tends to deviate from the mainstream because his most distinguished biographers see him primarily as a political philosopher. I see him as a political strategist, whose ideas were developed in specific contexts, usually in response to arguments he sought to counter and, in this case, political developments that he had not anticipated. His greatest gift was intellectual agility, not consistency.

29. Maier, *Ratification*, 155–211; Hancock's speech on recommended amendments is in Bernard Bailyn, ed., *The Debate on the Constitution*, 2 vols. (New York, 1993), 1:941–42. The proposed amendments are best discussed in Saul Cornell, *The Other Founders: Anti-Federalism and the Dissenting Tradition in America, 1788–1828* (Chapel Hill, N.C., 1999), 30–31. I embrace Cornell's estimate of 124 proposed amendments by the state ratifying conventions. There were actually more than 200 amendments, but many were duplications.

30. My interpretation of the Antifederalists—again, the term is mis-

representative—aligns itself with the landmark essay by Cecelia Kenyon, "Men of Little Faith: The Anti-Federalists on the Nature of Representative Government," *WMQ* 12 (January 1953): 3–43; a somewhat updated version of the same interpretation is in James H. Hutson, "Country, Court, and Constitution: Antifederalism and the Historians," *WMQ* 35 (October 1981): 337–68. See also Herbert J. Storing, *What the Anti-Federalists Were For* (Chicago, 1981). The central impulse of the Antifederalists was not democracy but an antigovernment ethos that had proved so effective opposing British policy in the prewar years. It was an inherently oppositional ideology with libertarian implications that distrusted any and all forms of government power. In that sense, it was inherently incompatible with a nation-size republic. It looked backward rather than forward, though eventually found its fullest expression in the government under the Confederacy in 1861–65. The Tea Party movement that emerged in the twenty-first century is a modern-day echo of the Antifederalist mentality. For a characteristically shrewd assessment of the Federalist Papers, see Bernard Bailyn, "The Federalist Papers," in *To Begin the World Anew: The Genius and Ambiguities of the American Founders* (New York, 2003), 100–125.

31. Chernow, *Hamilton*, 247; Elizabeth Fleet, ed., "Madison's Detached Memoranda," *WMQ* 3 (1946): 563.

32. Editorial note, *MP* 10:259–60; Editorial note, *HP* 4:287–301; Elaine Crane, "Publius in the Provinces: Where Was the Federalist Reprinted Outside New York City?," *WMQ* 21 (1964): 589–92; Larry D. Kramer, "Madison's Audience," *Harvard Law Review* 112 (January 1999): 611–99. The two-volume published version of the Federalist Papers became available in time to influence the debates in Virginia and New York, but chiefly, and ironically, as a target that focused the fire of the opponents to ratification.

33. GW to AH, 28 August 1788, *PWCS* 6:480–81.

34. *MP* 10:263–70, 477.

35. Warren Hope, ed., *The Letters of Centinel* (Ardmore, Pa., 1998), 69–70.

36. GW to Thomas Johnson, 20 April 1788, and GW to James McHenry, 27 April 1788, *PWCS* 6:217–18, 235–36. Washington concluded that Maryland's ratification, followed shortly thereafter by South Carolina's, "created a moral certainty of adoption . . . which will make all

except desperate men look before they leap into the dark consequences of rejection." As the Virginia convention gathered in Richmond, he was confident that "Virginia will make the ninth column in the federal Temple." GW to JM, 8 June 1788, and GW to Jonathan Trumbull, Jr., 12 June 1788, *PWCS* 6:321, 325.

37. JM to GW, 13 and 18 June 1788, *PWCS* 6:329, 339.

38. Marshall quoted in Jean Edward Smith, *John Marshall: Definer of a Nation* (New York, 1996), 118.

39. JM to GW, 18 March 1786, *PWCS* 5:94–95. On Henry as an orator, see Henry Mayer, *Son of Thunder: Patrick Henry and the American Republic* (New York, 1986).

40. TJ to JM, 8 December 1784, *RL* 1:353–54.

41. Smith, *John Marshall,* 123.

42. *DHRC* 9:952–53.

43. *DHRC* 9:959–61.

44. *DHRC* 9:1028–31.

45. *DHRC* 9:995–96.

46. *DHRC* 9:951.

47. *DHRC* 9:959.

48. *DHRC* 9:995–96.

49. *DHRC* 9:1506–15. Madison predicted that Henry would do anything in his power to throw sand into the gears of the new federal government, arguing that Virginia's representative "will commit suicide on his own authority." One of Henry's first acts was to block Madison's election to the Senate.

50. See Maier, *Ratification,* 345–400, for the best synthesis of the twists and turns at the New York convention. See also Linda Grant DePauw, *The Eleventh Pillar: New York State and the Federal Constitution* (Ithaca, N.Y., 1966). Governor Clinton and his followers made a point of rejecting the view that Virginia's ratification left New York with no realistic options. The new Constitution was going into effect, however, and as an editorial in the *New York Packet* put it, "Now, those who vote against the New Constitution vote themselves out of the New Federal Union." *New York Packet,* 15 July 1788.

51. "An Address to the People of New York on the Subject of the Constitution," 12 April 1788, *JP* 3. On Jay's diplomatic style of debate, see Maier, *Ratification,* 399.

52. Editorial Note, Jay at the New York Ratifying Convention, *JP* 3.
53. JM to GW, 21 July 1788, *PWCS* 6:392–93; JM to AH, 20 July 1788, *HP* 5:184–85.
54. The circular letter is in *DHRC* 23:236.
55. GW to JM, 23 September 1788, *MP* 11:262; GW to JM, 11 August 1788, *PWCS* 6:437–39.
56. JJ to GW, 21 September 1788, *PWCS* 6:527–28.
57. GW to Willliam Tudor, 22 August 1788, and GW to John Armstrong, 25 April 1788, *PWCS* 465, 226.

CHAPTER 7: FINAL PIECES

1. Pauline Maier, *Ratification: The People Debate the Constitution, 1787–88* (New York, 2010), 421–32, for the best synthesis of the post-ratification efforts by the opposition in Virginia and New York. For Madison's assessment of the political backlash from Henry and Clinton, see JM to GW, 17 August, 24 August 1788, *PWCS* 6:454–55, 468–71.
2. AH to JM, 23 November 1788, AH to Samuel Jones, 21 January 1789, AH to Pierre Van Cortlandt, 16 February 1789, and AH to the Electors of the State of New York, 7 April 1789, *HP* 5:235–36, 244–46, 254–55, 317–29; H.R. letters printed in the *Daily Advertiser, HP* 5:262–331.
3. GW to John Armstrong, 25 April 1788, *PWCS* 6:224.
4. GW to Charles Pettit, 16 August 1788, *PWCS* 6:448.
5. AH to GW, 13 August 1788, *PWCS* 6:444.
6. GW to AH, 3 October 1788, *HP* 5:223.
7. AH to GW, 30 September 1788, *HP* 5:221–22.
8. Henry Lee to GW, 13 September 1788, *PWCS* 6:510–12.
9. GW to Lafayette, 28 April 1788, *PWCS* 6:245.
10. GW to Henry Knox, 1 April 1789, *PWR* 2:20.
11. AH to James Wilson, 25 January 1789, *HP* 5:247–49.
12. My interpretation of Madison's mentality and motives at this propitious moment is based primarily on the correspondence in *MP*. Helpful secondary accounts include: Richard Labinski, *James Madison and the Struggle for the Bill of Rights* (Oxford and New York, 2006); Jack N. Rakove, "James Madison and the Bill of Rights: A Broader Context," *Presidential Studies Quarterly* 22 (1992): 667–77; and Kenneth Bowling, "'A Barrel to the Whale': The Founding Fathers and the Adoption of the Bill of Rights," *JER* 8 (1988): 223–51. Maier, *Ratification,* 443–68, provides a comprehensive synthesis.

13. The most accessible version of the circular letter is in *RL* 1:548–49.

14. JM to Thomas Mann Randolph, 13 January 1789, *MP* 11:416. See also JM to Tench Coxe, 24 June 1789, *MP* 12:257.

15. *RL* 1:590–611, which is the editorial essay that introduces the Jefferson-Madison correspondence in 1788–89, written by James Morton Smith. In my judgment, Smith's treatment of the issues at stake sets the standard for all scholars attempting to recover Madison's "original intentions" in drafting the Bill of Rights. If all of Smith's introductory essays in this three-volume edition were published as a separate book, it would constitute a major new biography of Madison.

16. TJ to JM, 6 February 1788, *RL* 1:529–30.

17. TJ to Francis Hopkinson, 13 March 1789, *JP* 12:557–58. Jefferson's draft of a "Charter of Rights" for France is in *JP* 15:167–68. For Jefferson's radical belief in generational sovereignty, see Herbert E. Sloan, *Principle and Interest: Thomas Jefferson and the Problem of Debt* (New York, 1995), which is a more elegant analysis of this utopian strain in Jefferson's thought than its title suggests.

18. I have discussed this utopian dimension of Jefferson's thinking at greater length in *American Creation: Triumphs and Tragedies at the Founding of the Republic* (New York, 2007), 100–105.

19. JM to TJ, 17 October 1788, *RL* 1:564.

20. TJ to JM, 18 November 1788, 15 March 1789, *RL* 1:567, 587.

21. JM to George Eve, 2 January 1789, *MP* 11:404–5.

22. JM to TJ, 29 March 1789, *RL* 1:609.

23. Address to the House of Representatives by the President, 5 May 1789, *MP* 12:132–34; Address of the President to Congress, 30 April 1789, *MP* 12:121–24.

24. The scale of Madison's editorial effort can only be appreciated by recovering all 124 amendments proposed by the state ratifying conventions. The best place to find them is Edward Dumbauld's *The Bill of Rights and What It Means Today* (Norman, Okla., 1957), 160–65.

25. Helen E. Veit et al., eds., *Creating the Bill of Rights: A Documentary Record from the First Federal Congress* (Baltimore, 1991), 263, 278.

26. Amendments to the Constitution, 13 August 1789, *MP* 12:333.

27. JM to Alexander White, 24 August 1789, *MP* 12:352–53; Maier, *Ratification*, 453.

28. For this classical view of the Bill of Rights, see Robert Rutland, *The Birth of the Bill of Rights* (Chapel Hill, N.C., 1955).

29. Veit, *Creating the Bill of Rights,* 64.

30. Amendments to the Constitution, 8 June 1789, *MP* 12:196–97.

31. *MP* 12:198–99.

32. *MP* 12:200–203.

33. *MP* 12:208.

34. Amendments to the Constitution, 17 August 1789, ibid., 344. See also Patrick T. Conley and John P. Kaminski, eds., *The Bill of Rights and the States* (Madison, Wis., 1992).

35. *MP* 12:207. See also Rosemary Zagarri, *The Politics of Size: Representation in the United States, 1776–1850* (Ithaca, N.Y., 1987).

36. *MP* 12:201.

37. The ongoing debate over the right to bear arms in our own time is obviously a deeply divisive issue that generates much shouting, foot-stomping, and even death threats. My point here is that for judicial devotees of the "original intent" doctrine, Madison's motives in 1789 are clear beyond any reasonable doubt. To wit, the right to bear arms derived from the need to make state militias the core pillar of national defense. In order to avoid reaching that conclusion, the majority opinion in *Heller,* written by Justice Antonin Scalia, is an elegant example of legalistic legerdemain masquerading as erudition. Madison is rolling over in his grave. For the history of the Second Amendment, see Michael Waldman, *The Second Amendment: A Biography* (New York, 2014), and Saul Cornell and Nathan Kokushanich, eds., *The Second Amendment on Trial: Critical Essays on District of Columbia v. Heller* (Amherst, Mass., 2013).

38. Veit, *Creating the Bill of Rights,* 175.

39. Ibid., 199.

40. JM to Richard Peters, 19 August 1789, *MP* 12:346–48.

41. Several historians have located the birth of American nationalism in the second decade of the nineteenth century. See Curtis Nettles, *The Emergence of a National Economy, 1775–1815* (New York, 1962); Steven Watts, *The Republic Reform: War and the Making of Liberal America, 1790–1820* (Baltimore, 1987); David Waldstreicher, *In the Midst of Perpetual Fetes: The Making of American Nationalism, 1776–1820* (Chapel Hill, N.C., 1997), which emphasizes the role of public rituals in creating a national ethos.

42. I have offered a fuller treatment of what we might call the Madison Problem in *American Creation,* 87–126. For a different view, see Gor-

don S. Wood, "Is There a Madison Problem?" in *Revolutionary Characters: What Made the Founders Different* (New York, 2006), 141–72. For the tragic consequences of Madison's shift to a states-rights position, see Susan Dunn, *Dominion of Memories: Jefferson, Madison, and the Decline of Virginia* (New York, 2007).

43. The following thoughts are mine alone. But three of the most distinguished historians of the founding era have influenced my interpretive instincts, often in ways they may not have intended. They are Bernard Bailyn, *To Begin the World Anew: The Genius and Ambiguities of the American Founders* (New York, 2003); Edmund S. Morgan, *Inventing the People: The Rise of Popular Sovereignty in England and America* (New York, 1998); and Gordon S. Wood, *The Radicalism of the American Revolution* (New York, 1992).

44. TJ to Samuel Kercheval, 12 July 1816, most conveniently available in Merrill D. Peterson, ed., *The Portable Thomas Jefferson* (New York, 1975), 558–59.

INDEX

abolitionism, xix, 146, 171

Adams, Abigail, 74

Adams, John, 6, 19, 87, 255n4, 261n1; as American minister to London, 74, 86; in Continental Congress, 9, 13, 14; elected vice president, 198–9; Jay's correspondence with, 91–2, 166; and Treaty of Paris, 68–9, 87

Alexandria (Virginia), 27

Alger, Horatio, 37

Allegheny Mountains, 12, 32, 72, 76, 90

American Revolution, 34, 41, 59, 83, 184, 219; consolidation of energies of, 24–5, 216; Constitutional Convention and, 103, 105, 120, 131–2, 139, 142–4; meaning of, xv, 157, 185–6, 213; military phase of, *see* war for independence; patriotic rhetoric of, 54; principles of, xviii, 16, 18, 76, 129, 142, 162; Washington as embodiment of, xvi, 196

Amsterdam, 68

Annapolis (Maryland), 62, 73, 98–100, 104, 107, 109, 111, 147

Antifederalists, 12, 161–2, 170, 179–83, 187, 271–2n30

Appalachian Mountains, 27; *see also* Allegheny Mountains; Blue Ridge Mountains

Aranda, Pedro Pablo Sandal, Count of, 68

arms, right to bear, 212, 276n37

Army, U.S., 241

Articles of Confederation, xvii, 27, 111–14, 117–19, 123–5, 159, 211, 221–31; Antifederalists' support for, 160–2, 179, 187; calls for reform of, 56–7, 59, 71, 91–3, 97–100, 102; ceding of states' western territorial claims under, 12–13; Committee of the States under, 227, 228; Congress under, *see* Confederation Congress; core values of American Revolution embodied in, 139, 142; drafting of, *see* Dickinson Draft; inadequacies of government under, 71, 91–3; lack of support for Continental Army under, 23–4, 53; need for replacement of, 103–4, 107, 109 (*see also* Constitutional Convention); raising revenue prohibited under, 35; ratification of, 5, 31; signatories to, 221, 229–30; state-based political architecture of, xi, xiv, 6–7, 25, 28, 123, 137, 148, 201, 218; systematic dysfunctions under, xv, 117, 127–8, 134, 140–1, 209–10

Bancroft, George, 141

Bank of the United States, 41–2, 46, 117

Beard, Charles, xiv, 126

Beekman and Cruger, 49

Bemis, Samuel Flagg, 261n1

FIRST FAMILY
Abigail and John Adams

In this rich and engrossing account, John and Abigail Adams come to life against the backdrop of the Republic's tenuous early years. Drawing on more than 1,200 letters exchanged between the couple, Ellis tells a story both personal and panoramic. We learn about the many years Abigail and John spent apart as John's political career sent him first to Philadelphia, then to Paris and Amsterdam; their relationship with their children; and Abigail's role as John's closest and most valued advisor. Exquisitely researched and beautifully written, *First Family* is both a revealing portrait of a marriage and a unique study of America's early years.

History

REVOLUTIONARY SUMMER
The Birth of American Independence

The summer months of 1776 witnessed the most consequential events in the story of our country's founding. While the thirteen colonies came together and agreed to secede from the British Empire, the British were dispatching the largest armada ever to cross the Atlantic to crush the rebellion in the cradle. The Continental Congress and the Continental Army were forced to make decisions on the run, improvising as history congealed around them. In a brilliant and seamless narrative, Ellis meticulously examines the most influential figures in this propitious moment and weaves together the political and military experiences as two sides of a single story, and shows how events on one front influenced outcomes on the other.

History

FOUNDING BROTHERS
The Revolutionary Generation

In this landmark work of history, Joseph J. Ellis explores
how a group of gifted but deeply flawed individuals—
Hamilton, Burr, Jefferson, Franklin, Washington, Adams,
and Madison—confronted the overwhelming challenges
before them to set the course for our nation. The United
States was more a fragile hope than a reality in 1790.
During the decade that followed, the Founding Fathers—
re-examined here as Founding Brothers—combined the
ideals of the Declaration of Independence with the content of the Constitution to create the practical workings
of our government. Through an analysis of six fascinating
episodes—Hamilton and Burr's deadly duel, Washington's
precedent-setting Farewell Address, Adams's administration and political partnership with his wife, the debate
about where to place the capital, Franklin's attempt to
force Congress to confront the issue of slavery and Madison's attempts to block him, and Jefferson and Adams's
famous correspondence—*Founding Brothers* brings to life
the vital issues and personalities from the most important
decade in our nation's history.

Biography

ALSO AVAILABLE

American Sphinx
American Creation
His Excellency

VINTAGE BOOKS
Available wherever books are sold.
www.vintagebooks.com